Playing the Audience

The Practical Actor's Guide to
Live Performance

Playing the Audience

The Practical Actor's Guide to Live Performance

by James B. Nicola

If the external characterization does not appear spontaneously, it must be grafted on from the outside.

—Constantin Stanislavski

APPLAUSE
THEATRE & CINEMA BOOKS

PLAYING THE AUDIENCE

THE PRACTICAL ACTOR'S GUIDE TO LIVE PERFORMANCE

BY JAMES B. NICOLA

Copyright © 2002 by James B. Nicola

Library of Congress Cataloguing-in-Publication Data
Library of Congress Card Number: 2002103402

British Library Cataloguing-in-Publication Data
A catalogue record for this book is available from the British Library

ISBN: 1-55783-492-x

Printed in Canada

APPLAUSE
THEATRE & CINEMA BOOKS
151 West 46th Street, 8th Floor
New York, NY 10036
Phone: (212) 575-9265
Fax: (646) 562-5852
email: info@applausepub.com

SALES & DISTRIBUTION
NORTH AMERICA:

HAL LEONARD CORP.
7777 West Bluemound Road
P.O. Box 13819
Milwaukee, WI 53213
Phone: (414) 774-3630
Fax: (414) 774-3259
email: halinfo@halleonard.com
internet: www.halleonard.com

UK:

COMBINED BOOK SERVICES LTD.
Units I/K, Paddock Wood Distribution Centre
Paddock Wood, Tonbridge, Kent TN12 6UU
Phone: (44) 01892 837171
Fax: (44) 01892 837272
United Kingdom

Acknowledgments

A deep debt of gratitude to Randi Jean Sobol, my primary confidante and sounding board during the inception of this book, and my informal-yet-intensive editor for the last two drafts. Also particular thanks to actors Bryn Gaddy Adamson, James Cleveland, and Mary Guzzy, and to speech professor Louis Freeman, all of whom drafted detailed notes.

Thanks also to all those readers—actors, teachers, stage managers, writers—who gave me feedback, including Bunzy Bunworth, Francys Olivia Burch, Kathy Conry, Patty Figel, Deborah Holmes, Virginia Bailey Parker, Lynne Nelson Rafferty, Bill Raoul, Peter Reznikoff, Donald Smyth, the students at the University of Oklahoma School of Drama, where I was able to use earlier versions as a textbook, and to Tina Balko, my mother, who had the patience to read the manuscript aloud to me—twice.

Additional thanks to the actors and students whose work appears as examples herein; to those who encouraged me with, "You oughta write a book . . . "; to teachers and colleagues who have shared their techniques with me, and to companies and classes who have inspired new ones.

Contents

INTRODUCTION

The theater is a lot like humanity: it needs your help.

Today we spend more and more time in cyberspace and less and less with other human beings. Instead of inviting friends over for an evening of cards, we play against the computer itself. Shopping centers the size of small towns have replaced the general store where we once gathered for gossip. The local switchboard operator, whose first name we used to know, has been rendered obsolete by computerized voices instructing us to "press the pound sign." Our age is one of fast cars, fast food, fast information, and fasting from human interaction. Ironically, this alienation makes our need for the theater's humanizing influence greater than ever, even as it is killing the theater little by little.

A lot of marvelous theater is being produced. My point is not that it is dying, but that it is being replaced, particularly by the all-too-convenient VCR. (Stores even market high-tech giant televisions as "home theaters," implying that the consumer is at the theater when he is really watching the tube.) The real danger lies in the changing constitution of the audience: raising future generations of couch potatoes will sound the theater's death knell. Many theaters are introducing outreach programs, earlier weekday curtain times, flexible subscription packages, and lunchtime short-play series to fill those seats. But as performing artists, we must do our part as well.

The typical American actor is ill-equipped to play to a house of more than six or ten rows; he can excel only in movies, television, or commercials—and perhaps in the small black-box spaces where he performed his thesis project. Training in the United States over the last fifty years has increasingly stressed acting for the camera at the expense of the stage. The strategy is understandable in such a highly competitive industry, for high-visibility alumni—celebrities—lure prospective students. And for those who want careers in television or film, the training is often quite good; but for the stage actor it is incomplete.

Is live theater obsolete already, a dinosaur best relegated to a bygone age? Cinema and television are the offspring of theater, after all. Is live theater so important?

To the latter question, I hope the reader answers with a resounding "yes." When we arrive at rehearsal, set foot onstage, or congregate to see a play, we are participating in an age-old tradition that has generated riots, deposed dictators, established national identity, provided solace in times of distress, and changed the course of history. Like religion, theater has been an organ to undermine tyranny—often right under the nose of the tyrant.

This link with religion makes sense. The first actor in ancient Greece was a celebrant of the god Dionysus; in the Middle Ages, morality plays were liturgical in nature, performed in churches; and even Stanislavski used the word *communion*. Today's actor, in contrast, typically pounds the pavement to audition for the latest soap opera, or just for a spot selling the soap. How did the actor devolve from worshiper to peddler? And must one be devout to be a compelling stage actor?

Well, no—and yes. The technique of live acting does spring forth from the special, communal relationship between living actors and spectators. *We are not really acting until we act on that audience.* Until then, there is only rehearsal. Yet the audience is not only under-emphasized in actor training; sometimes the slightest acknowledgment of them is actually discouraged. To deny the audience, we might as well replay a videotape every night.

Playing the audience does not necessarily mean playing *to* the audience (although it can on occasion), and certainly doesn't mean playing *down* to the audience—pandering—although portions of many great plays do precisely this. For the most part, we let the audience's laughter inform our work—invisibly.

Nor need we sell out to sheer commercialism and present only drama that is easy to understand or appeals to vulgar sentiment. Yet we should not be esoteric or elitist, either, content with only 2–3 percent of the population in attendance. Rather, through playing the audience we should strive to present even the most abstruse drama in a clear and exhilarating way to appeal to the entire populace. Reaching that populace is becoming harder and rarer. But for the theater to be vital, it must rise up out of the esoteric and into the popular; it is a populist medium, after all.

Playwrights have embraced the audience ever since the first actor spoke directly to the first spectator, of course. But more and more of late they have been lacing even naturalism with the surreal or the magical, creating worlds that exist only in their minds—and in the theater. Today's plays feature fantastical characters like angels, a swan in human form, and a young woman's soul trapped in an old man's body.[1] Wisely, playwrights have been relegating the strictly naturalistic story to the screen, having realized already that if theater-going were to remain too much like the movies, the audience might as easily drop by the video store.

Now it is time for actors and directors to meet the demands of playwrights. Just as Stanislavski developed his System to serve the naturalism ushered in by writers like Ibsen and Chekhov, it is only natural that playing the audience should now distinguish acting for the stage.

THE ART OF ACTING

This principle of participation is intrinsic to art itself. Even in painting and sculpture, art is not an object that is, but rather an act, which does; it only becomes art with the experiencing of it. It is the beholder's experience combining with the artist's creation that defines the act of art.

The value of *The Creation of Adam* lies in its power to flabbergast the multitudes assembled in the Sistine Chapel—still. Should the Vatican decide to lock the doors of the Chapel forever, it would cease to be a work of art, and become at best a work of *artistry*, at worst, just paint.

Although the *work* of art may be what is in front of you, the act of art is an activity,[2] which involves perceiving not just what is there, but also what is *not* there—a principle I call the "Other."

The last chapter of the ancient Indian text, the Diamond Sutra, says that there is no Form without Void nor Void without Form; the part of a cup that makes it a cup is actually the part that is not the cup. It is the void that can be filled that gives the cup its shape and function, and hence its "cup-ness."

Human beings are vessels, too. The theater is a celebration of, and investigation into, what we are vessels of—our humanity. Like a cup, the part of us that makes us human beings (besides our corporal form) is the part of us that is not here; not our physical body, but our metaphysical spirit; not our person, but our personality, or Self: the Other.

In the arts, the Other refers (among other things) to what the work calls to the mind and heart of the viewer besides what is in front of her. Academics may analyze a canvas's composition and brush strokes, but for five centuries what mankind has wondered most about is the enigma behind the Mona Lisa's smile. And when you read a novel or poem, or listen to music, the actual images that come to you arise from your own experience. The writer's words and the composer's notes trigger them, of course, but the artist's experiences do not actually become yours. *Experiencing what is not there* (in addition to what is) *defines the act of art.* The power of art, then, lies in how it acts on us in mysterious ways.

In drama, the Other entails everything besides the script itself. It includes, like the Mona Lisa's smile, the enigmatic spirit that infects everyone in the hall and leaves them altered once they leave it—the indescribable magic of the theater. You might think that magic is impossible to manufacture and manipulate, yet our craft is precisely this. Theatrical magic springs from the flow of impulses from stage to spectator and back again. This living, two-way current is alien to film and television, where audience and actor are essentially dead to each other.

Live acting, then, is not just about what you feel, it's about what you get the audience to feel; it's not merely emoting, it's evoking, provoking, invoking, and convoking. The secret to achieving all this lies not simply in performing in front of, but in participating with; not in what one says or does, but in what one gives; not in showing, but in sharing; not in what goes on inside oneself, but in what transpires *between* actors and audience.

Michelangelo was aware of this power of between; magnificent as all the Sistine Chapel's paintings are, the focus of the room is the very center of the ceiling, the point between God's and Adam's fingers, where he painted nothing. *The act of theater takes place in that space between God's and Adam's fingers.*

This spark between stage and spectator can be thought of as electricity. The actors come to the theater charged up for the evening's performance. The audience arrives charged to pay attention ("paying" attention implies that they expect something back). These two anodes generate electricity when the charge flows back and forth between them. The current may be invisible, but, like the life-giving spark in the Sistine Chapel, it has the power to make things happen. This is the power of the theater.

THE GOAL

We used to talk of an understood "contract with the audience" with unwritten clauses such as "the audience must be able to hear every word and see everything going on," and "every seat must be a good seat," and so forth. Playing the audience, we also aim to make the audience's experience *worthwhile, unique,* and *essential.*

For the first of these goals, think of when you read (or watch) a murder mystery: you trust that the author presents clues in such a way that you can figure out the identity of the murderer. The sequence of clues provides the mystery's structure—from the reader's point of view. You may even feel cheated in the last chapter if you find out that the inspector knew something that you could not possibly have known. As mystery novelist is to reader, so is player to audience. They trust that there will be a payoff at the end to make the two hours' traffic worth their while.

Second, to make the theater unique, that payoff should optimally be one that can be reached *only* through giving the play. The theater no longer enjoys a monopoly in mass entertainment; but we can establish a new, limited monopoly in doing what live theater does best: transporting live audience and actors, together.

Finally, for our audiences to consider the ritual essential, we must treat it as sacred. A viewer can put the VCR on *pause* any time to get a snack; the theater's audience should not even think about getting up until intermission. Our invitation must be so compelling that they cannot help but participate with fellow citizens in the communal explosion of joy, laughter, pain, and insight. The theater invites the spectator to reassess precepts, challenge prejudices, and leave the theater *changed*, however slightly, for having participated in the drama.

If we succeed in making the theater worthwhile, unique and essential, the public will come back again and again.

SUBSTANCE, SYSTEM, AND STORY

I have organized technique into four areas, or parameters, characteristic of all schools of acting (and of all the performing arts).

The Four Universal Parameters of Performance
- *Meaning,* investigating information from text and research (chapters 2 and 7);
- *Stakes,* personalizing that Meaning (chapter 3);
- *Connection,* what you do onstage from moment to moment (chapter 4); and
- *Shape,* or effective storytelling (chapter 5).

I have placed them in order roughly parallel to the sequence of the actor's process: you investigate Meaning and invest in Stakes before rehearsal even starts, for example. But the reader is encouraged to skip around from section to section, since these processes overlap. All four parameters deal not just with what actors do with one another, but also with how they involve the audience, or *theatricality* (chapters 1 and 6; chapter 7, resuming chapter 2's discussion, focuses on Language).

Meaning and Stakes provide the substance; Connection, the system; and Shape, the story. Without them, playing the audience can deteriorate into overacting, emoting, and mugging. With them, however, it makes for compelling, electrifying theater—once you know how to compel and electrify.

Moreover, this process binds everything you do onstage into a cohesive whole—the gift. Thus it can unify a company of highly disparate actors into one storytelling unit, regardless of their differing approaches, enabling the classical actor to work seamlessly with the Method actor in the creation of a single theatrical universe.

This book is intended to be helpful to both Method actor and classical, to novice or student and seasoned pro, especially one turning to the stage from television or film. It should help directors from these media, too, and those coming from acting or teaching. While it will not tell you how to direct, it may open you up to a new way of thinking about the theatrical experience, and suggest a few things you may want to test out in rehearsal, workshop, or class, ranging from specific staging ideas to the mystery of inducing inspiration itself.

Much of the technique merely constitutes what I have expected every stage actor to know; but many well-intentioned, dedicated actors do not. Some devices may be trailblazing, cutting-edge techniques; others may just codify what the great stage performers did before we learned to act for the camera instead of the hall. Whether in class, workshop, rehearsal or perform-ance, all these approaches (many of which, certainly, are not original) have been developed, tested, and proven to improve actors' work. Obviously, given the volatile nature of live performance, nothing is guaranteed to work every time. To play your audience well really requires instinct developed over the course of a career onstage. This book aims to give you a head start.

In the spirit of Stanislavski, *Playing the Audience* summarizes my own experiences over two decades of directing, performing, and teaching, which I offer to you as a practical guide to putting on really good shows. You will see that a great deal of work is necessary to keep your playing from *looking* like work. Then you get the audience to do *their* work by making it, like your own, as irresistible as . . .

   . . . play.

CHAPTER 1
THEATRICALITY

What we really do when we stage a play is orchestrate the journey of how we hope to play with the audience. This play—or interplay—is *theatricality*.

This word has been used as a pejorative, to suggest histrionics, overacting, chewing the scenery, showing off, and self-indulgence. I am using it to suggest the very opposite. Overacting for its own sake is virtually never a goal, with the rare exception of mime, burlesque, and certain other stylized methods of storytelling. In realistic drama, theatricality should be so subtle that the audience will not even realize they are being "played." Like heightened emotion, interplay wants to grow naturally out of the moment and be earned, not forced. The greatest technique is invisible. So for the most part, *don't let anyone catch you acting.*

The word *theater* comes from a Greek word meaning "a place for looking at something."[3] To take into account who is watching, then, defines the theater. Thus we face the audience, project to the back row, and so on. Theatricality means playing the audience—not necessarily playing *to,* but *with*—whether you let them know that you are doing so or not.

The point of the play is the play *of the play.*

Consideration of the audience will affect all your creative choices so that you present the most exciting theater possible.

COMPLICITY

The quintessential theatrical acting moment reputedly produced the longest laugh in live television history. Jack Benny, you may recall, always made himself the butt of jokes about being a skinflint. In one sketch from *The Jack Benny Show,* masked bandits knocked on his door and pulled guns on him, one of them saying, "All right, Mr. Benny, your money or your life." At which point Benny had no recourse but to turn to the audience to ponder his decision in the way only he could: palm on cheek, nonplussed. The studio audience chuckled, then laughed, then howled, then started chuckling, laughing, and howling again—and so it continued.

Why was this so funny? The silence asked the audience to understand his conflict: should he save his money or his life? Yet they could not help because they had no lines. So they were stuck at the impasse together. The silence got progressively funnier not because of what Jack Benny did, but because of the work he got the spectator to do: to look at the circumstances from his own point of view. Yet he hardly did a thing but turn his head and need their help—in absolute deadpan. Whatever you might think overacting could be, Jack Benny embodied the opposite; the audience did all the work. All he did was invite their *complicity*.

Complicity:
Each actor is in a relationship of complicity with the audience in putting on the play, and enlists their allegiance in looking at the world from the point of view of his own character.

(You may already be familiar with this principle in the form of rehearsal etiquette that says: Actors do not give notes to other actors. What one might think of as helpful actually tends to sabotage a fellow actor's independent complicity with the audience. At rehearsals, I even discourage the saying aloud of anyone else's text, for "to name it is to own it." If you have a great idea for another actor, suggest it to the director—in private.)

Beware of reducing theatricality to *presentational* as opposed to *representational* acting. The former suggests blatantly doing everything for the audience, perhaps at the expense of being true to life, like facing them directly and seeming to neglect the character you are addressing. The latter suggests trying to reproduce life onstage, as if being in character meant ignoring the spectator. Theatricality transcends the distinction between the presentational and the representational, exploiting both at the same time in order to be *invitational.* Jack Benny's invitation became irresistible because the complicity was so strong; then, the fact that everyone was in on the joke—both bandits and audience—became the joke.

Complicity is also why actors wait until the audience's laughter peaks before continuing with the next line. For the play's characters, nothing has been changed by the laughter. Why, then, do the actors hold up their dialogue when the audience laughs, undermining their characters' drive? Because the rule that says, "be true to your character" is superseded by one that says, "the audience must be able to hear every word." *The world of the play's characters defers to the audience experiencing it.*

Unless the fourth wall is actually broken, playing the audience does not mean breaking your communication with the others onstage; while addressing another character, you also speak for the audience's benefit, although you may not be looking at them. *You engage both the audience and the other character(s) at the same time.* Thus in three-quarters stance (once called "one-quarter open position"), your character may have no reason to open up to the audience; but you as the actor must.

Essentially, three-quarters position is a theatrical technique that helps you take the audience along. When you look at the other character, your body is still facing the audience; and when you look toward the audience, your body is still facing the other character. You are present as the character in the play and as the actor in the theater at the same time, and can play with both believability and complicity. The manipulation of this *dual connection* is the hallmark of live acting.

Thus you put on makeup, find the light, and play to the back row in a proscenium theater: If you play to the front rows, the folks in back see the shadow that your forehead casts on your eyes; if you play the back row, you include the entire audience, and your eyes are lit. Then the audience can see every little thing your character (who would probably rather hide) does.

Complicity, invitation, dual connection—all are really the same thing: your rapport with the audience.

THEATRICAL TRUTH

In addition to your character's objectives, you always play the *theatrical objective*: to win the audience, even if this means doing something your character would never do. But this makes sense after all, for a dramatic character does not really "exist" outside of the drama, which is born only when the audience arrives.

"Theatrical truth" is something of an oxymoron: a dramatic character is, after all, fictional. Our truth is not a mere factual truth. What we put onstage does not reproduce real life, but distorts it, through proportion, emphasis, shape, and so forth, to make a point. Stage life may derive from, but does not duplicate, Nature.

Naturalism does have its place in the live theater: when it suits how you want to affect the audience. But be wary of letting the quest for naturalistic veracity short-circuit a performance; on some level, never forget the spectator. In a lifelike production, you want your interplay with the audience to be unnoticed, but it is the paramount feature of live performance nonetheless.

When striving for this lifelike quality, it might help you to think in terms of *verisimilitude*. This word's etymology suggests what you are actually doing when you act: not being "real," but "real-like" (*veri-* + *similitude*). This is far more freeing than realism per se. The actor does not reproduce life, but creates and re-creates what we might think of as "Life in *Art*" (coincidentally, the title of one of Stanislavski's books).

Great plays exploit the distinction to the hilt. Hamlet gave his players the best advice ever: to speak the words "trippingly on the tongue" rather than "mouth" them; not to "saw the air too much with your hands, thus; but use all gently"; to "acquire and beget a temperance that may give [passion] smoothness"; and above all:

> Be not too tame neither, but let your own discretion be your tutor: suit the action to the word, the word to the action; with this special observance, that you o'erstep not the modesty of nature: for anything so overdone is from the purpose of playing, whose end, both at the first and now, was and is, to hold, as 'twere, the mirror up to nature. . . (III.2)

Hamlet had a specific goal in mind for which he wanted the players' acting to be so lifelike. He hoped that his uncle, King Claudius, seeing a public play with a story parallel to Claudius's murder of Hamlet's father, would "but blench" (blink or start) and give himself away. For Hamlet had heard

> That guilty creatures, sitting at a play,
> Have by the very cunning of the scene
> Been struck so to the soul that presently
> They proclaim'd their malefactions. . . . (II.2. 586ff.)

Hamlet knew that someone accused outright would muster his defenses, whereas if you could catch him just happening to see himself in a play—ah, well, that is theater.

So Hamlet wants his players extremely believable. Why then interrupt the performance time and again as a nasty emcee? To make sure the audience is following the story. More important than Claudius getting lost in the play is that he engage and react. This is also why the text of *The Murder of Gonzago* is in rhyme. Each interruption and rhyme reminds Claudius he is watching a play, not real life; these reminders make him feel safe enough to let his guard down.

Today, curtains dropping, blackouts, and applause function as similar reminders. Just when the audience becomes most involved in the plot at the end of Act I, they get reminded once more by the intermission. Are audiences supposed to "suspend disbelief" during the action of a scene, yet still clap at the end of it? Yes and no; part of them knows they are watching a play and that the suspense will be relieved. This knowledge provides that psychological safety net allowing them, like Claudius, to be "struck to the soul" during the scene, particularly when the action becomes acutely threatening, horrifying, or painful. (This is a lot like Brecht's theory, except he wouldn't want anyone jumping up.)

Theater does hold the mirror up to nature, but it might just be a fun-house mirror. The more distorted the mirror, the more theatrical the performance. Distortion = form. And form is something an artist purposefully molds, contrives, perfects.

Life onstage is not just like life off stage; it is formed life, conceived of passion, fertilized by imagination, and contrived by a storyteller for a purpose.

This purpose may be merely to entertain, but usually more is involved. Hamlet as the director tailored his players' "cunning" to get a jolt out of Claudius and avenge his father's murder.

"Truthful acting" signifies not so much a reproduction of real events, but actions, reactions and emotions that emerge from being truly connected and in the moment, given a set of circumstances that are not actually true. Theatrical truth lies not in the fact that what the audience sees happened once in real life, or that it is happening to real people, but that it is really taking place right now in the theater. The characters may be fictitious, but they are *here*. The audience knows the play is happening because they can see it happening.

And the path from actor to audience is a two-way street: the live theater audience is able to affect the performance as well as vice versa. If someone coughs, cries or claps, the actors hear. The pretense that the audience is not there would be a lie, for everyone onstage can easily see that the audience is, in fact, there. Live acting—theatricality—is based on the premise that the audience is present rather than absent.

And there really is no "fourth wall" keeping the actor and audience apart. Even though for the characters there may be a fourth wall, for the audience and the actors, there never is. Everyone can see quite clearly: there is no wall there.

Your given circumstances, then, are never merely those of your character in the script. They include the following truths that are born when your character hits the stage:

- *The audience is there.*
- *The actor is an actor, playing a character.*
- *That character is a playwright's contrivance.*
- *The blocking is a director's creation.*
- *The stage scenery has been designed, as have been the costumes, lights, sound, makeup, and technical effects.*
- *The script is, in fact, a play (i.e., a vessel for playing).*

To deny any of these theatrical truths is, quite simply, to lie.

Theatricality transforms the "untruthful" goal of creating the "illusion of the first time," and instead has us acknowledge the *reality of the only time* that these particular actors and spectators are gathered together in the same place.

Part of acting, let's face it, *is* pretending—but think of it not as deceiving, but as play-acting, or *playing.* Good acting is pretending with conviction, so that the audience will join in your make-believe and see you as your character. Think of *acting* as "to assume the action" of the character for the duration of the performance. This is perhaps why in Greek tragedy the murder of a king had to occur off-stage and be reported by some messenger: to "kill" a king onstage would have constituted de facto regicide, not merely a portrayal of it. In other words, the theatrical truth of ancient Greek drama was what we might call "*ultra*-verisimilitude" or "sur-realism" not in the sense of dream reality, but of higher reality.

This could explain Aristotle's "unity of time," confining epic tragedy's events to a single day or slightly more. In ancient Greece, any production's built-in lighting plot was the sun in the sky. For the plot to jump a day would have been an untruth, obvious to everyone in the audience. In its origins, the drama took place in the space and time in which the audience witnessed it.

It still does.

CHARACTER

Stanislavski's *objective* ("what does my character want?") is far more concerned with generating action than with pretending. His Magic *If*— "If I were the character in this situation, what would I do?"—has you tap into *I, character,* and *situation* to come up with what you *do.* So a character is someone that does, not merely something that is. Notice that the word *act* is right in the middle of the word *character,* reminding us that action is at the heart of it.

Character is defined by action.

The process of acting, then, is not fundamentally pretending, but getting the vessel of your soul to the point where you must take action. To *must* is one of the actor's most important tasks.

It is not enough to find the *must* in rehearsals, block the show, and repeat the form. To create something and then be done with it describes the process involved in essay, painting, sculpture or film; but in the theater, you are not finished with the process of creating your role until closing night. The actor must *must* every time he performs to give rise to every gesture.

Gesture

Gesture can refer to anything you do in performance, from traveling across the stage to raising an eyebrow. In film acting, gesture can be almost invisible, largely psychological and emotional—inner life. The cameraman provides close-ups, and later the director, editor, and composer put shots and sounds together to guide the viewer through the story. Telling a story onstage, especially in a large hall, entails an extra responsibility: making sure that the balcony does not miss what you are going through.

For example, in the movies, when detective Philip Marlowe gets a phone call from his client telling him that she is on Westlake, the camera cuts to a shot of his car driving through the streets of Los Angeles, then to a shot of the motel with the "Vac_ncy" sign blinking, then to a shot of the number 19 dangling from one of the doors. Next we see a fist knocking on the door, which opens, seemingly by itself. Then the camera enters the room, and finally the detective walks into view. The viewer provides the causal links and puts together the story that the phone call led Marlowe to drive to the motel and find a dead body. The actor need but think and the movie will convey the logical sequence of his thoughts. He does not even need to raise an eyebrow when he sees a clue; the film lets the viewer know that Marlowe is thinking something by a simple cut to his face, perhaps accompanied by a music cue.

Onstage, however, the phone call must be *perceived* as the reason Marlowe rises from his desk, leaves his office, gets in his car, and so on. Absent a cameraman or editor, the actor's gestures provide the causal links that take the audience along.

Appropriately, stars who played Marlowe in the movies could *do nothing* with great charisma—Bogart, Mitchum. In contrast, the Inspector in a stage thriller is invariably an eccentric personality who gestures frequently and floridly. This more histrionic sense of gesture functions as a sort of close-up, helping the audience see into the actor's mind. Deadpan like Marlowe's, which relies on the close-up to betray intent, tends not to work onstage.

> ***Every gesture is made to involve the audience in another facet of the inner life of the play.***

This principle does not provide a license to overact. As Hamlet said, "suit the action to the word, the word to the action." (The word "action" here suggests what we refer to as "gesture.") How do you know when it "suits"? A good beginning answer to this question is: when you can find the *must*. The best choices for gesture:

- involve your character taking action;
- require another character to react;
- move the play forward;
- help take the audience through that forward motion, or at least through what the character is experiencing; and/or
- make the text clearer.

If none of the above, the gesture should at least:

- make the moment deliciously interesting.

In other words, ask yourself: will it make the performance more colorful? and be worth it? Sometimes you will need vibrant, eccentric choices to flesh out your role. (Often they will end up being linked to your character's psychological makeup after all: whoopin', hollerin', and hyper-ventilatin' are not just what an actor will do to entertain, but what a character will do when stakes are high.) But beware of coming up with a colorful characterization that does not necessarily fit in the play; this could happen if too many of your choices convey mere "color" when the drama demands more substance.

> ***A must lies at the source of every acting gesture.
> But onstage every must embraces a tacit proviso:
> "I must" do such-and-such " . . . for the audience."***

In light of this, I often tell actors to "act *over* the audience." How?

For one, there is great theatrical power to be found in tactile connection: props you handle, furniture you pull out, other actors you graze or grab. Physical contact automatically connects you to your environment, and includes the audience even as you stay in the scene. By squeezing or stroking harder, or interrupting your pencil's tapping pattern, or breaking its point, you can betray an inner crisis without even looking up. Of course you must *need* to break that pencil point.

Every bit of blocking is a gesture; "cross down right" really means "desire to do something (you fill in the something) that *makes* you cross down right; then in the execution, either betray or hide that desire."

The actor has a lot more devices he can experiment with than fulfilling crosses, however. Keep this menu handy and feel free to add to it:

Ways to Betray Your Inner Life

- *Physically:* With outer appendages—tapping, drumming, playing with or touching props in revelatory ways; or through posture change; and so forth.
- *Vocally:* Stretching vowels, over-articulating consonants, raising your register to betray nervousness, lowering it to convey sultriness, and the judicious use of vocal life and *caesura* here and there (see p. 206).
- *Facially:* Rolling your eyes, smiling (but avoid mugging).
- Through *breath:* Remember, inhalation = inspiration. Try breathing in an idea—"in-spiring"—and you will be surprised how clear that unsaid thought can become. Think of Raymond Burr as Perry Mason, inhaling while interrogating a witness.
- Through *silence:* Especially when all eyes are on you and it seems you should speak.
- Through *charged stage business:* Turning your back to the audience (say, to hide), slamming a door (to vanquish).
- Through a *motif,* or repeated gesture, that you imbue with meaning: Captain Queeg's two steel balls in *Caine Mutiny.*
- Through *timing:* Sipping tea, puffing a cigarette, sitting or rising with meaning.
- Through *pace:* Talking faster to avoid some topic, or slower to underscore its importance. (For more on pace, see pp. 217-218)

Theatrical Paradoxes

Theatricality, then, builds on basic acting with a new set of theatrical circumstances, presenting a series of paradoxes.

- *You play the character while remaining yourself-the-actor at the same time.*
- *The audience is both present and not present.*
- *The author is both present and not present.*
- *The play takes place both onstage and in the audience.*
- *The play transpires not only in the time (and culture) of the characters, but also in that of the audience, the playwright, and the actors (any of which may be the same).*

Example. In Act II of Jean Giraudoux's *The Madwoman of Chaillot,* the well-spoken Ragpicker, the poorest of the poor, is asked by the four madwomen to defend all the evil people of the world in absentia in a mock trial. To do this he opts to speak as the Richest Man in the World, rather than as a lawyer, so that he can use the first person ("I . . ."). With this triple dose of charm— the actor playing the Poorest Man playing the Richest Man—he wins over certain swooning female characters and (one hopes) the audience, too.

In my production, the African-American playing the Ragpicker also served his own subversive voice. This was particularly evident in the beginning of his autobiography: "The first time money came to me, I was a mere boy, a little golden-haired child in the bosom of my dear family."[4] When he said "golden-haired," he elicited giggles in one moment and then sort of stared the audience down, miffed that his veracity as the Richest Man—and a blond—was doubted. His juggling of three roles at once, all three playing the audience, generated uproarious laughter.

SAFETY AND STING

All this fun was in support of Giraudoux's audacity in putting evil on trial— how subversive. Plato called Socrates, the philosopher who assumed this function, a gadfly. Giraudoux with *Madwoman* and Hamlet with his version of *The Murder of Gonzago* were pretty blatant in assuming this role, but usually the trick is not to let the audience in on the power of the gadfly's sting, so they will neither fear nor avoid it. Blithe romps like *Sugar Babies,*

Anything Goes, or any of the Marx Brothers' plays offer more than just irreverent fun: lacing their comedies are hidden manifestoes of anarchism as they "send up" authority, the class system, and even good manners.

Potentially, then, drama serves as society's moral arbiter, or gadfly. One might even think of theater as subversive by nature. If by chance you deem your current script tame and uncontroversial, it will behoove you to change that attitude. Even situation comedies like *I'm Not Rappaport* and *Social Security,* for example, challenge society's treatment of the elderly.

The more subversive a play, the more craft required to render it irresistible. This craft thrusts the playwright, actor, director, designer, and audience into a relationship of mutual complicity in each other's subversiveness.

Theater's dual role as moral arbiter and entertainer lies at the crux of another theatrical paradox: How do we serve the live audience while exploiting it, entertain while accusing, exhilarate while indicting? Theater intrinsically invites the audience to leave changed, but man's natural propensity is to resist that change which is, after all, traumatic.

Hamlet's audience was in fact duped into attending under false pretenses. If his play had accused Claudius outright, not only would the king have stopped it earlier, but Hamlet would be indicted for treason. Could we seduce Claudius into buying a ticket to *The Murder of Gonzago* today if he knew that our ulterior design was his own undoing?

We want the audience to come in and to come back, so we provide fun and safety to make it enjoyable and repeatable. How? For one, we invite rather than indict. This invitation can come in all sorts of guises. Hamlet deploys many of them: diversion, humor, charm, grace, lunacy, intimacy, vulnerability, need, and audience participation.

Example: Brian Bedford is not only charming, but also the consummate theatrical performer. In the Roundabout's production of *London Assurance* on Broadway in 1997, he would address the audience from time to time and elicit their response. At one point, the loudest laugher in the audience determined the location toward which he looked and gestured, as if to say, "See? She agrees with me! I'm right." This bolstering from the audience spurred him on to further audacities throughout the play.

In his first entrance as *Timon of Athens,* he opened his arms and beamed, delighted to see everyone, actors and audience alike. It was a warm, memorable outburst of grace and intimacy.

In needing the audience, you might go so far as to "break" the fourth wall, or even break *through* it. Take care, however, that the audience does not feel you are an invader but rather a welcome guest.

Example: In *The House of Bernarda Alba,* the insane grandmother, Maria Josefa, wakes up in the middle of the night hallucinating, seeing images of babies everywhere. In my production, once the audience realized that, in her mind, *they* were those babies, she went further, and crossed through the fourth wall into the center aisle. This gave them a case of the willies similar to the one her granddaughter Martirio was suffering onstage, trying to get her grandmother back to bed (Act III). The moment worked because Maria Josefa loved babies, and hence, the audience. The willies were tempered by warmth. My actor would even see if she could get away with caressing one "baby" in the front row; but this was not possible at every performance, for you cannot force, nor re-create, rapport. Each night, the actor had to win the audience before she could play with them so aggressively, enlisting all her grace and daftness to do so.

Of course in some productions, particularly of naturalistic plays, you should not look at the audience directly, never mind approaching where they sit. But even without visibly acknowledging them, their reactions will inform your performance rhythmically and psychologically, for they are part of your theatrical circumstances.

When the play finally gets to the stuff that's hardest to take—the muck and mire of human horror—then we apply the Aesop Effect:

Let the spectators figure out how the moral pertains to themselves, rather than rubbing their noses in it.
Invite rather than indict.
Enthuse rather than accuse.

Hamlet's invitation was irresistible, and Claudius bit, betraying his guilt all by himself by suddenly stopping the show; no treasonable indictment was necessary. Before Claudius realized what Hamlet was up to, he could have been enjoying the play as much as anyone. Hamlet exploited theatricality to expose the jugular vein of truth. You can, too.

The safer the audience feels, the more involved they will get. Think of taking the audience on a roller-coaster ride. If you don't fasten their safety belts, they will fasten their own. But once they are buckled up and on the way, you can have fun together. Try giving them a glimpse of the loop-de-loop ahead; if you make it a real doozy, you generate incredible suspense. Maybe you even need their help to navigate it successfully.

Sometimes the audience does more than merely take the ride. In *Peter Pan,* you require the children in the audience to clap their hands for Tinker

Bell's life; *The Mystery of Edwin Drood* has a different murderer every night, depending on how the audience votes. In other words, the audience actually helps build the roller coaster's scaffolding as the ride proceeds.

But there are many other functions to assign the audience, which they are most eager to fulfill. Just as Maria Josefa did in *Bernarda Alba,* you can cast them in a role.

CASTING THE AUDIENCE

A novelist, facing the blank page, will often get her juices flowing by ascribing to her reader a specific identity. Radio announcers and voice-over actors visualize a real person so they can talk to someone other than a cold microphone in a sound booth. Stage actors apply the same principle.

In direct address, no contrivance is required on your part to talk to the audience, for that is indeed to whom your character is talking—the living, present spectators. Your soliloquy will be more effective, though, if you determine a specific rapport with them that will propel your speech, and then assign them an attribute to establish that relationship. Do they approve of your actions? Or are they disappointed in your shortcomings?

Or you can go further and actually cast them in a role. You might (1) cast them as your best friend and confidant, your shoulder to cry on, your enemy and accuser, or as both the little devil and angel tormenting your conscience (they sit on your left and right shoulders, respectively). If you are portraying Don Juan, play to an audience of philandering husbands rooting for you. If you portray one of the women he seduces and then jilts, your audience may comprise sympathetically forlorn lovers.

If you think your character just has to be talking to himself, then (2) cast the audience as the Self whom you are addressing. Actually visualize a hall full of people who are you. You render your soliloquy intimate and theatrical at the same time, because talking to the audience = talking to yourself.

You can also (3) play the geographical layout of the audience as a spatial diagram of your logic, especially when your ideas are complex. For example, the left and right can be cast as liberals and conservatives. In a large hall, try playing your character's references to God as if He lives in the balcony; ditto when your dialogue mentions "grace," "goodwill," or such personifications as a muse of fire.

If it helps, think about the technique in this way: (4) treat the audience as if they were agents of your imagination, sitting inside your mind, but let your mind—and heart—expand to fill the entire hall. The theater is, after all, a metaphor for the Soul of Man: why not exploit it as a metaphor for yours?

Alternatively, if your production "uses" a fourth wall, you can (5) place that fourth wall behind the back row, rather than in front of the first row, so that you define the audience as an extension of the scenery. It is rather obvious to play the whole hall as spectators or jurors at a trial, or guests at a wedding ceremony, when the script so suggests. But you can also play them as something other than an audience, letting the balcony "play the role of" a mountain, treating the back row of the orchestra as the road to Moscow.

Or (6) complete your fourth wall by putting objects on it that allow you to look toward the audience. The typical example is to put a mirror or window downstage, so that your character can just happen to look in it (or through it) at moments when you want the audience to read your mind, without violating the world of the play. When looking at a mirror on the fourth wall, the audience readily accepts that your character sees her reflection, while *you* see them. We often place an imaginary mirror behind the back row of the audience so that you, while looking downstage, can believably "see" the other actor standing on the side or even upstage of you— he looks toward them, where the mirror is, in order to see you. If you ever rehearse in a dance studio, practice using the mirror.

The script will offer suggestions for roles in which to cast the audience. When a dramatic character talks about society, mankind, or any subset thereof, the playwright expressly wants you to provoke the audience to a reaction, either agreement or reproof. So (7) try addressing these comments about the audience directly to them, even if not written as direct address per se: they sit most eagerly as the living metaphor for "society" and "people out there." An actor in Shakespeare's company could refer to "the world" quite easily by addressing the entire Globe Theater; so can you.

All seven of these devices are but the practical application of Stanislavski's observation that the eyes are the window to the soul.

Find ways to share the back of your eyes with the audience to involve them, especially at your character's richest moments.

See if you can get away with looking right at the audience during those moments. If you cannot, try looking in their direction without letting them know you see them. If that still does not work (your director will be your guide), then at least lift your head up and breathe so that the audience can see what you are thinking.

The following menu is a good starting point for the sorts of instances when you may want to try playing the audience, overtly or invisibly.

Play the audience:
1. *When playwrights tell you to, at moments of*
   - *direct address, soliloquy and asides.*
2. *Charged subtext and other huge unsaid things: when you want the audience to read your mind or need their particular attention, allegiance, or participation because the dialogue entails:*
   - **irony,** *or other moments when your inner meaning contrasts with the text;*
   - **conjecture,** *so the audience sees the possible future;*
   - **memories, nostalgia, stories,** *and* **anecdotes,** *so the audience sees the past;*
   - **missing characters** *whom you discuss but are off stage at the time, or who may never appear in the play;*
   - **apostrophe,** *when you address someone who is not there—either a real person or a*
   - **personified abstraction;**
   - *other* **references absent** *from the stage, images you want your audience to picture;*
   - **intangibles** *or other* **abstract thoughts,** *so the audience sees your images palpably;*
   - *situations where* **humor or ludicrousness** *is in your mind (e.g., Jack Benny, see pp. 1-2);*
   - **rhetorical questions,** *which you want the audience to answer;*
   - **silent crises** *during which you need the audience's help, including minor moments when your character changes in circumstance or resolve;*
   - **philosophy** *and* **social commentary:** *when referring to "the world," "humanity" or portions thereof, like "men and women";*
   - **platitude, epigram,** *and* **wit,** *which are brief instances of such commentary.*
3. *Any other time it works.*

Knowing when it works is problematic. This is the point where the director steps in, and later, audiences. On Broadway, once those preview audiences start coming, shows can change drastically, or even close. This is because the audience does half the work: the experiential part. The actor can invite all he wants, but Invitation is a two-way street. If you challenge, coerce or intimidate them unduly or too soon, they may decline to get involved. Don't invade—invite.

***Invite the audience;
then let them
invite you
to play them.***

Then, over the course of the evening, let this interplay grow.

Example. The Importance of Being Earnest opens with Algernon comparing himself to other pianists:

> I don't play accurately—any one can play accurately—but I play with wonderful expression.

The "any one" who is missing from the stage—the accurate piano player—is a perfect role in which to cast the audience. But this fourth sentence of the play is perhaps too soon to demand active role-playing of the spectators, who are busy assimilating the dramatic circumstances and the funny English accents. They may need a few moments to fasten their seatbelts, look at the roadmap, and adjust the rear-view mirror. So we scored the first beat of audience interplay later (the twelfth speech of the first scene) after Algernon and his manservant, Lane, established a bit of context:

> Algernon: Is marriage so demoralizing as that?
> Lane: I believe it is a very pleasant state, sir. I have had very little experience of it myself up to the present. I have only been married once. That was in consequence of a misunderstanding between myself and a young person.

We wanted the audience to "see" the young person Lane had once married. Therefore our Lane placed the image of his wife in the audience. In fact, he was to find her sitting in the audience somewhere if he could, as if she were present watching the play.

We learned from the opening preview that placing the image of her in the front row (which sat on the same floor as the stage in this 99-seat theater) did not work. Even though the person he chose that night happened to be someone the actor knew personally, no one else in the audience was aware of that fact. Out of fear of being singled out later, the nearby spectators proceeded to sit on their hands—literally. This defensiveness quickly spread to the entire audience. For subsequent performances, therefore, Lane was to start looking for his wife toward the back of the audience. If some female spectator were to respond invitingly, he could then play her—

warmly—as the spouse in his memory. In other words, he (1) invited the audience to (2) invite him to (3) play them.

In Act II we went a little further. The spectators were transformed into Cecily's flower garden. She actually crossed to the front row to water their feet at the top of the act. Later, Gwendolyn went down the center aisle a few rows to observe the "tiered garden" (the rows of chairs) while inhaling their intoxicating aroma. Being from the city and unused to such flowers, she coughed—a joke which eased the tension of anyone in the flower bed who took exception to her proximity.

Once the audience had already been walked among and sniffed by the actors, it became relatively easy for them to get actively involved in the plight of the lovers in Act III. For several moments, the actors addressed—faced—the audience during the escalating argument. Almost as overtly as Brian Bedford in *London Assurance* (see example, p. 11), they appealed to the audience to root for their triumph over the class system that was keeping them apart.

Note the growth of interplay over the course of the evening. Handling the audience requires delicate treatment over the course of the show's run, too. For example, just as you learn your lines in order to forget them, try also to forget what the audience did last time. Let them provide reactions as spontaneous as you hope to make your performance; you, in turn, must play their reactions, not those of last night's crowd, for *you can't force a rapport with the audience.* To assume that the audience will react in a certain way is presumptuous and can even prove embarrassing. Some audiences will applaud, for example, when the star enters, some not. If you react dishonestly you might come off as pompous. Similarly, avoid laughing at your own character's jokes, or crying when you want to evoke sympathy.

Never do the audience's work for them.

Besides, crying (and even laughing) at yourself evokes pathos, not sympathy. Holding your head up through the storm of life imbues you with dignity which the audience will respect. This respect forms the basis of empathy—complicity.

More to the point, if you do too much work, the audience will quickly realize that they need not do any. You have excused them by encouraging them to sit back and merely watch instead of inviting them to participate. It will be very hard to jump-start them into fifth gear once they have been idling in neutral for most of the evening. Again, don't accuse, but don't excuse either—enthuse!

Casting *to* the Audience

In casting the audience, you make them your best friend, lover, jailer, or whatever. In casting your inner life out *to* them, you can invite them to play— themselves. Still, be specific with what you want from them, and then do not get upset if you feel you are not getting it. Fortunately, the theatergoer's natural propensity for empathy is strong.

Casting to the audience is like a fisherman hoping for a bite. The fisherman fashions his lure bright and attractive: you do the same.

Example. In Tommy Tune's production of *Cloud Nine,* fifteen parts were played by seven actors, each changing roles at intermission. Act I is a comic farce, taking place in a British colony during the Age of Imperialism, which the play indicts. Act II, taking place a century later with the same characters only a few decades older (through the magic of theater), is a contemporary feminist comedy where each role eventually soars in an introspective soliloquy. One actor, E. Katherine Kerr, played three parts: two in Act I, and one in Act II as the newly-divorced Betty, housewife and mother, who had been wronged time and again by her philandering husband in Act I.

In her Act II soliloquy, Betty confides in us about how recently she has started to "touch herself down there." This public admission of masturbation is nothing compared with what we have been through by this time in the play. (*Cloud Nine* unashamedly exploits the brazenness of a sex comedy, but it is ultimately about the unbridled, self-embracing human soul.) When Kerr began this speech to the audience, she was open to—and probably looking for—a response from us. In fact, she made me giggle, at which point she turned to smile directly at me sitting in the front row. I took the bait and she hooked me. This made me laugh more. And so it continued, her gracious discomfiture just about sending me to the floor in hysterics; the rest of the audience soon followed. Staying in character, she let the spontaneous rapport stop the show for a moment. When the audience calmed down, she proceeded with her monologue. What Betty had learned was how to love herself, and therefore how to give herself as well. As she finished, she glanced back at me with a smile before leaving the stage.

This turned out to be the climax of the play (in the American version). Seconds later during the curtain call, all fifteen characters bowed, one at a time. Each actor had to exit after his first bow for a quick costume change so that his second character could bow. Kerr's three characters bowed first, eighth, and fifteenth, the last being Betty's—and she took that bow right to me.

The performance exploited the peculiar love that exists between actor and spectator, anonymous yet real. I have never met this actor, but her performance showed me what theater can do.

So try to offer as much of yourself as you can, and accept back from your audience all that they offer you. But remember, more than what you do, live acting involves what you get the audience to do. Do not shy away from asking them to do more, and earn their compliance, or complicity, through increasingly infectious and intimate interplay.

Inner Dialogue

Complicity dictates that a good portion of your character's agenda will be to conceal your ulterior designs from the other character at the same time you as the actor betray them to the audience in the most intriguing way you can. Your rapport with the audience over the course of the performance might be thought of as *inner dialogue*. While inner monologue (see p. 41) brings *you* through the psychological flow of your character, inner dialogue brings the *audience* through the psychological flow of your interplay with them.

Think of the time you got an unpleasant phone call, say, from someone who talks too much, and your best friend was in the room. Your friend saw all your facial gestures—rolling your eyes, moving the receiver a few inches from your ear—which the listener on the other end of the line did not. He could both hear what you were saying and see what you were thinking. Onstage, all you have to do is place that best friend in the audience to generate the same kind of intimacy—and duplicity. The trick is: the guy on the other end of the line will be doing the same thing. Think of a split-screen shot of a phone call in a movie or television show like *Mad About You*. In Peter Ackerman's play, *Things You Shouldn't Say Past Midnight*, a 3 A.M. conference call between three apartments exploits this very device to hilarious ends.

Whether you look at the audience or not, your task is still to make the back row feel like that friend who is watching you talk to someone else on the phone. *Intimacy (with the audience) plus duplicity (with the other character) make a scene theatrically rich.*

There are two parts to inner dialogue: (1) what you ask, and (2) what the audience responds—and both parts remain unstated. It shapes everything you do (physically, emotionally, psychologically, vocally, theatrically, rhythmically) to provoke the reaction you desire from the audience, even when you do not acknowledge them. You can think of it as tacit promptings that apply to every moment you are onstage, such as:

- "You're with me, right, audience?"
- "You see things from my point of view now, huh?"

- "Can you believe he just said/did that?"
- "Can you tell me what I'm supposed to do now?"

In other words, inner dialogue orchestrates your appeal to the audience.

In children's theater and boisterous comedies, these concerns may be stated in the dialogue. Think of a children's play where Goldilocks is hiding while the Three Bears ask the audience: "Where did she go?" Half the audience is howling and pointing; the other half is saying "shhhh" because Goldilocks herself had already begged them: "Please don't tell."

This talking back is par for the course in children's theater. But when the audience does not talk back out loud, you still want them to respond silently, with inner dialogue. In this way:

All theater is children's theater.

Sometimes you can convey your inner dialogue blatantly, looking right at the audience: in a burlesque or spoof, you might point at your fellow actor, raise a brow, and purse your lips. Usually, though, you betray it subtly, while just happening to be looking in the audience's direction.

You can invite the audience to undergo their part of the inner dialogue without even looking toward them. Simply process your part: really think through it. Then breathe deeply, speak clearly, and think specifically, and chances are that the audience will participate in your thoughts and plight.

Inner dialogue actually derives from what we do in real life all the time: try to provoke a particular response from our listener. Oscar Wilde inflected his voice upward even when he spoke in declarative sentences, as if his inner dialogue were "what do you think about that?" or "don't you agree?" or possibly "I do hope that now you find me irresistible." Think of "half a question mark" after the following epigram—not quite asking, not quite declaring: "Work has always been the bane of the drinking classes[?]. . . " The ellipsis (". . .") is where you ask for a response.

People from the upper Midwest or Canada achieve a similar effect by adding "eh?" to a declarative sentence. And many young people now follow the Californian habit of inflecting upward, particularly when not wanting to hog the conversation or come off as bossy. Thus someone who says, "Like, the other day I was going to the grocery store? . . . " might really be asking, "You do want to hear this, right?" And a downer like "You are wrong!" might be disguised as, "Like, I'm not sure that's a very good idea?"

Inner dialogue fills everything you say or do with a specific intent. When you factor in the live audience as "one of the people listening to you," it provides you with a powerful and versatile tool for achieving heightened theatrical life economically, because it expressly activates your two-way current with the audience. And since it is unstated, any thought is fair game as long as it works.

Inner dialogue can even be your own rather than your character's, such as when the villain in a stylized melodrama encourages the audience to boo and hiss (for certainly the character wants to win the audience).

Example. In my production of *The Sunshine Boys,* the actor playing the buxom blonde in the vaudeville sketch in Act II had to struggle to maintain her dignity, because the script treated her as a sex object. So every time Neil Simon had the two Sunshine Boys break character to kvetch about something, she broke character, too, and let everyone know what she thought about the whole situation. Even though her character had no lines outside of the sketch itself, her inner dialogue featured such tacit observations as "Can you believe they used to write material like this? . . . These guys are so unprofessional, aren't they? . . . " and "Grace under pressure, right, audience?" Without taking any undue focus, she triumphed as the superior one in the scene.

If you have difficulty acknowledging the audience in your thoughts, then try simply talking to that other self inside your own mind. Construct a multi-part inner monologue between two (or more) conflicting facets of your psyche. Go through both parts so that (1) you allow the audience to follow your flow of thoughts, and (2) you make even introspection active and suspenseful rather than passive and pensive. The resulting unstated text would become the soliloquy or asides you would say if only you had the lines. (Soliloquy is not inner dialogue, because it is stated, but it might be thought of as "outer inner dialogue." Conversely, inner dialogue might be called "silent soliloquy.")

The Appeal of the Ineffable

Sometimes a dramatic moment will defy articulation in any words at all, even to yourself. Instead of silent soliloquy, the moment calls for raw, nonverbal emotion. How could you possibly state the unstated of something as powerful as Edvard Munch's painting *The Scream?* Words simply will not do.

So how do you act compellingly in moments when you don't even entertain a thought?

Perhaps you have had an acting teacher point out the area between your lower stomach and sternum, your physiological center. According to Eastern traditions, this center is also where your psychic center (or soul) might be thought of as "situated." Nearby are located your heart, lungs, diaphragm, pelvis, stomach, and bowels—your viscera, or guts. Metaphorically, we refer to these guts (along with brain, blood, sweat, and tears) as your *creative furnace*. Playing from the viscera may seem like a terribly amorphous concept, but those who practice Eastern disciplines like yoga or who have had some training in the Suzuki acting method understand that it takes a long time to be able to engage your center naturally, and then to share it thoroughly. When you see an actor who can do this, though, you know it. A theatrical actor can get his guts to fill the entire hall with an ineffable appeal to everyone in that hall.

Example. The quintessential illustration of what I am talking about was Frank Wood's performance as the *Side Man* on Broadway. Jazz musicians are not usually known for their gift of gab, at least not in their relationships with spouses. Every time his wife started a fight, he would try to say something in response, or think something, but his jaw would just drop and his eyes light up in utter, unutterable, frustration. He was trying so hard—to be a good husband and father, to be kind, to be reasonable, to be communicative—but all that came out was piercing silence.

Great moments of great performances flabbergast. The appeal of the ineffable also informs a thousand little thoughts and reactions over the course of the play. In life, some of our deepest thoughts are not verbal. So as you get more in character over the course of a run, and as you amass more experience over your career, you may not need to assign words to every moment when you want the audience to share what you are going through.

SCORING

To share your inner life with your audience, you convert what you think, feel, or want into something you do. Stanislavski used the term *scoring* to refer to the process of structuring that inner life as a sequence of psychological actions which you then transform into physical actions and activities—gestures.

For an exclusively inner-to-outer process to work requires a lot of time and trust. Arthur Miller, in his autobiography *Timebends,* discusses the producer's doubts about Lee J. Cobb's abilities before the opening of *Death of a Salesman.* For some of the best actors, impressing is simply not a goal of rehearsal. Cobb and director Elia Kazan had impeccable timing, however, and come opening night the play was a great success.

Respecting this inner-to-outer process in others—possibly in you, dear reader—how can I invite you to become the most exciting actor you can possibly be? By suggesting that you augment your approach. Remember that your theatrical objective mandates involving the audience; feel free to score gestures to serve not just your personal process, but also your audience.

How your character tries to influence other characters in the play furthers dramatic action; how you-the-actor affect the audience, we might call *theatrical action*.

Stay active with your audience at all times.

Harold Baldridge, director of the late Sanford Meisner's Neighborhood Playhouse School, has been known to give such result-oriented notes as "it needs pizzazz there," "vary your tactics," and "pick up the pace." I was delighted to hear these suggestions and told him so. He responded, "Oh—well, the audience is coming."

Example. The Montana Repertory Theater employs a few students and recent graduates in its touring production each year. When I directed *The Sunshine Boys,* a student played Ben, the perfect straight man to his curmudgeonly Uncle Willy. Before blocking the first scene, I first encouraged him to execute the Stanislavski-based process he had studied, scoring inner actions and gestures, by himself; I would then help mold what he came up with. But rehearsal hours were ticking by and he was not coming up with a thing. After talking to his professors I realized he wasn't going to. Apparently the more experienced students and recent graduates had not been available that season; this student, a junior, was still young creatively. He was in over his head and we had a show to get up.

In the first scene, the nephew unpacks groceries for the reclusive uncle while trying to get him to agree to see his old vaudeville partner Al, with whom Willy has been feuding for years. The mechanics of Ben's task gave us a creative option: choreographing a series of percussive physical actions to the text. Each clang of a can on a counter, slam of a cabinet, and even the moment he banged his head on the refrigerator door, was timed (not unlike Homer Simpson's "d'Oh!") to come between particular words, at moments of exasperation at Willy's cantankerous one-liners. Once he got the rhythm of those 20–25 cues in his body, he devoted rehearsals to listening, varying reactions, building, and fighting not to be daunted. Opening night, more than one of his teachers asked me how I got him to act.

> *"If the external characterization does not appear spontaneously,*
> *it must be grafted on from the outside."*
> *— Constantin Stanislavski[5]*

Say you have determined seven moments of inner action in a scene. If seven interesting gestures appear spontaneously every time you act the scene, then your instrument is already a wonderful conductor for your inner life: you may be one of those blessed actors who have to be careful not to over-act. But if nothing happens, and your audience (or director) has no sense of your seven inner actions, and your performance is uninteresting, then other measures are called for.

See if you can get your character to, perhaps, giggle through moment 1, breathe deeper at 2, kick something at 3, bite your lower lip at 4, raise your voice at 5, look up toward the audience at 6, and puff your cigarette at 7. Then there is always the cough, the stutter, the inhaled-thing-not-said, the silence when you should speak, the rolled eyeballs, the forced smile, the vo-cal life ("mm hmm"). Be careful of one such device becoming your trade-mark, or you could quickly become a caricature of yourself. (One Tony-winning actor too often stretches her tongue to tap her upper lip, though her range is far beyond that.) Remember to (1) engage your entire instrument, including your viscera; and (2) trust the audience to "get it." Captain Queeg had a lot more going on than just fondling some steel balls, but all he had to do was fondle those balls.

Of course it is best if the seven gestures spring forth naturally during the course of rehearsing the scene; then you just need to try to regenerate them every time. But in the absence of that, you might try "grafting."

Scoring Audience Events
1. Mark *your script at each event for your character.*
2. Choose varied *devices to involve the audience at each event.*
3. Distill *them to the ones you really need.*
4. Discard conscious knowledge *of technique to make your work invisible and your performance organic.*

Example. To illustrate, we turn to Act I of Ibsen's *Hedda Gabler.*[6] Soon after the newlywed Tesmans arrive home, they receive a visitor in Mrs. Elvsted, an old schoolmate of Hedda's. Mrs. Elvsted announces that a friend of Mr. Tesman's from long ago, Eilert Lövborg, is back in town. She begs Tesman to receive him warmly. Hedda sends her husband off to the next room to write Lövberg an ingratiating note so she can have a moment alone with her old school chum.

But exactly how chummy were they? The scene is fraught with intrigue as Hedda strokes and flatters her guest to pump her for information for some mysterious reason. Eventually Mrs. Elvsted even confides that she has left her husband:

HEDDA: (*after a short silence*) And what are your plans now? What are you thinking of doing?

MRS. ELVSTED: I don't know yet. I only know this, that I must live here, where Eilert Lövberg is—if I am to live at all.

HEDDA: (*takes a chair from the table, seats herself beside her, and strokes her hands*) My Dear Thea—how did this—this friendship—between you and Eilert Lövberg come about?

MRS. ELVSTED: Oh, it grew up gradually. I gained a sort of influence over him.

HEDDA: Indeed?

MRS. ELVSTED: He gave up his old habits. Not because I asked him to, for I never dared do that. But of course he saw how repulsive they were to me; and so he dropped them.

HEDDA: (*concealing an involuntary smile of scorn*) Then you have reclaimed him—as the saying goes—my little Thea.

MRS. ELVSTED: So he says himself, at any rate. And he, on his side, has made a real human being of me—taught me to think, and to understand so many things.

HEDDA: Did he give you lessons too, then?

MRS. ELVSTED: No, not exactly lessons. But he talked to me—talked about such an infinity of things. And then came the lovely, happy time when I began to share in his work—when he allowed me to help him!

HEDDA: Oh, he did, did he?

MRS. ELVSTED: Yes! he never wrote anything without my assistance.

HEDDA: You were two good comrades, in fact?

MRS. ELVSTED: (*eagerly*) Comrades! Yes, fancy, Hedda—that is the very word he used!—Oh, I ought to feel perfectly happy; and yet I cannot; for I don't know how long it will last.

HEDDA: Are you no surer of him than that?

MRS. ELVSTED: (*gloomily*) A woman's shadow stands between Eilert Lövberg and me.

HEDDA: (*looks at her anxiously*) Who can that be?

MRS. ELVSTED: I don't know. Some one he knew in his—in his past. Some one he has never been able wholly to forget.

HEDDA: What has he told you—about this?

MRS. ELVSTED: He has only once—quite vaguely—alluded to it.

HEDDA:	Well! And what did he say?
MRS. ELVSTED:	He said that when they parted, she threatened to shoot him with a pistol.
HEDDA:	(*with cold composure*) Oh, nonsense! No one does that sort of thing here.

You are playing Hedda.

Step 1. See if you can find all the playwright's clues that point to huge unsaid things that you will want to play with the audience, and mark them with a pencil. When you have finished, read on.

For those unfamiliar with the end of the play, factor in this additional knowledge: Hedda has doomed herself to a life of relative poverty now that she has married a mediocre academic. Act I ends with her turning for consolation to her father's old pistols. In retrospect, then, you know that Hedda is in fact the mysterious pistol-wielding woman in Eilert's past.

Now revise your choices to make sure they elicit this particular sense of intrigue. In doing so, remember that events between Hedda and the audience occur not only when she is speaking, but also during Mrs. Elvsted's lines.

In Mrs. Elvsted's first line, for example, through her declaration of how important Eilert is to her, she unwittingly declares herself a threat to Hedda. There is now conflict of which only one of the characters is aware. Hedda's sitting next to her and stroking her hands is a physical action to betray excruciating jealousy and desire to control. Then her use of the ironic "my dear Thea" diminishes her unsuspecting rival. The two dashes: "—how did this—" and the euphemism "this friendship" reveal the volcano of jealousy in Hedda. Mrs. Elvsted's casual declaration, "I gained a sort of influence over him," must generate a huge covered reaction from Hedda, who despairs of ever having any influence over anybody. Ibsen's prescription for Hedda's cover is the euphemism, "Indeed?" Hedda, as cool as she can be on the outside, is actually wretched inside.

All these moments are a lot like Hedda's "having a friend over" while she is "on the phone" with Mrs. Elvsted; that friend is the audience.

Think about the inner dialogue you want to evoke during audience events you have identified, and continue revising your markings for the rest of the scene. Then read on to see one possible solution, starting with the sixth line in the excerpt. At the risk of being too detailed, I have marked (some of) the playwright's clues, besides his obvious stage directions, and my assessment of them in brackets {}.

MRS. ELVSTED:	He gave up his old habits. {*Clue:* **Euphemism; Hedda *is* "his old habits!"** *Audience:* **"Did Eilert renounce Hedda totally?"**} Not because I asked him to, for I never dared do that. But of course he saw how repulsive they were to me; and so he dropped them. {*Hedda:* **"Repulsive! We were wonderful together!"** *Audience:* **"Ah, now the conflict is clear—debauchery versus propriety. And Mrs. Elvsted doesn't even know that her enemy is the person to whom she is speaking!"**}
HEDDA:	*(concealing an involuntary smile of scorn* {*Clue:* **Stage direction prescribes huge unsaid thing.** *Audience:* **"Hedda could kill right now."**}). Then you have reclaimed him—as the saying goes {**forced politeness in conversation**}—my little Thea. {*Clue:* **Ironic again.** *Audience:* **"Why must Hedda's past affair with Eilert be secret? What is she plotting?"**}
MRS. ELVSTED:	So he says himself {*Hedda:* **"Ouch!—She has rehabilitated him without even trying to!"** *Audience:* **"Ah, he is now following Mrs. Elvsted's moral lead."**}, at any rate. And he, on his side, has made a real human being of me—taught me to think, and to understand so many things.
HEDDA:	Did he give you lessons too, then?
MRS. ELVSTED:	No, not exactly lessons. But he talked to me—talked about such an infinity of things. And then came the lovely, happy time when I began to share in his work—when he allowed me to help him!
HEDDA:	Oh, he did, did he? {*Clue:* **Understatement.** *Audience:* **"It seems he did not allow Hedda this privilege during their debauched affair."**}
MRS. ELVSTED:	Yes! He never wrote anything without my assistance. {*Hedda:* **"Does he actually need her more than he did me?—ouch!"** *Audience:* **"Eilert veritably *belongs* to Mrs. Elvsted and Hedda can't bear it."**}
HEDDA:	You were two good comrades {*Clue:* **Euphemism.** *Audience:* **"Hedda is trying to demote their relationship to a platonic one if she can."**}, in fact?
MRS. ELVSTED:	*(eagerly)* Comrades! Yes, fancy, Hedda—that is the very word he used! {*Clue:* **Repetition and exclamation marks.** *Hedda:* **"!%*$#@^&!, she really is replacing me."**}—Oh,

	I ought to feel perfectly happy; and yet I cannot; for I don't know how long it will last.
HEDDA:	Are you no surer of him than that? {*Audience* **and** *Hedda:* **"Maybe there is hope that their relationship is not so firm."**}
MRS. ELVSTED:	(*gloomily*) A woman's shadow stands between Eilert Lövberg and me. {*Hedda:* **"Of course there's another woman—me!"** *Audience:* **"Is this why Mrs. Elvsted has called on Hedda?"**}
HEDDA:	(*looks at her anxiously* {*Clue:* **Another charged stage direction**}) Who can that be? {*Audience:* **"The way Hedda just said that—now I'm certain the woman in Eilert's past is Hedda!"**}
MRS. ELVSTED:	I don't know. Some one he knew in his—in his past. {*Clue:* **The dash makes Mrs. Elvsted particularly mysterious.** *Audience:* **"What did Mrs. Elvsted just keep herself from saying?"**} Some one he has never been able wholly to forget. {*Hedda:* **"Ah—thank goodness!"** *Audience:* **"So there is still a trace of Hedda's fingernails left in Eilert."**}
HEDDA:	What has he told you—{*Clue:* **This dash betrays more involvement than friendly interest.** *Audience:* **"Hedda is soliciting information to plot something."**} about this?
MRS. ELVSTED:	He has only once—quite vaguely—alluded to it.
HEDDA:	Well! {*Clue:* **Interjection.**} And what did he say? {**Cool yet passionate interest at the same time.**}
MRS. ELVSTED:	He said that when they parted, she threatened to shoot him with a pistol.
HEDDA:	(*with cold composure* {*Clue:* **Stage direction.** *Hedda:* **"I must cover my reaction."**}) Oh, nonsense! No one does that sort of thing here. {*Clue:* **Hyperbole and exclamation mark; this is a blatant lie—but the audience does not know this for sure until the end of the act; Mrs. Elvsted in fact never finds out.**}

Note that what is not said takes up more room on the page than the lines themselves. With just about any good play from Ibsen's time till now, that will be the case. All the bold-faced comments are not conjecture, but rather emerge naturally from the text itself. So if you add one more of these unstated details each time you rehearse the scene, you will render the script as rich as the playwright conceived it.

Step 2. The script is so charged that you could almost do nothing and the unsaid will be clear—if the audience pays attention to every word. You have a slew of methods at your disposal to compel them.

For one, remember that Tesman is in the next room, and that this conversation is not for his ears. If you try placing that room behind the audience, then every time you look to make sure he is not coming in, you also let the audience get a good view of your eyes, and therefore a glimpse of your crisis.

For another, Ibsen already tells you to stroke Mrs. Elvsted's hands. By interrupting the pattern of stroking, and squeezing tight, or stopping suddenly, or patting instead of stroking, you can betray one of your sudden inner crises by trying to cover it. What if at some point you stood behind your "friend" to brush or even braid her hair? Then the audience would see everything that registers on your face without Mrs. Elvsted's seeing a thing. Maybe you get a little manic with one braiding twirl. Then, to compensate, suddenly you pet her over-kindly, like a puppy.

I leave it to you to supply each event with a specific gesture to evoke an audience response. Vary your choices. Then run the scene a few times.

Step 3. Next, eliminate what you find you don't really need after all, or what the audience won't need. If you can't execute your choice without its looking like one, it's probably too much.

Step 4. Try forgetting your work, or at least don't think about it; trust that a residue of the charge will remain nevertheless. (Stroke Mrs. Elvsted's hands when staged to, of course; but you should *need* to do so.) In a chemical reaction, the catalyst you add makes the other compounds react together to make some new compound, but you get that catalytic chemical back in the end. In dramatic terms, that chemical reaction generates the Catalyst Effect:

If you
(1) rehearse a staging choice at a moment you have
identified as an event, and then later
(2) eliminate it, that choice acts as a catalyst,
leaving an automatic, invisible-yet-sensible spark of interplay
without your having to do anything at all.

Your Hedda will be left with a series of events when you plan to play the audience. Remember: at each of these moments, you must need to play them.

* * *

Orchestration of audience events may sound like a lot of connecting the dots from one "bit" to the next, and not like the free-flowing process that turned you on in acting class. But when you think about what goes on in a rehearsal period, isn't such a list of moments and devices—cross here, rise there, turn left, cough—exactly what staging a show entails? and precisely what the stage manager records in the prompt book to maintain the show over a run (e.g., putting in replacement actors)? This orchestrated sequence of choices is the form of the show. The trick is to go through that form night after night, without its appearing orchestrated at all; and to make the life onstage as full and spontaneous as possible.

Simply repeating the form is not enough. You tap the inner life to find the *must* that will re-evolve the outer gesture, which in turn communicates something else. This process is one way in which Theatricality incorporates and builds upon Method acting: we use the Method to create a living, breathing performance *with* our audience, not in spite of them.

Of course a healthy process is integral to cultivating an excellent product, but process serves product, not the other way around. We can even violate a principle from our training when it makes for a better show. Process gives us tools, not rules; and the occasional rule is a tool, not a master. In other words:

The actor's product is the audience's process.

"Playing the audience," then, does not mean merely playing the audience. It means that you have a lot to say, and a lot you must not say, to everyone in the hall; and that when you say it or don't say it, you do so infectiously, with conviction, persuasion, and panache—theatrically.

SMOOTHNESS

Needing the audience does not necessarily mean playing them as overtly as Jack Benny. Hamlet coached his players to "acquire and beget a temperance that may give" their acting "smoothness." This applies to playing the audience. Beginners often work a scored audience event in distinct steps: "Now I am playing the other character/ Now I am playing the audience for a beat/ Now the scene resumes and I am playing the other character again." This shows the seams instead of the scene. (For naturalistic dramas, in other words, it is bad.) Rather than falling out of the scene to face out, as in a quick aside, try to let the rising stakes make you turn toward the audience in a gently evolving phrase (if you turn at all). While you may be looking away from the other characters, stay connected to them in every other way but with your eyes. Let smoothness and aplomb camouflage your craft.

You need not write the word *coffee* in bold letters on the mug; just make delicious coffee with an irresistible aroma, and serve it hot.

CHAPTER 2
MEANING

Meaning involves more than word definitions. It entails first a phase of *comprehension,* which refers largely to what the play does mean; then a phase of *analysis,* what it might mean; and finally how to get that information to inform your work, *interpretation,* or what the Meaning does. Comprehension is largely objective; analysis, subjective; and interpretation, creative.

In other words, Meaning involves understanding and then conveying that understanding from the page to the stage. Even the word *information* suggests more than mere data: it means "something that forms or gives form to." Remember this as we discuss Meaning, then: it all goes toward shaping—informing—your performance.

ACTABLE ANALYSIS

Comprehension is gleaned from various sources of character information:

1. *what your character says;*
2. *what your character does;*
3. *what other characters say; and*
4. *what the playwright says.*

In period plays like classics or other difficult pieces, the list typically expands to include mandatory research:

5. *what the playwright tells you to go find out.*

Sometimes the meaning is not obvious, or several meanings are possible. Different actors will come up with different interpretations, after all. So analysis includes, among other things, figuring out what your character is not saying—and why. A play's themes may also affect your choices for your character, who could even be ignorant of them. Only you as the actor cannot be ignorant of them. Thus the above list expands to embrace:

6. *what you happen to find out;*
7. *what the playwright hints at, including his themes;*

8. *how your character says what he says (language—see chapter 7);*
9. *what your character does not say (silence)—and why.*

As you can see, there's more to Meaning than word definitions.

Moreover, to endow a role with all the mystery and complexity of a living organism, and make it a personal creation at the same time, the actor must be free to imagine with abandon and to explore caprices whose validity need not be "proven." So interpretive gestures can be derived from and justified by the text—or not. Thus we expand our list once again to embrace:

10. *whatever works.*

Lest you think that this gives you free reign to do whatever you want, think again. When not derived from the script, interpretation needs to be supported by or at least consistent with it so as not to become nonsense.

The actor's analysis is not the same as the academic's, for while the latter *observes* the world of the play, the former *lives* in it. Certainly actors with a good academic foundation are much quicker to realize when a capricious choice is weak, inconsistent, or destructive. But keep the proper priority in mind as you read on: actable analysis—mining the Meaning—is never undertaken for its own sake, but always with a view to how it informs your work—and play—with the audience.

Analysis is not the goal, then, but the means. It is actable when it helps you come up with what you're going to do onstage. What is not useable is often best thrown away. Beware of becoming enamored of an idea that may be more suited to an essay than a performance. You might have known actors who have imposed Freudian interpretations on their roles, and then proceeded to act their analysis instead of the actual scene as written. Hamlet and Gertrude are not Oedipus and Jocasta. Understanding the Oedipus complex might free you up to tap some inner ugliness, but you can neither serve nor stage the Greek myth. I am not prescribing that you avoid these thoughts entirely, but once you have them they are best forgotten: they will still enrich your characterization, but automatically.

Actable analysis involves pulling the script apart, recognizing and interpreting clues both in the text and between the lines, and putting it back together again not just intellectually, but into the very blood and guts of your character so that the lines become your own.

Putting an automobile or a clock together requires knowledge not just of all its parts, but also of the intangibles: logic, causality, and mechanics. The mechanics of a play are:

11. **dramatic craft,** and
12. **human nature.**

Objective Information

The first four sources of actors' information come from the text itself, which is your best creative friend. But while the first two sources—what your character *says* and *does*—are pretty self-explanatory, the next two require a little putting of two and two together.

What Other Characters Say: Stage Directions in Dialogue

Other characters' dialogue is teeming with information for you to incorporate. Obviously, you should note when others' lines provide basic information about your character's history, personality, or circumstances. At times dialogue prescribes specific actions and reactions. At the most basic level, if another character asks yours to "sit down," this suggests that you were not sitting down the moment before (with rare, *rare* exception). Clues in the dialogue will inform not only many of your physical gestures but also your mood, attitude, point of view, or general deportment. Since everyone in *As You Like It* refers to Jaques as "melancholy," your Jaques had better be—or have a fabulous reason for being otherwise.

You should assess this information through the *filter of the speaker's bias,* for others may be misrepresenting you by mistake, design, or delusion. Iago, for example, lies about Othello. The audience's complicity in his lies involves them in his treacherous aim, which is the dramatic action.

At times, a character may not even know he is mistaken about another. How do you know when a character is, in fact, lying, or mistaken? Sometimes you simply do not know, which is one reason many plays support vastly different interpretations. The rule of thumb:

> *Assume a character is saying what he means*
> *and means what he says, unless:*
> • *the script provides evidence to the contrary;*
> • *that act of misrepresentation propels the action.*

Even innocent misrepresentation can move the action forward. Moreover, you should not simply discard false information about your role—especially when provided by another character of dubious integrity—as this may confuse the audience. Rather, the deception should prompt further investigation as to why that other character misrepresents yours, for this too is intriguing. In Wilde's *An Ideal Husband*, the apparently amoral gadabout is actually the highly moral savior of those with a terrible secret in their past. Here, a character's dubiousness helps to furnish the point of the play.

In addition to providing facts about your character's life, or attitudes others may have toward your character, authors once established general information like time, place, and atmosphere directly in the dialogue, since their productions did not enjoy much in the way of sets and lights.

Example. Newlyweds Juliet and Romeo lovingly bicker about whether the bird they hear is a lark or a nightingale; but they are really discussing what time it is. Romeo has just been banished for killing Tybalt accidentally and must escape before daybreak. The nightingale would signify time for another kiss (or whatever); the lark, a morning bird, that it is time to part:

Juliet:	Wilt thou be gone? It is not yet near day:
	It was the nightingale, and not the lark
	. . . .
	Believe me, love, it was the nightingale.
Romeo:	It was the lark, the herald of the morn
	. . . .
	I must be gone and live, or stay and die.
Juliet:	Yond light is not day-light, I know it, I:
	Therefore stay yet; thou need'st not to be gone.
Romeo:	Let me be ta'en, let me be put to death;
	I am content, so thou wilt have it so.
	. . . .
	Come, death, and welcome! Juliet wills it so.
	How is't, my soul? Let's talk: it is not day.
Juliet:	It is, it is: hie hence, be gone, away!
	It is the lark that sings so out of tune.
	. . . .
	O, now be gone; more light and light it grows. (III.5)

In all of literature we can hardly find a more passionate discussion of the hour. But pay attention to the *facts* as well as the emotions: this is the first morning after their elopement.

What the Playwright Says: Stage Directions

Not all stage directions are the playwright's. Before the early 1980s the acting edition would record stage directions from the first production as prescribed by the director and noted down by the stage manager for submission to the publisher. They would not necessarily be the playwright's ideas, nor would they always enjoy his sanction. And so actors are usually taught to cross out the stage directions in the script in favor of developing their own physical actions with the director. This is wise for the most part, especially for such picayune instructions as "cross left to sofa" when your sofa is on the right.

But some stage directions also provide much-needed clues. If you're supposed to be looking out the window, that would explain why you're talking about whom you see there. And a scripted pause requires you to investigate the dramatic action of that pause (we will discuss pauses later). So you may want to keep a clean copy of the script handy, just in case you reach an impasse in making sense of what's going on.

How do you know whose stage directions they are? When they involve character description or mood, or contain particularly beautiful prose, published stage directions will usually have come from the playwright's pen. For instance, popular reading editions of Ibsen's plays were published, like novels, before they were ever staged (often issued just before Christmas to make them best sellers). Since he wrote to be read, not just performed, he may have written more stage directions for the reader than would be necessary for the actor. Tennessee Williams's stage directions are particularly known for their poetic language, Shaw's for their verbosity.

EXTENDED TEXT

We turn now from objective to subjective information, from what is said to what it means. Analysis requires choice to render it actable: deciding on the meaning's importance and relative importance to your character. This phase of mining the Meaning involves a matter of opinion.

For the most part, a character says what she means and means what she says. Certainly adhering to literal meaning exclusively can make for boring theater, so sometimes you will want to deviate from the rule, while at other times you will *have* to. But you are not necessarily a better actor when you violate it for no good reason. When can you mean what you are not saying, or say something that you do not mean, and still enhance rather than undermine the text?

A rich script is laced with myriad clues that do not necessarily provide answers, but shine a light on where to investigate. A playwright leaves many clues ambiguous on purpose, cueing the actors and director where to flesh out the characters not just with analysis, but with life. (Tennessee Williams said that a character that is not ambiguous is not complete.) Learning to identify such a clue is half the battle. Fortunately, since he wants you to find his ambiguities, he supplies ample arrows to point you in the right direction, suggesting your agenda while leaving the interpretation itself to you.

I proffer the term *extended text* to refer to whatever you infer from or ascribe to a script other than the text itself. In life there is always a lot more going on than merely what we say. The ratio of what we think versus what we say may be 3-to-1 or even 10-to-1. Since characters in a play are in some sort of crisis, the ratio can be even higher. In addition to what lies behind and between the lines, extended text includes what happens before and after each scene, plus the character's history—psychological, emotional, educational, and so forth. So extended text encompasses the rest of the story, the entire unsaid, within the scene and without. It may be derived directly from the text or applied to the character from research, rehearsal, imagination, or instinct.

Adjustments and Secrets

I have seen actors go overboard writing volumes on their character's history, including events thoroughly extraneous to the play. These copious notes remain on paper as homework, often far too complex to travel from page to stage. Nevertheless, an extensive biography may be helpful, rooting the actor securely in the role. So if it works for you, or even if you think it does, go right ahead; but take care not to allow a plethora of details to get in your way, obscuring the forest for the trees.

Remember that the director, by casting you, no doubt wants you to use your own self as the point of departure for the role, sometimes in ways you will not even be aware of. You then need only to find the one, two, or possibly three *adjustments* to help transform you into the role. (See Building from the Neutral, p. 148.) The most effective adjustment is not necessarily a quality, but a circumstance you assume as fact.

Declarations like "my character would never do that" generally indicate that you have not yet assumed the adjustments necessary to take you from yourself to the role. This is why Stanislavski eventually departed from the premise of starting with merely "yourself" to build your character, in favor of starting with *"yourselves"*—including imagined, potential selves. Your Macbeth must be ambitious enough to murder a king, though you never would.

Often the script will be blatant in mandating an adjustment. At other times, the author can be a bit less obvious, wanting you to conceal something and keep it a mystery. The event may be a past secret that is finally revealed at the climax—culpability, paternity, even incest.

You may be looking for an adjustment that is not prescribed by the text at all. Try one, then another, until you land on the one that suddenly opens the whole role up to you. Then be sure to discard unsuccessful ones. When you can, draw upon your own life to flesh out the role so that these discretionary adjustments will ring true. The less fiction you assume, the clearer and more believable your work will be. Why make acting harder than it is?

Strive for the fewest adjustments possible.

Example. Ibsen paints a rather complex and ambiguous character in Hedda. We know that she was her father General Gabler's favorite, that she used to pull Mrs. Elvsted's hair in school, and that she is fond of pistols. If, with all that Ibsen provides you, it is still impossible to make the leap to having to shoot yourself at play's end, then try some adjustment. Maybe (1) you not only played with guns as a teenager, but actually shot birds, squirrels, and the like. Or (2) your chemical balance is off kilter; had you lived today, you would be on medication. Be careful of the second, though: Ibsen's point may be undermined if Hedda is having a nervous breakdown, while it is strengthened if she is perfectly rational.

If either of these works, then you're home and may need nothing else but what the script gives. Otherwise try a third and a fourth. Say that your Hedda suffers from social claustrophobia and cannot bear being touched, so you take a step away whenever someone comes toward you, particularly your husband. Perhaps, too, you constantly straighten your clothes, wipe your hands, or pick lint off yourself (whether or not there is lint). By the end of the play, when Judge Brack blackmails you into becoming his whore, you will be bursting out of your skin. What else could you do but kill yourself? (Since you have already assumed the script's adjustment that you are also an aesthete, you do so beautifully.)

There is the famous case of Laurence Olivier playing Iago as a latent homosexual. This adjustment was reputed to backfire dreadfully. It may flesh out the psychological complexity of the role very well, however; your Iago might be able to "pass for straight," no one else knowing what desire might lurk within. Again, let the choice serve you, rather than you serving it.

So making strong choices does not necessarily mean talking about them and then slavishly implementing them, but using them to help play your actions. In fact, the more experienced my actors, the less I want them to tell me their choices. I much prefer seeing life onstage as the audience does, unaware of actors' intentions. Besides, discussing choices is something a character truly would never do. Occasionally rehearsal hits an impasse and choices need to be voiced, but otherwise:

Actors' secrets work best when kept secret.

Adjustments, like those for Hedda, should require acting with your guts. The more personal and dangerous you make them, the less work you will have to do onstage. The best adjustments are so powerful that they act on you—effortlessly—and then get you to act on others.

Sometimes the effect can be overt, but an adjustment need not read visibly at all. Some adjustments simply help you embrace the circumstances of a scene; others, to achieve a mood, rhythm, or other subtle quality. And they need not be intrinsic to the circumstances of the play, as long as they work. Typically, for instance, the American actor has difficulty playing the posture of a king, since ours is a country with no royalty (officially); but if you were to stand, walk, and boss others around *as if you were a six-year old*, you would be amazed at how effective a king you can appear. Every six-year old, after all, lords it over his own world.

How do you know if an adjustment works? First, during rehearsals, see if it helps you to act, and others to react to you, in a way that makes the next action happen. Second, you can ask your director, without necessarily telling him what your choice is. And third, during performances, the audience may let you know.

Relationships

Going beyond your own adjustments, think about *pairs* of characters:

- Where and when did they first meet?
- Exactly how do they feel about each other: hot or cool, intellectual or passionate, bothered or indifferent?
- If their first scene together in the play is their first meeting ever, then exactly what has each heard about the other(s)?

And so forth. The answers, when not overt in the script, are invariably suggested. These impressions about each other will affect your encounters. Body language, facial expression, and rhythm of speech will differ depending on, say, whether you are apprehensive with each other or relaxed.

If the scene involves characters who are already acquainted, go further than just imagining their previous meetings—try acting them out. In particular, try *improvising* the first meeting of two characters (see Structured Improvisation, pp. 152-154). Some actors remain unaffected by improvisation and consider it nonsense, and to tell the truth, it is often practiced without application to scene or character. But it can be of tremendous help in, among other things, specifying physical behavior with one another. For instance, a married couple has a history of corporal knowledge ("one flesh"). It does not necessarily follow that they go around kissing or touching each other all the time; but perhaps they *could*. Sometimes deportment is a matter of knowing each other so well that you can take each other for granted. Improvising physically could help establish intimacy psychologically.

Often a relationship takes precedence over either character and effectively functions as the protagonist with its own will, objective, and the primary through-line of the drama. Think of a two-character play. The relationship requires its own history and future, crises and resolutions, and so on. In *A Coupla White Chicks Sitting Around Talking,* as in *Thelma and Louise,* the protagonist has got to be the title role—the couple.

Example. In *As You Like It,* cousins Rosalind and Celia have become inseparable, especially since the ouster of the old Duke, Rosalind's father. In I.3, the usurping Duke Frederick, Celia's father, banishes Rosalind most harshly and unexpectedly. Personalize the history of your friendship, and your fathers' estrangement, to convincingly portray the depth of your affection and the awkwardness of your current situation. Then you will not have to pretend to act, but rather can automatically *react* to the crisis of losing each other.

Celia makes a surprise move: she exiles herself voluntarily in order to stay with Rosalind. This reaction may defy all reason, but must make perfect sense to the heart. In effect, the friendship has a will of its own, as if it were a single character. Celia cements the bond by saying to her cousin, "Thou and I am one," one of the most passionate uses of the word *am* in all literature. (Notwithstanding that there was no standard English grammar yet, Shakespeare nonetheless chose "am" so that the listener would hear Celia's action of fusing *thou* and *I* into *one.*)

In Elmer Rice's *Street Scene,* Nikolai Gogol's *The Inspector General,* Friedrich Dürrenmatt's *The Visit* or Ben Jonson's *Volpone,* you will find little dialogue between the various pairs of neighbors. These few exchanges stand for relationships that have grown over years. As actors playing the townspeople, develop your history with each other so that your few moments together create a believable village. Stanislavski was amazed at how expertly the choruses in operas could do this and come across as lifelike to the audience.

The fewer the clues in the script, the greater the demand on actors' invention to create a role—or a relationship.

The Young Man from Atlanta does not even appear in the play of the same name, but affects everyone in it; the others, then, must create *him*.

Inner Monologue

The extended text that goes on in your character's mind during a scene, yet remains unsaid, is *inner monologue.* It is the nonverbal content that either complements the text or fills a silence. Think of the "dance" we do in a bar or museum before initiating conversation with an attractive stranger, or the politics of unspoken subterfuge that might characterize a highly charged board meeting. Inner monologue makes ordinary dialogue dramatic, both in life and onstage.

While much of your inner monologue will consist of sheer invention, a playwright will prescribe a good portion of it. Comb through the script for clues as to not only what you are thinking, but also when. The clue may lie several acts away.

Example. At the end of *As You Like It,* Orlando tells his future father-in-law that when he first met Ganymede in the forest, "Methought he was a brother to your daughter." (V.4) Yet nowhere in his previous scenes with Ganymede (Rosalind disguised as a lad) did he say, "Have we met before?" or "Are you related to . . . ?"

To the actor, this line is a shining bright indicator that should affect what Orlando thinks when he first meets Ganymede in III.2. During this first meeting, Orlando's sudden question "Where dwell you, pretty youth?" acquires rich meaning. The word *pretty* can be charged with particular interest, for his attraction to the youth is seeded with the potential of more than just making a new "male" friend. The actor can experiment with various solutions as to what precisely he is thinking, when he thinks it, and why he does not say it out loud until V.4. (Some have used these two lines to help justify Orlando's knowing Ganymede's true identity all along.)

In coming up with your inner monologue, however, I offer several caveats:

- Inner monologue is more than just a list of thoughts or images: it includes the logical links between them, the *flow* of thoughts.
- Think of inner monologue not just as inner thought, but as *inner action*.
- Inner monologue should propel the text rather than interrupt it.
- Beware of defending, indulging, concentrating on, or being distracted by your inner monologue at the expense of listening to other characters. Inner monologue should free you, not make you tune out.
- Beware of dangerous subtext.

Subtext, Action Statements, Attributed Verbs

Subtext refers to the unsaid that lies under the text, as if hidden by it. (When a character keeps a secret in one scene but reveals it in another, the hidden agenda might be better styled as *delayed text*.) Healthy subtext consists of *action statements*. The line "You are sitting in that chair" has no dramatic meaning if the audience sees that the "you" is sitting in a chair. If, however, you imbue that line with the action of "I want that chair," or "I already told you to come here, I'm not going to say it again," or "You sit around all the time and it's not healthy: change your ways," then the line takes on dramatic force. A passive line becomes active.

In fact, whenever a line seems flat and inactive, the playwright has provided you with a BIG CLUE that something else is going on. He wants you to find the action of the line: that's how playwrights write plays. In the opening of *The Merchant of Venice*, Antonio's friend tells him "You are sad/ Because you are not merry" not to state the obvious, but to tease Antonio as effectively as he can. He is acting on the other character to make him laugh.

Associated with action statements is the technique of attributing a verb to dialogue. Verbs such as *state, explain, inform, say, enjoy* are weak; *cajole, demand, insist, belittle, denigrate, revel* are more specific, active, colorful, and playable.

Action statements and attributed verbs crystallize the process of getting your character to the point where he must say the line, rather than merely saying it because it is the next line. They specify your intent and activate the words. You can make lists of possible action statements to try with various speeches even before rehearsals begin; later, your director (and sometimes another character, while playing the scene) should let you know which ones work and which do not.

The best kinds of subtext are action statements
***and attributed verbs that make the line* active.**

Subtext can be a dangerous concept, though, if actors feel obliged to come up with complicated subtext that is simply not there, jamming in choices that clash with the script. Certainly "playing an opposite" is a valuable experiment, and when orchestrated sparingly can add wonderful spice to a performance or even provide the solution to a problematic role. And irony may be the only valid interpretation of a particular line. But when creativity supersedes clarity, the spectator tunes out.

For instance, if you are playing the butler, it is going to be tough to assume the subtext that you are secretly a serial killer—and try to do in your boss at every waking moment—unless it is also the playwright's agenda for you. Such a choice may be suggested by the text: if, when you exit, another character says, "What's wrong with your butler, Reginald?", then, sure, the choice makes sense of this line. But if the script makes no mention of snarling at your master and threatening him with a knife, you might be confusing the audience and should probably try something else. An indefensible choice that gets in the way should generally be eliminated.

Sometimes, however, all it needs is another adjustment to temper it, the juxtaposition of the two making your inner life vibrate. Assuming a secret like "I desperately need to keep this job and so cannot let anyone know that I am a serial killer" may make your performance appropriately colorful instead of confounding. Alternatively, you may need to go further to make your choice work, particularly if a daft and dangerous butler is what the play needs. Remember, though, to maintain a balance between your creativity and the playwright's.

Anticipation and Surprise

One of the most overlooked yet informative components of inner monologue is anticipation. Every time you say (or do) something onstage you should have a notion of the specific impact you expect it to have on others. Do not confuse this healthy, natural anticipation with the mistake of anticipating (as the actor) how the scene will turn out (for the character) ahead of time; I am talking about precisely the opposite. The outcome should surprise your character, who generally anticipates something that does not end up happening.

In everyday conversation, such anticipation is automatic: we expect to succeed in asserting our will (or in deflecting someone else's) even when the situation is not rife with conflict. For example, if a fun-loving friend of yours starts an exchange with, "There were these two guys . . ." you expect that he is about to tell a joke, probably with a convoluted set-up and a groaner of a punch line. He, meanwhile, assumes that you are going to let him tell his tale, and will be thrown off if you say, "Is this going to be a long one?" The juice of daily conversation lies in this frustrating and colorful agenda of the unsaid.

Likewise, a character in a play does not say something simply because it is the next line, but in order to achieve his will of the moment, or *local objective*. So in scoring your inner monologue, think about:

- ***what you expect to provoke, or assert, and***
- ***how other characters expect to provoke you.***

Then in performance:

- ***assume you will accomplish your local objective, and***
- ***forget knowledge of subsequent action so you will be surprised by others' noncompliance.***

Of course, you cannot do your fellow actors' work for them. As they surprise you, your responses are generated anew, in the present, for you must deal with the ever-changing circumstances of the scene. As you interact with others, your anticipations will change from moment to moment—and from performance to performance. Stage life is like a hot potato tossed back and forth: keep the audience guessing who will be the next to catch it, and how.

Silence

There is great information to glean from what your character does not say. A silence can even be more dramatic than text once you figure out a dramatic reason for it. Do not assume that your character is not thinking a lot or not doing anything just because he is not speaking. He may even be about to speak. Determine why you remain silent until your cue. Think of some reason other than "it's written that way": it could be out of circumspection, or because you cannot get a word in edgewise, or something more interesting. Having the character not speak when it looks as if he should is one of the ways a playwright prescribes where to investigate what's going on.

When Addressed (Two Characters Onstage)

In Strindberg's *The Stronger*, one of the two characters has all the lines: the silent one is the stronger . . . or is she? Well, that is the riddle of the play.

When one of two characters has the long speech, remember that it is what the listener goes through that advances the plot, for she is generally the one being affected. The twist in *The Stronger* is that the silent one goes so far as to act on the speaker. But for the most part a speaker does not say what she does not already know.

If you play the one addressed, score the inner monologue of your silence, the *phrase of listening*. The speaker is trying to convince you of something, or get you to do something. Determine why you do not say anything; if you are silent for 83 lines, find 83 reasons. Then make your reasons active. Your reactions will serve as catalysts to the speaker, causing her to augment her intensity, alter her approach, or change the subject entirely. Some of your reactions can be almost invisible—almost.

> ***Think of silence as dialogue without words.***
> ***A monologue is really half of a dialogue.***

Example. In I.7 of *Macbeth*, Lady Macbeth spurs her husband on to do the dastardly deed of murdering King Duncan. Macbeth has asserted earlier in the scene that they "will proceed no further in this business." When he preempts her with "Prithee, peace," she does not do what he asks, but rants for a while to get him to listen. Then:

Macbeth:	If we should fail?
Lady Macbeth:	We fail!

            But screw your courage to the sticking-place,
            And we'll not fail. When Duncan is asleep—   (1)
            Whereto the rather shall his day's hard journey
            Soundly invite him—his two chamberlains
            Will I with wine and wassail so convince,
            That memory, the warder of the brain,
            Shall be a fume, and the receipt of reason
            A limbec only; when in swinish sleep
            Their drenched natures lie as in a death,
            What cannot you and I perform upon
            The unguarded Duncan? What not put upon his
            Spongy officers, who shall bear the guilt
            Of our great quell?

Macbeth:	Bring forth men-children only;
	For thy undaunted mettle should compose
	Nothing but males. Will it not be received,
	When we have mark'd with blood those sleepy two
	Of his own chamber, and used their very daggers,
	That they have done't?

At "And we'll not fail" (1) she stops having to appeal to his courage and proceeds to specify her plans. In the middle of this line of hers, Macbeth changes. Simply the fact that he remains silent (instead of trying to silence her again or questioning her) shows that he is now considering the possibility of not failing.

By the end of her speech, he has become so affected by her "undaunted mettle" that he actually joins in plotting how to frame the guards. If the actor can involve the audience in Macbeth's transformation from adamant resister to reluctant draftee to active co-conspirator—a growth that takes place during her lines—they will be waiting with bated breath to see him soon surpass her in evil.

Action between two characters, in other words, is reciprocal: like alternating current, it goes both ways.

> **The Principle of Electricity:**
> **It is not what a single character does but**
> **the electrical charge between that generates and**
> **clarifies the dramatic action.**

When Overhearing Others
Example. In III.2 of *As You Like It,* when Rosalind (disguised as the boy Ganymede) finds her heartthrob Orlando in the forest, Celia, once introduced, is quiet for about 150 lines. Why? You decide. Perhaps Orlando's presence titillates Rosalind-in-drag so that she/he puts on a great show for Celia to watch. (Rosalind was awfully sad back at court in I.2; now she is anything but.) Or your Celia may simply be so overjoyed for Rosalind's restored spirits that you would not think of interrupting her.

In IV.1, Celia is again a quiet observer for a long time as the "lovers" get carried away. When Orlando leaves, however, Celia erupts, scolding her cousin "You have simply misused our sex in your love-prate. . . ." This line represents quite a change in tone and attitude from her silence, and from her last line many minutes earlier. Even if your Celia is merely teasing, earn that eruption by orchestrating the buildup during her silent observation. Cousin Rosalind may be forced to work hard to keep you quiet while Orlando is there, even having to put her hand over your mouth.

With very little text over the course of the scene, your Celia can convey a series of careening moods from entertainment to dismay to exasperation, resignation, and finally surrender.

At last the moonstruck Rosalind wafts off, to "find a shadow and sigh till he come." Celia's subsequent punch line "And I'll sleep," which scans like a burlesque rim shot—"Buh-DOOM *CHICK*"—does not work quite so well if you have been cool throughout the scene. This line suggests that by now you should be so exhausted that you need the sleep. Let the ending of your silence, then, inform its phrasing, with a beginning and middle leading to that end.

By the way, the lovers' next meeting is chaperone-less. This later scene can—and should—take on a new tone, whether more honest, erotic, dangerous, passionate, or all of these. Something causes both lovers to give up the ruse:

Orlando: I can live no longer by thinking.
Rosalind: I will weary you then no longer with idle talking. . . . (V.2)

Without Celia for the first time, they are about to confess their feelings; meanwhile they do an awfully good job of teasing each other, making for a sultry scene indeed.

- *There is information not only in what characters say but also in when they say it.*
- *A corollary source of information, then, to "what your character does not say" is "what your character does not say . . . until later."*
- *Phrase a silence with a beginning, middle, and end.*
- *The presence of a silent character alters the other characters onstage.*

Pauses

Many actors pause to get to the point of having to say the next line; their work shows. The actor who keeps the text going instead of pausing laboriously is the more compelling actor. Inner monologue should not stop the dialogue, but rather generate it.

Strive to act on the text: let your inner life color the playwright's words rather than interrupt them.

Do not construe the ellipsis (. . .) or dash (—) as pauses. Both of these punctuation marks suggest something unsaid, but not necessarily a length of time. The ellipsis indicates something omitted. It could involve simply a deflection to a second thought, part of the first thought remaining unstated. The dash can suggest a similar actual interruption mid-thought or a change in the person addressed; sometimes it merely betrays an editorial preference. Rather than a stop, try either of these clues as a ricochet, which conveys the same dramatic flow more intensely.

Occasionally, however, the dramatist writes the word *pause* into his stage directions. Such a scripted pause is a phrase, which is characterized as a gesture with a beginning, middle, and end. The end of one phrase sparks the beginning of the next. When a playwright scripts a pause, he is not merely suggesting the rhythm, he is cueing you to the *dramatic rhythm*—that something must *happen* in that silence. Think of the pause as a silent phrase whose "text" must nonetheless be filled. The previous line must *require* the brief silence to get to the next line.

This does not mean that the actor need always reveal the inner life of the pause to the audience by mugging or telegraphing. In an absurdist or existential play, absolute emptiness may be exactly what is required: ultimately there may be nothing to wait for in *Waiting for Godot*. The challenge is to make silent moments juicy for the audience.

Example. Chekhov orchestrates this blankness as one character's insensitivity to the despair of another. From the juxtaposition of two contrasting moods emerges his sense of comedy.

Uncle Vanya is depressed over his brother-in-law the professor's beautiful new wife, Helen. While taking tea outdoors in Act I, he raises his voice to belittle the academic to his mother, who dotes on her scholarly son-in-law:

Vanya:	We can't all be non-stop writing machines like the learned professor.	(1)
Mrs. Voynitsky:	What exactly do you mean by that?	(2)
Sonya:	Grandmother! Uncle Vanya! Please!	(3)
Vanya:	I am silent. Silent and repentant.	(4)
	[*Pause.*]	(5)
Helen:	It's a perfect day. Not too hot.	(6)
	[*Pause.*][7]	(7)

Vanya:	It's a perfect day. For a man to hang himself.(8)
	[*Telegin tunes the guitar. Marina the nurse walks*
	about near the house calling the hens.] (9)
Marina:	Chuck, chuck, chuck. . . (10)
	(trans. Ronald Hingley, adapted)

Chekhov takes the scene from spitting (1–2) to scolding (2–3) to silence (4–5) to serendipity (6), and then to silence once again (7).

During the first pause (5), how does the hitherto quiet Helen get to the point of having to speak? When she does, it is to say nothing at all but comment on the weather (6), certainly a trivial topic. Her impetus to speak may not be revealed so much in what she says as in the fact that she must say something because, as is often the case with Chekhov, the silence is so stultifying. She may be speaking to cut through the horrible tension in the air, or to avoid having to introspect about her miserable existence.

Vanya's subsequent declaration of suicidal despair (8) is rendered utterly comic by the nurse's insensitive sound effects (10). Admitting that you want to kill yourself may be something extraordinary to (most) American ears, but here, threatening suicide seems as commonplace as arguing or gathering runaway chicks. The emotional music of this sequence essentially runs: (8) "I want to kill myself," (9) twang of out-of-tune guitar, (10) "Here chicky chicky!" Chekhov has scored the sounds and the sense; the actors provide the substance, and then let the unsentimental rhythm do its part, automatically rendering the scene pathetic—and comic.

More recent plays may actually be characterized by the silences, as in Harold Pinter, Samuel Beckett, and Richard Nelson's exquisite, excruciating *Goodnight Children Everywhere*. In a Pinter production where the pauses are hollow, someone in the audience falls asleep. Be careful not to let the "ball drop," but keep it afloat. If the electrical charge from the stage dips, the audience loses interest, and you have to work awfully hard to get their attention back. In the meantime, they may have missed an important moment. So during a silence, keep the "ball in the air": *let something loom over the audience.*

During a pause
- *have a heck of a lot more going on inside you than when speaking, and*
- *find a way to communicate your inner life to the audience, even without words, so as to make them care enough to pay attention.*

A scripted pause can be as short as the time as it takes you to inhale. How long? The answer is a unit not of time, but of dramatic action: A *pause* must convey an action, so it has a beginning, middle, and end. A *beat*, on the other hand, is generally but a moment—a beginning, a middle, *or* an end. (I am referring to "beat" as a stage direction, not breaking down a scene into beats, an entirely different word.) A moment can last a split second or be stretched as long as the audience is kept in suspense. Say your character is sneaking around where she shouldn't be; then the door starts to creak open slowly, so that she freezes. Then the door stops. Nothing happens for a second . . . five seconds . . . twenty seconds. . . . The second that the audience no longer cares about who's there—or the moment right before—is when something else should happen.

Determining the substance of the silence, then, enables you to play the audience with aplomb.

Exercise: Scripting the Silence. Write out your character's inner monologue during the pause with three things in mind, making sure that

1. something happens during that silence
2. in the form of a beginning, middle, and end
3. that will generate the next line of dialogue.

I offer two caveats. First, write the script of silence out *in pencil,* and feel free to amend it during the rehearsal process and even during the run of the show. Why? Because as you rehearse, you get closer and closer to the role. Ultimately you want it to be your character's script, not yours, and he may have a better idea in the third week of rehearsal than you had in the first week.

Second, think of the inner life not as introspective, but as "extrospective." Remember, the best inner monologue is inner action—even better, though, is outer action momentarily averted. Let your character have so much to say that he cannot decide what to say, or such a dangerous thing to say that he must censor himself. Thus you create intrigue about all those fiery unsaid thoughts. No thought creates no action; passive thoughts tend to make an actor look like he is working hard; but active thoughts, so provocative that they must be restrained (at least for the moment) make for exciting theater. To keep that ball in the air, you may not need to make your inner action obvious, but betray it just enough to keep the audience engaged.

There are of course rhythmic silences a playwright scores without using the word *pause.* If you have no dialogue while eating breakfast, and the next line is the maid's who now clears the dishes because you have finished, a rhythm has been prescribed. Most rhythm-of-life pauses you think you need today, however, your character will not need tomorrow. So for heaven's sake, don't set your pause-filled rhythm in stone: you may simply not yet be reacting fast enough. At early rehearsals, you need this time to explore a particular reaction. By performance, though, you will be able to react without the pause.

In general, the most effective vessel for inner action is not silence, but text; you can convey a lot more color, emotion, and innuendo with words than without. So be suspicious of an unscripted pause. Ask yourself:

1. Do I absolutely have to have the pause?
2. Does removing the pause diminish the play for the audience?

The answer to the above questions is almost always no. With a classical play, by the way, I rarely stage more than three unscripted pauses per act that are to be repeated every performance. These become grand pauses occurring at grand moments.

- *The word "pause" and the punctuation marks "..." and "—" are bright clues that something unsaid is going on. Only the word "pause" (and sometimes "beat") mandates any length of time.*
- *A pause is a phrase with a beginning, middle, and end.*
- *Unscripted pauses are difficult to earn; in wordy plays like classics, they are almost always unnecessary.*
- *Earned pauses (not scripted) should invariably occur at events so huge that they cannot help but dumbfound the characters onstage.*
- *Whether scripted or unscripted, a pause warrants investigation and investment to make it a dramatic moment that not only intrigues, but can be achieved only through silence.*

Discursive Speech

Say your character does not answer a question that has been posed to him. By having him deflect—either silently or with words—the playwright generates both conflict and suspense: conflict, as the asker requests a response that you decline to furnish, setting the two speakers at odds with each other; and suspense, as the audience anticipates finding out why you avoided the question, and what your answer will be.

Instead of remaining silent, your character may smoothly steer the conversation to a new subject, avoiding the conflict. No character changes topic on a mere caprice. Such a non sequitur suggests a moment of drastic inner action. Your inner monologue should convert each non sequitur into a spark that will hold the audience's attention.

During a long speech or soliloquy, sometimes the playwright seems to have you ricochet haphazardly from topic to topic all by yourself. Craft your inner monologue to bind these desultory thoughts with a cohesive purpose to keep the audience with you. To do this: (1) link the thought behind one line of text to another that you may not say until much later, and (2) figure out why you proceed with the seemingly unrelated next line, making each detour from the main point sensible and *necessary*.

To hold your audience while you go off on a tangent, you put the previous topic "on hold," reassuring them, "we'll get back to that point later, folks." When you finally do return to the original topic, each detour has prolonged the audience's anticipation of your getting to your point, giving your arrival all the more impact and flair. Watch footage of Victor Borge at the piano, stretching out long moments of not playing anything for bit after bit, laugh after laugh, all the while stringing the audience along in anticipation of what he *is* going to play.

Example. Late in Act I of *The Madwoman of Chaillot,* the title character talks about life to the young man, Pierre, who has just tried to commit suicide, and whom she romantically insists on calling "Roderick":

> To be alive is to be fortunate, Roderick. Of course, in the morning, when you first awake, it does not always seem so very gay. When you take your hair out of the drawer, and your teeth out of the glass, you are apt to feel a little out of place in this world. Especially if you've just been dreaming that you're a little girl on a pony looking for strawberries in the woods. But all you need to feel the call of life once more is a letter in your mail giving you your schedule for the day—your mending, your shopping, that letter to your grandmother that you never seem to get around to. And so, when you've washed your face in rosewater, and powdered it—not with this awful rice-powder they sell nowadays, which does nothing for the skin, but with a cake of pure white starch—and put on your pins, your rings, your brooches, bracelets, earrings and pearls—in short, when you are dressed for your morning coffee—and have had a good look at yourself—not in the glass, naturally—it lies—but in the side of the brass gong that once belonged to Admiral Courbet—then, Roderick, then you're armed, you're strong, you're ready—you can begin again. (from the Maurice Valency adaptation, p. 47)

To this, Pierre responds, "with tears in his eyes," "Oh, Madame . . . ! Oh, Madame . . . !"

Now what in heaven's name moved Pierre to tears? None of the Countess's morning ablutions could appeal to a young man climbing the corporate ladder. What were his inner thoughts while listening to her?

She goes on for a long while discussing the morning paper, former neighbors, fruit salts, her corset, and the morning walk. Only much later she sums it all up with, "You see, then, Roderick. That's life. Does it appeal to you now?" Pierre replies, "It seems marvelous." Certainly he is not going to start copying Madame in his own morning ritual. It is not the details of her day, but her joie de vivre that fills him with raison d'être. (OK, it's a French play.) All her ramblings are actually related to the topic sentence, "to be alive is to be fortunate."

It is this inner monologue to which Pierre responds. What he and the Countess have in common is a fragile will to survive. Pierre is the survivor-in-training, while the Countess is experienced; she strengthens his will by sharing not just her experience, but her delight. This sharing is what the magical scene is really about. The speech's discursive structure unveils its spiritual meaning.

If the character does not return to the original topic, keep investigating. You will almost always find that the play returns to that topic later, in some fashion. The reason for the delay may be the point of the play.

Keep in mind, too, that a character who can keep the through-line of a speech going ad infinitum betrays not only a great intellect, but also personal values and passion for the tangential topics.

To the actor, there is really no such thing as a non sequitur. Discursive speech suggests a soul that is full almost to the point of bursting.

Thought Groups

Circle abrupt transitions in your script, then, and try to find the links. But for verbose characters, also try to link related thoughts into groups. As your marks on the page become your work on the stage, an enigmatic character who seems to be unfocused, neurotic, or demented, might turn out to be in love, a visionary, or both—like Benedick in *Much Ado About Nothing*:

Example. After Benedick overhears his friends discussing Beatrice's secret love for him, he addresses the audience:

> . . . They seem to pity the lady: it seems her affections have their full bent. Love me! Why, it must be requited. I hear how I am censured:

(1) they say (1ª) I will bear myself proudly, if I perceive the love come from her; (1ᵇ) they say too that she will rather die than give any sign of affection. (1ᶜ) I did never think to marry; (1ᵈ) I must not seem proud: (1ᵉ) happy are they that hear their detractions, and can put them to mending. (2) They say (2ª) the lady is fair,—(2ᵇ) 'tis a truth, I can bear them witness; (2ᶜ) and virtuous,—(2ᵈ) 'tis so, I cannot reprove it; (2ᵉ) and wise, but for loving me,—(3) by my troth, (3ª) it is no addition to her wit, (3ᵇ) nor no great argument of her folly, (4) for I will be horribly in love with her. (II.3)

You will have great difficulty in moving this portion of the soliloquy along if you think that every punctuation mark delimits an entirely new thought. Most of the passage summarizes what "they say" both about Benedick and about Beatrice—but they have said it, and he has reacted to them, *already*. At the colon (1) you are already thinking about the subsequent list of faults that you are accused of, and what you are going to do about them. That brings you all the way to the decision (1ᵉ–2) to "put them to mending." At (2), you are about to summarize her plusses and minuses; but these are not new thoughts to you either, for you have courted the woman before. So your Benedick need not stop to think, you need merely share with the audience, asking for help in figuring out what you are going to do.

Instead of there being twelve or fifteen thoughts in the above passage, by grouping them together you find that there are only a few, and really only one new: "I will be horribly in love with her." And even this arrival is set up as early as the third sentence's "It must be requited." Each thought is actually nascent in a previous one; for the single driving force behind the speech is *that he is already in love with her*. Benedick uses the soliloquy not merely to make a decision, but for the audience to help him finally be himself.

So sometimes the main subject of a character's inner monologue is something he has not yet realized, at least not in words. The best thoughts, like the best emotions, are ineffable. This does not mean that they are not specific; they are just so rich, so flabbergasting, so awe-inspiring, so wonderful and horrible, that words barely suffice in clarifying them. So you keep talking.

A playwright's use of punctuation marks, by the way, will help you organize your speech into thought groups. A colon (:) instructs the speaker, "relate how the second clause follows from the first"; it functions like an arrow propelling forward. A semicolon (;) says, "relate how the clauses are like two sides of the same coin, or equivalent elements of a list"; it functions like the fulcrum of a seesaw or rung of a ladder. Both colon and semicolon suggest you keep on talking instead of pausing to think; it's up to you to figure out how. This requires mental energy as hot as sparks, for your character, in crisis, is operating far more quickly than you need to—yet. Turning your inner gears relentlessly may work you into a frenzy, but it will also endow you with momentum, clarity, and maybe even the charm of Benedick.

Pre-Beat and Post-Beat

Inner monologue—what goes on between the lines—has a corollary in what goes on between the scenes, called *pre-beat* and *post-beat*. These two components of your extended text are so essential that you cannot act competently without them. How can you begin without knowing where the starting point is?

The playwright does provide clues. If a scene starts with characters in the middle of a task or conversation (*in medias res*, in Latin, which means "in the middle of things"), then he is pretty blatantly requiring you to fill out the moments of unscripted prior dialogue and activity—the pre-beat—that got them to the scene.

Sometimes just knowing your pre-beat will not suffice, and you must make choices that will reveal it to the audience. At other times, the play may want to keep the audience wondering what has happened. By specifying your pre-beat you can make that first moment gripping even before any context has been established.

The pre-beat of the entire play has been referred to as the back story, the external plane, the facts, or the pre-story. All amount to pretty much the same thing.

> ### Types of Facts
> - **Facts that the script stipulates directly (given circumstances)**
> - **Facts that the script suggests (implied circumstances)**
> - **Facts you make up on your own (imputed circumstances)**

After deciding what the facts are, convert them into stage life that is as interesting and active as possible.

Example. Uncle Vanya opens on Dr. Astrov having tea with the Nurse. First she tries to get the doctor to drink. Then he changes the subject with, "How long have we known each other, Nanny?" Sounds ordinary: but do not be misled by this cup-and-saucer dialogue. Chekhov does not start the dramatic action with this moment; he starts it earlier, before the rise of curtain. Astrov's pre-beat should make this moment the very point at which the play must start. This pre-beat involves first being summoned (what was he doing when interrupted?) and then, on arriving, being forced to wait, and wait, and wait.

He may be trying to remain patient and hold his temper (for his crotchety patient refuses to see him) or to drown out the boredom, or he may be resigned to the absurdities of life. But he wants something more than merely to rehash the history of his friendship with Nanny. (Soon the audience learns of another reason he likes to linger at this household: Helen, his patient's pretty young bride, will be returning from her stroll any minute now.)

So specify your minute or two (or more) of life prior to the scene, and the goal with which you enter. Otherwise you will merely look like an actor making an entrance, not a character diving into a situation. When the scene opens with your character mid-conversation, think too about why the playwright started the scene there.

Similarly, when you exit (or when the scene ends with you onstage), what is going to happen next; where are you going, and what do you aim to accomplish? This choice is your post-beat. Exit with an objective that drives you offstage. Optimally, this exit will leave the audience rooting for you to succeed, and looking forward to your next appearance.

Episodic Structure

Episodic structure signals you to fill in the "scenes between the scenes." When two characters appear together in scene 2 with their relationship at point A, and not again until scene 5 when they have arrived at point E, the playwright has scored an ambiguity for you to specify: What were points B, C, and D?

When the plot spans years, as in Jon Robin Baitz's *A Fair Country* and George Kaufman and Edna Ferber's *The Royal Family*, the mandate to fill in the missing events becomes obvious. But a playwright's use of time can be more ambiguous. The relationship between Macbeth and his wife involves more than just the five scenes in which we see them together. Their marriage plummets from mutual dedication to cold alienation, all between their scenes. Furthermore, while the real Macbeth reigned seventeen years, Shakespeare's character reigns however long you choose, as the Bard compressed real time into dramatic time to intensify the action. It's up to you to specify your dirty deeds between the scenes of Acts III–IV so that your lords rise up against you and move the plot along to Act V.

An event of a new thought, changing emotion, or sudden resolve may happen during a scene, yet remain unstated. In Act II of *The Heiress*, the title character is jilted by her gold-digging suitor on the night of their anticipated elopement. In Act III he is back to woo her again. But in the years between the acts, she has grown. Although she never states it in the dialogue, her resolve has changed since their first courtship. You can fill your audience with anticipation by letting them know that you have decided something, but not what, until the very last moment of the play. You might not even decide what you do at the end *until* the end.

PROBLEMS THAT DEFY ANALYSIS

More than once has some talented and conscientious actor asked me, during an early rehearsal, "Can we cut that line? It's so confusing." I let him neither cut the line nor worry about solving it. Certainly the character does not know there will be a problem, so why should the actor belabor it? If, rather, he remains open and lets himself be surprised by what leads up to the difficult moment, then eventually, at some rehearsal, the line suddenly emerges organically—and maybe even reveals more about the character than either of us could have imagined. Ironically, the most confounding line or transition may provide the very clue that you have been needing all along to flesh out your character.

Analysis functions as the touchstone that converts obstacles into watersheds and binds seemingly desultory information into the workings of a single soul. If your part comprises a bit of this, a bit of that, and a bit of another thing, it is when you solve how these components fit together that you have figured out, in large part, what makes your character tick.

Sometimes, though, analysis reaches an impasse and can only yield to instinct. As you rehearse, remember that the tools of analysis are there to help you interpret the play; but the play is there for the living audience. I confess that when I directed *The House of Blue Leaves* I loved the play but had no idea why John Guare wrote it—until opening night, when we finally gave it to the audience.

If we cannot solve a play's mystery, perhaps our character can't either. Maybe our responsibility is not always to analyze the drama, but occasionally just to experience it, over and over. Then again, the solution to a problem may lie somewhere outside the script, in research.

RESEARCH

Delving into sources outside the script can enable you to stand in the shoes of your character without having to pretend so hard to be standing there. In other words, the library provides power. So let "the world be thine oyster" and go have adventures. Remember, though, that like all technique and homework, Research is shy: it does not like to be shown off, but prefers to remain unseen and unnoticed. All it desires is to enable the actor to work *less*.

Of course you want to look up all unfamiliar words, but you do more than just (1) know what you say; you also want to (2) own it, and then (3) make it vivid for the audience. Moreover, facts and definitions are not sufficient; you also (4) penetrate their impact on your characters, which is particular to their culture, not necessarily to yours. Conduct research, then, so that you can effectively (5) live as the character in the world of the play.

Milieu

Cultural milieu provides dramatic circumstances—facts—that are not necessarily specific to the plot. Dress, manners, mores, and culture should reverberate in everything your character says, does, thinks, and feels. If Hedda Gabler were alive today, for example, she could just get a job. Or could she? This is one of the questions in re-mounting such a classic. And what values cause her to exit violently instead of finding some alternative? Why could other strong women of the nineteenth century—Georges Sand and George Eliot—not have been her role models? The answers are not all in the script. For one, unlike many contemporary Americans, she undoubtedly cares very much what other people think, notwithstanding her debauched past and ongoing recklessness. So she is an individual, but no rebel. On the contrary, bred to value respectability, inside her burns a furnace with no vent.

Ibsen gives us only a facetious explanation of why she married Tesman in the first place. But think of the time and of her father: more shameful would have been to end up a spinster. Celibacy was no option for a proud woman who craves influence in society. So she weds, miserably; Hedda Gabler is replaced by Hedda Tesman; and the play begins.

When a playwright writes "Norway, 1890" or "Revolutionary Virginia" or "A rural Irish pub, today," he is asking you to mine all the information you can about those times and places from sources outside the script. Ask yourself what your character's education and upbringing would have been. Find some of the literature, mythology, folklore, customs, social structures, and news events of the period: these would have informed how your character sees things. Diaries of contemporaries are even more valuable than historical writings, for they provide subjective accounts, whereas historians generally strive for objectivity. Knowledge of facts is mandatory for both artist and academic, but knowledge of feelings and attitudes has a particular value for the actor, who must charge his heart and soul as well as his mind.

An actor playing Blanche DuBois does not have to fly to New Orleans to ride on the streetcar named Desire (which I hear is no longer operating, anyway). If she were to visit the French Quarter, however, she would not have to imagine the trip for the audience, but only recall it. Since a trip to New Orleans may be out of the question, you can at least simulate the experience by substituting the seedy neighborhood nearest you. (Do go with a friend, though, and watch your back.)

There is nothing like inviting a full-blooded *guest* to rehearsal who might have known people like the characters in the play, or even been one. If you are playing a soldier in David Rabe's *Streamers*, the Vietnam War was recent enough that you can interview veterans; for Lanford Wilson's *Fifth of July*, you would also want to find some peace activists. For older plays dating back several generations, find whomever you can. Migrant workers make great guests at rehearsals of John Steinbeck's *Of Mice and Men* or *Grapes of Wrath*; better still if they were around during the Depression. At the other end of the social spectrum, if you are in Philip Barry's *Holiday* or *The Philadelphia Story*, try to find Philly Main-Liners who might remember the 1920s and 30s. If you cannot, the country club set is still alive and well in any city, just waiting for you to exploit them for your research. You may have to dress up to meet them.

Certainly a picture can be worth a thousand words. But a visit—or visitor—may be worth a thousand pictures.

Intelligence

Actors who tend to think of acting more as feeling than as thinking frequently overlook the necessity of personalizing a character's intelligence. An author designs his characters' specialized language to be intrinsic to the plot and theme. If you are playing a police investigator, a doctor, or a migrant worker, invest in the jargon enough to make it your own daily shop talk. Again, the process of personalizing technical language entails more than knowing your terminology, but also being able to *convince* with it. This personalization will get you that much closer to what's really going on, and to your character's soul.

Sometimes the specialized language is not professional.

Example. In Act IV of *Long Day's Journey into Night*, Jamie quotes from Dowson and refers to Swinburne. These poets were commonly known to the literati of the first two decades of this century, including Edmund, the poet in the family. To play either role, familiarize yourself with their poetry. Without doing this, you may still be able to convince someone you know who Swinburne was if you are a great actor, but you will be lying. You will also miss the point. The Tyrone brothers got their values in part from having an actor for a father and a morphine addict for a mother, but also from literary *décadents* who were being read and emulated (the English ones were emulating the French). Now it starts to make sense why Jamie spends all his time in bars and bedding babes, while Edmund, who is tubercular, romanticizes such behavior. The pair of them integrate Decadent and Poet, Reckless and Recluse: two sides of O'Neill himself.

Does this insight not make playing those boys easier?

Unnecessary lying makes acting harder.

Manners

A character's education includes breeding. The French have an expression (and Flaubert a novel), *Sentimental Education*. In the United States we are barely familiar with this expression, which refers to rearing in all ways but intellectual—manners, morals, breeding, and the ways of the heart. In terms of what is actable, breeding is perhaps the single most salient feature of a social class and a civilization. I can tell a Frenchman in New York from fifty feet away, for instance, because his lips are barely open, his body is mostly still, and I cannot hear him. The American in Paris, in contrast, tends to move his mouth, head, and arms quite a bit, and talk loudly. Start a lifetime habit of people-watching, and take notes.

Unfortunately for the actor, the age of deportment is dead. Today we sit, walk, and talk with such relaxation that it borders on slovenliness. I am not indicting the culture of the day, but if you take on these habits unknowingly, they will make acting difficult. It takes but a moment to learn how to slouch, but if you slouch normally, you will need a lot of rehabilitation to play someone who doesn't.

The actor can transport us to a time when common people took pride in elegant manners, posture, and conversation. Remember the salon scene in *The Music Man*, replete with recitations and tableaux—in Iowa. After the Civil War, books on manners outsold the Bible as the middle class strove to penetrate the upper class.

Today you can track some of these sources down. Parents or grandparents may be happy to share their knowledge. There are still finishing schools in existence. Study the few remaining members of the aristocracy who make public appearances, or find film footage of them from before World War I. Barring that, watch Christopher Plummer a lot.

Again, your research must not merely include the factual but also infuse the physical and visceral. When you look at paintings or photographs of the period, try to enter them, not merely observe. When you read manuals instructing you in the proper way to shake hands or make introductions, shake hands and make introductions. An actor understands a Restoration play significantly better once she has wielded a fan and endured a corset for a day. Don't just read: practice.

In addition to deportment, manners encompass values. A woman smoking a cigarette, or getting a job—or a divorce—in 1900 would be taking drastic action, while in 1970 she would not. At a soirée, to introduce oneself to someone of a higher class, like a duchess, or to walk in front of her instead of behind, would have constituted a tremendous faux pas and warranted shunning. ("Who invited that one?")

Receiving

As *Lady Windermere's Fan* opens, the butler, Parker, asks the title character, "Is your ladyship at home this afternoon?" But she clearly is at home. What gives? Is he being funny?

Not merely: In the nineteenth century the question meant, "Are you home to visitors," or "Are you receiving callers?" Society ladies kept certain hours of the week when they received; they were not expected to be available to visitors at other times. It was neither rude nor hypocritical to say you were not at home when you were physically there. To our ears the line is funny, but it is also genuine. Oscar Wilde's point may have been that the *age* was funny.

The importance of receiving permeates Western literature before our era. In *Hedda Gabler*, Mrs. Elvsted's stakes in requesting that the respectable Tesmans receive Eilert Lövborg are huge. If they do not, he will have no entry into society and can live only as an outcast.

> ### Manners are a question not just of style,
> ### but of what is really going on in the play.

Example. A gentleman paying a call would hang on to his hat if he expected his visit to be short, but hand it to the butler or maid if he expected to stay for a while. Why then does Ibsen mention in his stage directions that Judge Brack hangs on to his hat in every one of his scenes, even in long visits with Hedda?

A gentleman would also be required to call at the front door and be announced. But Brack, in Act II, slips in the back door. What is the action behind his rudeness?

He is controlling Hedda, letting her know that he has access to her house and to her, any time he wants it, from any entry, regardless of propriety. Ibsen drives the point home with Hedda's line, as she points a pistol toward him at the opening of Act II, "This is what comes of sneaking in the back way." In the conservative Norway of 1890, this is how a writer could get away with prurience.

In Brack's last scene, still with hat in hand, the seed of what might have been playful naughtiness sprouts into sheer evil: he blackmails her. His control of her becomes complete and unbearable, leading her to the ultimate action of the play.

Between the Victorian era and the 1950s, by the way, the etiquette of the upper classes did not change as much as you might think. Each century before the nineteenth had its own variations, outlined in Joan Wildeblood's invaluable book, *The Polite World*. For the nineteenth and early twentieth centuries, I highly recommend Daniel Pool's *What Jane Austen Ate and Charles Dickens Knew*.

Historical and Literary Sources for Characters

When you play a historical character, to a certain extent you present the documentary as well as the drama. If you are playing *Abe Lincoln in Illinois* or *Henry V*, put yourself in the shoes of the title character; look into the Scopes Monkey Trial as you tackle Lawrence and Lee's *Inherit the Wind*.

But keep in mind that a dramatization is not a documentary. Writers of historical plays distill and distort the factual truth for dramatic ends. *The Diary of Anne Frank* is a selected interpretation of her diary, which was in turn a distillation of her life. You are not a journalist or historian, so present the play, not the biography. As with analysis, let your research serve your acting choices, rather than vice versa.

Biographical roles notwithstanding, even a fictional character may be based on historical fact—or on literary antecedents. If you are cast as the detective in Agatha Christie's *Black Coffee*, check out her novels and short stories that feature Hercule Poirot. The actor playing Mrs. Erlynne in my production of *Lady Windermere's Fan* read about the beautiful Victorian actor Lillie Langtry; Oscar Wilde based his character on this famous mistress of the crown prince, and wrote the role for her to play as well. The notion of the *demimondaine* (mistress of an aristocrat or noble, or high-class pros-titute) is largely unknown in the United States.

Since theatrical truth is born from human truth, the practical actor is always a student of human nature. The correlations you discover between real life and your character's may surprise you.

Example. A graduate student of mine was playing a character that seemed to her to be rather arch and two-dimensional: Dionyza in Shakespeare's *Pericles*, a role not unlike the Wicked Stepmother of fairy tales. Pursuing this line of research, she constructed a collage of wicked stepmothers from various genres, including Disney stills and illustrations of witches from chil-dren's literature. Then a friend sent her a newspaper clipping about the mother in Texas who allegedly hired a hit man to murder her daughter's cheerleading rival at school, an exact parallel to what Dionyza does. The collage allowed her unabashed versatility, while the news story rooted her in truth, making her performance at once believable and creepy.

It may be that your character was inspired by a prototype. To play a role that derives from the Harlequin, the Henpecked Husband, or the Shrewish Wife, it helps to have an understanding of those commedia dell'arte charac-ters (sixteenth to eighteenth centuries). Jarry's *Ubu* plays (late nineteenth century) were originally written as puppet shows, replete with the slapstick of the Grand Guignol (France's Punch and Judy); this knowledge makes their physical violence, well, approachable. You should not necessarily play the prototype instead of your character, but your awareness may inspire you to experiment with the heightened slapstick of pratfalls and fisticuffs.

The greater your literary and historical awareness, the more clearly you can understand and communicate the heights, depths, and nuances of any play.

Character Names

It is not always obvious what to research. Sometimes you think you already know a word's definition and are not aware that it carries additional layers of meaning. Such is the case with a proper name. Remember that a play-wright chooses or invents his names for people and places. A character is never simply a person, but embodies a metaphorical aspect as well.

Every character is part allegory.

The older the play, the more obvious this allegorical aspect is likely to be. In Medieval drama, for example, characters were blatantly named Everyman or Lust. In Shakespeare's *Twelfth Night*, your Toby Belch had better do the same (i.e., belch). Point up the mercurial aspect of Romeo's friend Mercutio, evident in the very shape of his speech (see Parallel Structure in chapter 7, p. 188-190); maybe he's bipolar.

During the Restoration (late 1600s) we meet characters named Mirabell ("looks beautiful") and Lady Wishfort (who, now past middle age, can only "wish for it" in *Way of the World*). Even today, a character named Hope (*Anything Goes, Sweeney Todd*) would suggest—what else?—hope.

Sometimes it is only the choice of name that illuminates this symbolism. In Inge's *Bus Stop, Bo* suggests both *beau*—handsome one, or suitor—and *bovine*—a clumsy bull; and that's who he is. *Cherie* evokes (1) cherry, slang for virgin; (2) the French *chérie*, a loved one; (3) the juicy fruit that is both sweet and tart, which is sort of her personality. *Grace* is self-explanatory. Names offer a point of departure for creating your role.

Sometimes the information is almost subliminal. In Arthur Miller's *All My Sons*, Joe Keller's name suggests that he is an "All-American Joe, the Killer" while his son, Christopher Keller, is actually accused in the play of being too much like Christ, and the son of a killer ("Christ of a Killer" becoming "Christopher Keller").

Sometimes the play's title is the clue. In Tennessee Williams's *Orpheus Descending*, no character named Orpheus appears per se—but there is one. Orpheus warded off hell's demons by enchanting them with song. The singer in the play is the protagonist, Val, so he must also be part Orpheus, an enchanter—which, it turns out, is how to play him. Meanwhile, the ensemble is charged to create not just a believable southern town, but also a hell on Earth. This Orpheus, unlike the myth, may not get out of hell alive.

Even if you think you already know what a name means, it behooves you to open the dictionary.

Example. Returning to *A Streetcar Named Desire*, you may already know the word *blanche* as French for "white." Certainly the character Blanche does fabricate at least a veneer of virginal innocence, which will develop into the bitter irony of the play. Her last name, DuBois, is French for "of or from the woods." Williams seems to be making her out to be a fairy tale creature like Snow White or Sleeping Beauty, and she can certainly be thought of as lost in the woods both morally and mentally.

Don't stop there. Since a role is defined by action, let's look up the verb *to blanch*:

transitive
1.	To take color from; to bleach.
2.	To whiten, by covering to cut off direct light.
. . . .	
4.	To loosen the skin off by scalding.
5.	To cause to turn pale.

intransitive

To turn white or become pale.[8]

These definitions conjure applicable qualities—and actions. Number 2 is particularly appropriate when you remember that she cannot bear a naked light bulb. In their climactic moment (scene 9), her erstwhile suitor Mitch turns on her, "I don't think I ever seen you in the light! That's a fact! . . . You never want to go out till after six and then it's always some place that's not lighted much." He then rips the paper lantern off the light bulb, "un-blanching" our heroine.

So indeed it is "all in a name," but a name may describe not just what someone is, but what someone does.

CHAPTER 3
STAKES

We now turn from investigating what the play means to investing in how much it means—to your character and to you. Stakes involve personalizing your role so that you live your life onstage as your character; then that character says the next line, does the next cross, and plays the audience, because she must. By the time of performance, of course, you should be able to *must* pretty relentlessly.

Stakes inform every aspect of what you do and how you do it, including, for example, diction and projection. When you have to communicate, you do so clearly and compellingly. (You got to *gotta*—or *nada*.)

To be a brilliant performer, though, you will fulfill more than the character's stakes. You will also have some of your own, informed by the vision and passion of the director, the playwright, and yourself.

SPECIAL VS. CASUAL

Film acting is often characterized by its casualness; the director and cameraman are there to render it special. In television, there may even be a laugh track to help. But in the theater, no dialogue is merely casual. If some of your character's words seem to be ordinary, then look to the *situation* for what is extraordinary. Then if you think that both the words and the situation seem ordinary—think again. Your task is to find out what makes them special enough to have warranted inclusion in the play.

Special does not necessarily mean non-naturalistic or stylized. Yet even in a naturalistic play when your character needs to *appear* casual, you will make him interesting—nay, compelling—not by overacting, but by heightening your Stakes.

"It was Awaaaaay!"

One evening my roommate went to the (late, lamented) Boston Garden with some friends to see a hockey game. Sitting in front of her was a little kid, about eight years old, with his father. The boy was decked out in a Bruins cap, a Bruins jacket and Bruins patches, with a Bruins souvenir program and Bruins pennant—Bruins everything—and cheering enthusiastically, to say the least. At the period break, one of the grownups asked the friend next to him if he had gone to the game last night. The little boy, overhearing, turned to this total stranger and bleated, "It was awaaaaay!"

Consider these three words as if they were the entire text of a character. Through his delivery (together with the costume), we know everything we need to know about the little boy. The most important thing in the world to him is: the Boston Bruins. The second most important thing: the Boston Bruins. His pet peeve: people who do not follow the Bruins closely enough to know that the game last night was in Detroit, yet still feel that they are entitled to occupy a seat in the Garden and actually speak as if they were fans. In other words, the little boy did not say, "It was away" casually, to convey information. He said, "It was AWAAAAAY" to suggest: "You ignoramus, you're not a real fan, everyone knows that the game was away last night, what are you even doing here?" With just three words, he conveyed his soul.

When a playwright puts dialogue down on a page, he places his character in a dramatic situation at least as personal and passionate as that of the little boy who cried "It was awaaaaay!" Your goal, then, is to burn inside to the point where you simply have to speak, like our dauntless Bruins fan.

The Rich Objective

You may recall these three fundamental actor questions:

1. *Who am I?*
2. *What do I want? and*
3. *What am I willing to do to get it? (or How far am I willing to fight for it?)*

These questions provide a sort of formula for personalizing the character's stakes. Number 2 is called the *objective,* one of the radical contributions of Stanislavski's System.

As Stanislavski points out, a scene changes tremendously when one objective is substituted for another. There may be no single right choice. An interesting character will often have more than one objective at a time.

In *A Chorus Line,* there is no mystery about what everyone is auditioning for as they sing "I really need this job." Composers and lyricists call such tunes "*I want*" songs.

In straight plays there is more dialogue, and more time for complexity. But the objective is usually not "cut and dried," even in musicals. In *South Pacific,* Nellie Forbush sings "I'm Gonna Wash that Man Right Outa My

Hair" to help herself do just that. Yet isn't her real desire precisely the opposite? In Nellie's case, one desire drives the mind while an opposing one rules the heart. When two objectives directly clash like Nellie's, you have come upon a paradox. Paradox or inconsistency does not mean that your work is incorrect, but that your character is becoming human.

The primary dramatic action of *South Pacific* can be thought of as Nellie's conflict with her own prejudices. She is in good company: other classic vacillators include Benedick (love for Beatrice vanquishes chauvinism), Macbeth (evil suppresses conscience), and Hamlet (action over inertia). Inside each soul brews a tempest of conflicting objectives that they struggle to sort out; soliloquy or song is their request for the audience's help.

Even characters who do not appeal to the audience directly can unite conflicting objectives. Does Stanley Kowalski want Blanche *out*, or does he just *want* her? Does Blanche want to keep Stanley *away*, or just *keep* him? What does she want at the core: love, dignity, survival, or to defend her illusions? These complexities are resolved differently by different actors, and so performances of *A Streetcar Named Desire* vary.

Certainly you *layer your objectives,* but which takes priority? One's overall thrust in life, or in the play, is called the *super-objective,* while various minor objectives of the scene or of the moment (local objectives) may either contribute to that super-objective or delay it (*tangential objectives,* i.e., those that interrupt the main thrust of the moment for some detour). During a scene, one local objective may be superseded by another as the wills of various characters clash. And during the course of the play, the same may happen to your super-objective, although you could construe this as your character's finally realizing what she really wanted most all along.

Is "what do I want?" an unimportant question because the answer can be so varied? Precisely the opposite. Without any objective, your character has no force of will, the play enjoys no spark of conflict, the scenes remain bereft of drive and the hall devoid of electricity. If, on the other hand, you have a few objectives that conflict with one another, your character may not come off as clear to the audience—yet—but will at least come off as interesting. When conflicting objectives generate huge storms within you, your struggle to resolve them will even win the empathy of the audience.

To illustrate, Dorothy wants (1) to get to the Emerald City, and later (2) to get the broomstick of the Wicked Witch of the West, but both serve as means (3) to get back to Kansas. The first two are local objectives, the third her super-objective. Each time she stops along the way to befriend and pick up a fellow traveler, objectives 1 and 3 are temporarily deferred by a tangential objective: "I want to be kind to those in need" or "I like to make friends." There is no reason at first for her to suspect that the Scarecrow, Tin Woodman, or Cowardly Lion is going to be able to help her get to the

Emerald City, or to Kansas; only incidentally do they end up helping her get that broomstick.

This network of conflicting objectives earns a rich payoff at the climax. By the time she is about to leave Oz, it is hard for her to say good-bye to all her new friends. Her inner conflict pits the objective of going home against that of keeping her friends; she cannot have both. This is what makes the moment of parting so bittersweet.

In contrast, Macbeth achieves his first objective, the throne, by the end of Act II. So what objective do you put into play for the remainder of the drama? His subsequent through-line (three acts' worth) no longer traces the path to the throne, but how his character changes in order to keep it: the growth of his malevolence, his courage to face death, and ultimately his emptiness: "Life's . . . a tale/ Told by an idiot, full of sound and fury,/ Signifying nothing." Your newfound objective at play's end might be "to meet my fate" or "to fulfill my role in life to the end," or something better you decide on. Layer his objectives as you will, but at no time need you subvert his initial one: "I want to be king." He confronts Macduff in battle because he wants to stay king, not because he wants to abdicate.

The more mysterious a play on first reading, the more important it becomes for the actors to put strong objectives into play early in the rehearsal period, yet with an open mind. Later you may exchange one objective for another, or alter the priorities you have assigned them. Your goal is for your super-objective to fill your subconscious. This process takes time. During performance this subconscious anchoring frees your conscious mind to roll with the punches and juggle ever-changing circumstances.

While use of the objective simplifies and clarifies your work,
the richness of an interpretation springs forth from:
(1) a multiplicity of objectives in conflict with one another; and
(2) the character's figuring out for herself what she wants most.

As with Nellie Forbush, number 2 often provides the principle dramatic action of the play.

Hidden Objectives

Every once in a while you come across a situation where there seems to be no objective, and it appears that the character is "simply talking." In life, we are not obliged to have an objective at every moment; but, again, a play is not life, but formed life. The moments in life when one would have no objective are not the moments the playwright has included in his play.

Neither in life nor in drama do we necessarily reveal our objectives; sometimes we even hide them from ourselves. But make sure to choose one as the actor, even if you decide that your character is not conscious of hers.

When a choice is not obvious, then, find the *hidden objectives*. Be specific or (trust me) the audience will fall asleep.

> ### *When no objective is stated per se,*
> ### *it is even more important to assume one.*

In three typical types of situations, you will frequently need to dig deep to come up with an objective: expository dialogue, ancillary characters, and existential plays.

Expository Dialogue

In the first scene of a parlor drama, a few characters—often the maid and the butler—discuss the goings-on in the house to set up the entrances of the principals. It seems that your character is merely conveying exposition. But don't settle for "merely": find an objective.

Example. Consider Act I of *Hedda Gabler*, where Tesman's Aunt Julia and Bertha the maid discuss recent events, setting up the title character's entrance. How do you get the audience to apprehend the details in the dialogue before they are given any context with which to listen? (Bertha and Julia are indeed establishing that context.) Each actor must assume urgent stakes that make her own immediate needs pressing, at least to herself. If the spectator can detect a sense of crisis in these two women, his curiosity will be piqued enough to grasp the facts.

Bertha's objective can be stated: "I want to keep my job." How badly? Make a choice: maybe your kid brother needs that operation. Therefore, you become inordinately anxious to do good so as not to get fired. Through you we might see how Hedda makes the people around her walk on eggshells, foreshadowing the impact of her entrance a few minutes later.

Aunt Julia appears less vulnerable—at first. She is jockeying for position in the newlyweds' lives, which she cares about deeply. How deeply? You, as Aunt Julia, decide. Hedda has no intention of giving you any position at all, and dismisses you rather perfunctorily, pretending to mistake your hat for a servant's. What a shot!

These two characters do more than provide exposition for the main plot. They go through their own little one-act drama, complete with a beginning, middle, and end. This end, in turn, is the beginning of the rest of the drama, as Hedda effectively pulls the rug out from under Aunt Julia and takes over the play's agenda.

Good exposition is not merely narration. Strong objectives—Stakes—can charge seemingly boring exposition with volatility and transform it into an explosion, overt or contained. If you really can't find an objective other than "to deliver the exposition," that objective in itself may suffice if you are passionate about it. Bill Irwin's adaptation of Molière's *Scapin* went so far as to drop a sign down that read "Exposition"—which got a good laugh.

Ancillary Characters

Even ancillary characters—servants, messengers, spear-carriers, townspeople—are in some crisis. If the playwright does not give you an explicit one, he is giving you a mandate to create your own. Otherwise, there would be no dramatic reason for you to be onstage. Of course the director will not be able to give you the focus downstage center, but your character should want just that: As far as you are concerned, the title of your play is *I Deliver the Message* or *Spear Carrier Number Two Saves the Day* (or, in a tragedy, . . . *Doesn't Save the Day*). Alas, you must let the director stage you where she needs you to be for the clarity of the overall story, not just your own.

But let every Chorus, Spear-Carrier, and Townsperson take note: There is no such thing as an ancillary character from that character's point of view, which is the point of view from which you must look at your world. Even characters who never speak contribute to the action. Therefore there is no *just* commenting or *just* being onstage when something happens. The practical actor never uses the word *just* as an adverb, anyway; he makes his work special, not casual. As Stanislavski said that " 'in general' is the enemy of Art," so I offer the following:

"Just" is the enemy of Special.

When the script provides nary a clue, score your inner monologue by assigning life history, world vision, and objectives, just as fully as you would any other character. If a character does not speak at all, his dramatic through-line will be conveyed exclusively through this inner monologue. Determine not just what he thinks and how he listens, but what he does and how he acts, so that your choices become playable.

Onstage Representative of the Audience (ORA)

Your Spear-Carrier, in other words, has been created for a dramatic reason: find it. When not intrinsic to the plot, you will at least contribute to how the viewer watches the play, as an Onstage Representative of the Audience (ORA), observing the drama as one slightly removed from the action. Since the audience may empathize with you, you can facilitate or bolster their reactions.

Why do we repeat tragedy night after night, year after year? So that maybe it will not happen at this performance. The more we awaken that hope in the audience, the more alive we make the play. If, when Medea murders Jason's children (and hers), you, as one of the Chorus, are as aghast as the spectators at the discovery, then they realize that they are not alone in their feeling of repulsion. Instead of alienating the audience, the production embraces their humanity—through you. You could go further: actively hope that she won't do it, and invite the audience to share in that hope. You could even try to stop her: and if you get the audience trying to stop her, too, then you have truly done something theatrical.

A similar principle holds when a play gets particularly rambunctious, rude, or lewd. You can generally get away with even the dirtiest joke if someone onstage reacts like a normal person or prude, for then even the normal persons and prudes in the audience will know that it is OK to feel skittish or offended; after all, the joke was offensive. Hence the incorrigible Marx Brothers have their Society Lady, Margaret Dumont, reassuring her audience, "You're right: they *are* ill behaved." Ancillary characters allow the audience to react to their fullest without feeling alienated.

Keep in mind, too, that characters who never speak do not know that they are not going to speak. The fact that they are often on the verge of speaking may provide an essential ingredient of the dramatic tension. (See Silence, pp. 44-51.)

Example A. In *The Winter's Tale,* King Leontes, struck by a fit of irrational jealousy, imprisons his wife, banishes their son (who then dies), and orders their daughter put to death, without any evidence of Queen Hermione's wrongdoing. In III.2, not even he can interrupt as Paulina lambastes him for his cruel, blind acts. Paulina even risks being tried for treason with her sharp tongue. So why do the rest of the lords remain silent? Since they are duty-bound to the king, they should protect him and at least silence her. But they know she is right. Whose side are they really on?

Best if at any moment they are on the verge of doing something: either stopping Paulina, or speaking up to support her. The latter, however, would constitute treason, so their heads keep their hearts from talking. What inner conflict! Paulina's speeches are designed to stir not only Leontes, but you, one of the courtiers. She probably wins some of your fellow lords over to her side. Threat of rebellion is imminent—but not without you.

If all the lords find physical life to betray these stakes, the scene will be rife with crisis. You might even make the audience feel like jumping into the fray.

Example B. The Mute in *The Fantasticks* seems to be merely a theatrical contrivance, a sort of "living set-piece," but might assume any of the following objectives:

1. to present the play incredibly well, and thus serve as a sort of stage-manager/taskmaster to the other characters, making sure they enter on time, stick to the script, and so on;
2. to manipulate the audience into rooting for first one family, then the other, as an ersatz activities director;
3. to hurry up the resolution and the ending to the play so he can go get a beer;
4. to participate in the action as a "human" character instead of being doomed to remain a mere theatrical entity (cf. Pinocchio);
5. to push for a happy ending—and perhaps a group hug.

Once you flesh him out, your Mute can "say" as much as any Chorus could, and although you can give him no lines, you can give him drive—and a soul.

Existential Plays: The Absurd and the Clown

Existential plays, whether comic or tragic, treat the emptiness of life. They include those of realistic writers, like Chekhov and Eugene O'Neill, and also the Theater of the Absurd—Ionesco, Sartre, Beckett, Pirandello, and much of Stoppard and Albee. In the Absurd, the play underscores the pointlessness of life or mocks social forms in a ridiculous or perverse theatrical universe. At first glance these authors' scenarios often seem plotless, and their characters, objective-free. But look again.

Waiting for Godot, with its stark existential landscape (a bare tree in a bare theater), is perhaps the archetype of a play whose characters have, arguably, no will. To make the script a play, the actors must choose an objective. It could be as simple as "I want to wait," or the stronger "I want to find out who or what Godot is," or the subtler "I want to survive." The objective "I want to find out what we are doing here" would be the exact opposite of "I want never to find out what we are doing here," yet both may be playable. How to decide?

Sisyphus, a character from Greek mythology, provides a clue. He was doomed for eternity to roll a boulder up a hill, let it fall, and roll it up again. Camus, in the last line of his famous essay *The Myth of Sisyphus*, points out that we "must imagine Sisyphus happy." So if you are playing Vladimir or Estragon in *Godot*, you might try as your objective "I want to be happy," "I want to be able to think I am happy," or "I want to be entertained; I want to play." Your objective need not always be stated aloud in rehearsal, especially when the play is cast with the likes of Bert Lahr, Zero Mostel, Steve Martin, or Robin Williams, all of whom have done *Godot*. The very being of these consummate clowns overflows with joy, color, and comedy; they were born to entertain, and that might be all that is needed to make *Godot* work. (Perhaps it was knowing this that led director Alan Schneider to keep Lahr from "talking about" the play during rehearsals.)

Why this link between the Clown and the absurd? Because the Clown is essentially an existential creature. He, like Sisyphus, achieves no change in the world situation—neither his audience's, nor his own—and one can barely picture him engaged in the humdrum routine of being the breadwinner, husband, and father. *I Love Lucy* was so funny, in part, because who could really imagine someone as zany as Lucy Ricardo as a housewife and mother? We are all part Sisyphus, and the Clown amuses us by rendering our existence palatable as we bide our time between yesterday and tomorrow.

More than clowning is required in these plays, however. A class of student actors performed some scenes from *Godot* competently enough for students, but they made the play as interesting as boulder rolling. So I led a discussion with the question, "How can you personalize the situation in the play to intersect with your own lives?" The students took it from there. Almost everyone offered a private story about waiting in vain for the phone to ring, having hopes dashed, or suffering the stark landscape of their particular childhood. Tears were shed, epiphanies were had, and the next week's performances of the same scenes were both heartrending and hysterical.

The best stakes, then, are drawn from life experience with which you identify. In fact, naturalism and absurdism are born of the same source. The subtitle of *Jack or the Submission* is *A Naturalistic Comedy*. Ionesco's point is not that his nonsensical universe is not real life, but that it is: you figure how. An absurd universe is a glimpse of human nature reflected in a fun-house mirror.

Since the playwright already provides that distortion, if you try to play "absurdly," you often end up undermining the playwright's common sense; if you play with utter conviction and believability, then you show the world we live in for what it is: absurd.

Nonsense is serious stuff.

In the naturalistic idiom, O'Neill turns the clown into the poet. Some of Edmund's dialogue in *Long Day's Journey into Night* is the very anthem of existentialism, as he "stumble[s] on to nowhere, for no good reason." (Act IV). Be wary of approaching this play as just a very long look at family life. Even the title betrays the diseased family's common objective: surviving one more rotation of the earth. Treat the objective "I will last," though, not as a cop-out, but as valiant—the mission of a hero. Without objective, the play is just talk, talk, and more talk; with objective, it can attain the heights of triumph and the depths of tragedy and pathos.

No Objective?

Mysterious and esoteric scripts, like much of absurdist drama, may defy you to determine an objective. You may be tempted to experiment without one, hoping it will be revealed to you by the sheer act of saying the words in the circumstances of the play. This may be an informative experiment if the objective "drops in" by itself, unforced. Eleonora Duse would evolve the blocking by repeating text over and over until she had to do something. One can imagine her gestures all the more powerful for their sparseness. But having no objective by the time of performance is not an option. Moreover, this objective-free process may be problematic for your fellow actors in rehearsal: how can they possibly react when you are not imposing your will on them? It will be more effective to engage some objective, even if you exchange it later for a better one.

Duse, Lucille Ball, and Bert Lahr would automatically be worth the audience's dollar. The rest of us must find a way to infuse objectives into mysterious, nondramatic, or nonsensical scenarios in order to provide dramatic momentum; otherwise we may have very little hope of keeping the audience awake.

Textural Objectives:
Values, Peeves, and Passions

Consciously or not, we all embrace a value system of (among other things) passions and peeves: what we esteem most highly, or what turns us on; and what we oppose most vehemently, or what disgusts us. For the little boy at

Boston Garden who blurted "it was awaaaaay," perhaps all his passions were the Bruins.

For a character, these values carry the force of objectives and create the texture of life. During the course of the play they may generate a brief detour or two from your main through-line of action. Dorothy stops for fellow travelers because even though she wants to get back to Kansas, she can't help befriending creatures in need. There would be no dramatic texture to *The Wizard of Oz* if she were not kind in this way.

So for any role, try listing your five (or so) pet passions and peeves. Let at least one or two of them be indefensible, not expressly mentioned in the script: sometimes the silliest one will turn into an anchor for your characterization.

Example. In the Off-Broadway production of A. R. Gurney's *The Cocktail Hour,* the mother's first entrance was striking, and telling: She travelled all over her living room and adjusted virtually every object a millimeter or two while engaging in delightful conversation. It was as if cleaning, ordering, and controlling her environment to the *nth* degree were her normal demeanor. This flourish of an entrance let the audience instantly experience the burden of having been raised in that home. It certainly made my jaw drop.[9]

So peeves and passions are your stakes in living from moment to moment as a full human being. Incorporate them so that you wipe with your particular brand of propriety, primp with your own vanity, and flick the ash of your cigarette with your special nonchalance.

VISION

The Playwright's Vision

Perhaps more important even than the objective is the question:

"Why are we doing this play in the first place?"

Not all plays germinate from the same seed as *War and Peace*: but from the point of view of their creators, they at least match Tolstoy in depth and importance. Whether or not they involve the act of war, *great plays feature great fights,* ranging from family, class, race, and political struggles to those of the heart. Your task is to figure out how to get the audience to fight alongside you.

So much of the twentieth century's drama can be styled *theater of ideas.* This label is odd in a way, for when is a play not about an idea? But these plays often seem to be generated from an idea rather than from a real-life situation; they may not pretend to even a modicum of believability in the naturalistic sense. Sartre's *No Exit* takes place in his version of hell, Genêt's *The Balcony* during his mythical Revolution, and Tennessee Williams's *Camino Real* on life's *real*, or "royal," road—his view, perhaps, of purgatory. Sometimes, then, it is only by understanding the playwright that you can even begin to be passionate about the play, and get your audience to be too.

To mount a classical play, it will help to complete the following analogy:

The playwright's audience was to his play then as today's audience is to what *now?*

Coming up with the *what* is the task of rehearsal. You want to have already gotten familiar with the other three variables—the play, society then, and society now. Think of it this way: what was the author trying to say to his audience; and what do you want to say to yours?

So check out a playwright's other works, a biography or two, writings of those who influenced him, and accounts of contemporaries who knew him. All can be invaluable.

Example. Shaw was a radical of his day: a humanist and social reformer in a conservative society. Higgins (Shaw's semi-autobiographical role) expresses his own egalitarianism as he remonstrates to the bawling Eliza late in *Pygmalion:*

> The great secret, Eliza, is not having bad manners or good manners or any particular sort of manners, but having the same manners for all human souls: in short, behaving as if you were in Heaven, where there are no third-class carriages, and one soul is as good as another.

When you realize how singular this egalitarian vision was in 1912, you can see Higgins as not merely arrogant, but also wonderful—which is no doubt how he sees himself.

The author's point of view might have to be gleaned in subtler ways. Perhaps your character is based on someone he knew, or someone famous. Perhaps he wrote in reaction to something else, a clue that may help you see the world of his play.

Example. Chekhov, in his pastoral comedies, was reacting against Russian drama like that of Turgenev. So in performing *Uncle Vanya: Scenes from Country Life* it is important that the production not start out as overtly ridden with plot intrigues as Turgenev's *A Month in the Country.* By including the subtitle in his play, Chekhov invokes the earlier piece as a lens through which to view his own work. He wants us to notice that his vision departs from his predecessor's. Unlike *A Month in the Country*, no tryst is consummated in *Vanya,* though a few are craved.

In fact, Turgenev was something of a gigolo himself: understandably, his characters inhabit a world full of adultery and intrigue. Chekhov was tubercular; his characters (at least some) inhabit a world full of—nothing at all. It is this sense of frustration, despair, and emptiness treated comically, wherein lie the soul of Russia and, arguably, the greatness of Chekhov's works.

For the director, familiarity with the playwright's other work is mandatory; for the actor, it can be revelatory. Try reading some of Chekhov's short stories, which are valentines to the Russian people. These tone poems and character studies expose human frailty and peccadilloes, but at the same time reveal a sense of universal glory in the human condition. So with your next sigh in a Chekhov drama, you might reveal a guileless soul in abject despair.

I offer here the old saw regarding what the actor should do to cover in case he ever goes up on his lines during a performance: "In an Ionesco play, just repeat the last line you said; in Mamet, just swear; in Chekhov, *sigh.*" But whatever you do, do it with Stakes!

The Play's Vision

The Fallacy of Intent

By identifying the vision of the play as opposed to that of the playwright, I am distinguishing what she might have said after writing it from what's in the script itself. In a way, the script takes on a personality of its own and becomes its own author and defender. The author can later have a change of heart or mind; but once the play has been published, or released, she has let it go. It is when the imagination of the actors and director marries the invention of the playwright that the scripted character is born as a living organism.

So keep in mind the "fallacy of intent." You are not obliged to uphold what the playwright said her intent was, nor what was deleted from a previous draft. You are only obliged to serve what finally appears as the play itself. The playwright's views expressed outside the script may shed light, but you get to choose whether to apply what you discover. Research, remember, is to serve you, rather than you serving *it*, even when it comes from the author's pen.

In an afterword, Shaw tries to describe what happens after the final curtain of *Pygmalion*: Eliza will eventually marry Freddy and support him, Colonel Pickering helping to establish her in a flower shop. Alan Jay Lerner, in a note to the reading edition of *My Fair Lady*, confesses: "Shaw and heaven forgive me!—I am not certain he is right." Unlike a librettist or lyricist, of course, an actor does not alter the text. But there ends his responsibility to the playwright. I am not saying that Eliza will not end up with Freddy; they are fictional characters, after all. But in his creative state, Shaw wisely left the future relationship between Higgins and Eliza ambiguous in the play (as opposed to in his notes); and from this very ambiguity arises the play's eroticism. Besides, we all know that the character of Henry Higgins was close to Shaw himself: how could he have been objective about Higgins's future? (By the way, the movie *Pygmalion* ends like the musical—or vice versa.)

Every playwright carefully orchestrates ambiguities. But even though he may suggest how to render them specific, the responsibility for doing so lies with the actor and director.

The Production's Vision

Ensemble Techniques and Spell-Casting

Sometimes the ensemble takes on a personality with a voice of its own which, like that of the playwright or the play, can inform your interpretation. This will be particularly true of productions that are staged without a fourth wall or that are otherwise non-naturalistic.

How does an ensemble's personality inform your own stakes? The answer is as varied as the numerous directors and ensembles with which you will work.

Example. My *Hamlet* toured for a season before a week of brush-up rehearsals leading to a New York run. Over the course of that season, the form solidified, but the purpose of the piece atrophied. The actors knew their lines and what they meant so well that they spoke too rapidly to be understood. The blocking was tight and efficient but the performance was pointless.

During the brush-ups, then, we focused not on the blocking or text, which the actors knew very well, but on the ritual of casting a spell for the audience. *Performing a play is not merely* like *casting a spell: it* is *casting a spell.* We cast spells in life all the time, from saying a prayer, to knocking on wood and avoiding cracks in the sidewalk, to cheerleading at ball games. In the theater, a spell cannot be cast until you actually decide to do so.

The addition of a candle helped. The ensemble lit it and placed it onstage during their group warm-up huddle long before the audience arrived. At this session, each actor contributed some episode, from his life or from the media, of what is "rotten" in the world today as it was "in the state of Denmark." This ritual personalized the evening's performance in no uncertain terms, individually and as a group.

When the actors went back onstage at the top of the show (but before the house went fully dark), they each took a moment to look directly at the audience, embracing the pain of the world, or channeling it, or just saying hello. This action initiated the rapport with the audience. The cast's purpose was to incant the spirit and story of Hamlet in the hope that mankind today (the audience) might not be doomed to repeat the tragedy.

Their final pre-show action was to blow the candle out. This business represented—metaphorically, it re-enacted—the murder of Hamlet's father prior to the first scene of the play. It also symbolized the extinguishing of any light in the world, like hope, goodness, or even God (often represented by the Eternal Flame).

The performance, now emerging from this snuffed out candle, transformed into something approaching a kind of a mystical experience—a result particularly apropos to *Hamlet*, which is, after all, a ghost story.

Spell-casting may seem an odd notion to you, but I assure you it is not an uncommon technique. If it helps, think in terms of a blessing instead of a spell.

My company of *Macbeth* consulted a local witch to bless the space with us at midnight on the new moon prior to opening, in the hope of beating the alleged curse that has followed this play for centuries. (Attendance was not mandatory; but eerily enough, there were exactly thirteen people at this event—a lucky number indeed.) The theater was located on what had been sacred Native American burial grounds, so they didn't want to take any chances. They also (of their own volition) burned sage backstage throughout the run of the play; I am told that sage was also burned backstage during Robert Falls's *Rose Tattoo* on Broadway.

Now, this may seem like a lot of hogwash to you, but don't knock it till you've tried it. These two plays have characters who are witches, and *Hamlet* features a ghost, but all plays involve the human spirit trying to get somewhere or do something. Treat that spirit with reverence and awe, and your payoff, I assure you, will be unpredictable and worth your while—and your audience's.

Your Vision

A friend of mine says that he looks at every day of life as part of an apprenticeship to the day we die. To the actor, analogously, every life experience is fodder to nourish each performance. The charisma with which you captivate your audience is a product not just of your work onstage, but of this life experience.

So besides reading, questioning, listening, and traveling, do not be above, say, joining the Peace Corps. How else could you really personalize Brecht's war-torn, morally ambiguous, economically deprived worlds of *The Good Person of Szechwan*, *Mother Courage*, and *The Caucasian Chalk Circle*? You can't; you can only pretend to. The more you live and see and care, the more you will be able to make the audience believe.

CHAPTER 4
CONNECTION

Electricity, of course, is invisible; but you can tell it's working when the flashlight goes on or the motor starts to hum. Likewise, although no one can really tell a beginning actor how to "connect," one can notice when she fails to do so. Like riding a bicycle, you can talk about it to death, but you can't do it until you do it. Then, as you do it over and over again, it becomes part of your natural stage demeanor. The task is one of ultimate complexity, and utter simplicity. So although I cannot exactly define the stuff of Connection (for there is no stuff to it), I will discuss its effect on various facets of the performance—turning the flashlight on—and offer some exercises to practice achieving it.

Some of these exercises have been designed for rehearsals, others for class or workshop with no particular script in hand. Yet even these have proved useful to the rehearsal process from time to time when it became clear that a company needed one of them. When a scene is not quite working, it may be hard to identify *what* is needed, but these exercises will give you a few things to try.

We connect in many ways:

- *to the space, including both*
    - *the hall (and the audience) and*
    - *the theatrical world;*
- *to other actors;*
- *to the circumstances of the play, including*
    - text,
    - tasks, *and*
    - other impulses;
- *to the moment; and*
- *to your entire acting instrument, including both*
    - inner life *and its*
    - physical expression.

Moreover, you want your battery to keep the performance's motor running continually, generating not just occasional sparks of electricity, but a constant current. So this parameter also entails:

- *transforming the need to communicate something—*
  Meaning and Stakes—into an active impulse; and
- *linking each moment to the next.*

MAGIC AND FRUSTRATION

Connection is what paves the way for magic to come-a-visiting; it is also what makes acting so mysterious, for the medium that conducts theatrical electricity is intangible. You cannot measure this electricity as you can voltage. And usually the audience only notices when the connection is broken, like when the flashlight goes off.

There is the story about a particular performance of Laurence Olivier's when everything just happened to click, both onstage and with the audience. Everyone in the theater could tell they were participating in a unique, almost miraculous experience. But backstage after the show, he was miserable. Someone asked him why he was so upset when he had just given such an extraordinary performance. He replied, exasperated, "Because I don't know how I did it!"

This kind of other-worldly brilliance is so fragile, so transient, that it cannot be duplicated at will. While you the actor are in control of your lines and blocking, you cannot be in control of this magic. All you can do is let yourself be a little bit out of control, or open to its possibility. Open does not mean undisciplined: the trick is how to be out of control properly. And when you are performing at your best, you won't notice how you are doing it.

Is an actor like Olivier great because his work was consistently fine, or because every once in a while it was unforgettably fine? Probably both. Technique refers to two different processes: it is what you rely on when inspiration is lacking, so that your performance will reach 95 percent of your potential 95 percent of the time; it also refers to how you encourage that inspiration to drop in so that you operate at 105 percent as often as possible.

Reapplying the pre-orchestrated form of the production—text, blocking, rhythm—you hope to achieve a magical performance. "But if I repeat exactly the same performance," you may ask, "how is that remaining open?" The subtle distinction: You don't actually repeat the performance; you repeat the form. Etymologically, *perform* = "by or through the form." You the actor are to a great extent in control of that form, while you the character—are not!

The suspense of not completely knowing what is about to happen is precisely what makes the theater great. In control yet out of control, re-creating rather than repeating, each moment generating the next rather than last night's performance generating tonight's, letting it happen again for the first (and only) time rather than making it happen the way it did last time: these qualities make a performance dynamic, full of the spark of life. For putting up with the frustration, every so often the theater rewards an actor with an evening of magic.

So the act of theater can be likened to giving a gift, but the gift is in the giving.

***Being truly present* is *the present*.**

CONNECTING TO INNER LIFE

Emotion Memory

You may already be familiar with *emotion memory,* the mapping of personal experience into the character. The process entails recalling some emotional event from your past by finding a device to trigger the feeling. Do not underestimate the power of smells and sounds (like songs).

Keep in mind, though, that the technique's value derives not from being conscious of tapping your own life, but from your character's being able to tap it automatically. You may recall your tears at your grandfather's funeral to inform your character's tears onstage, but your character cannot actually be mourning your grandfather. Similarly, you may be an angry feminist, but your Joan of Arc should be fighting the English invaders (and the French clergy) as opposed to today's male-based power structure. Your own feminism may inform your acting, but not necessarily rule it (unless, of course, it happens to work). Personalization techniques like emotion memory are tools to root your character in human truth and to strengthen her conviction, not to confound her situation with your own.

The Siphon

To connect to your inner life, Stanislavski offers the elegant metaphor of the siphon: You can't force the emotion up from the tank; rather, you tap it gently, or organically. His Magic *If* provides the tube. (See Character, pp. 6-7.)

In other words, Acting ≠ Emoting. Far more fundamental is belief in your specific circumstances; the appropriate inner life should follow automatically.

An ounce of believing is worth a ton of emoting.

Besides, your character is not thinking of the feelings you need to summon for the part. *An emotional state is never the goal of the character.* With rare exception, a character wants to avoid those feelings. Monitoring inner life constitutes falling out of character and, ironically, damps those very feelings.

If you cannot yet laugh hysterically or cry on cue, work toward embracing the full circumstances of each role: laughter and tears should follow. Meanwhile, you have many methods at your disposal for deepening your emotional capacity, including:

- Study emotion memory intensely, which implies that you also:
- Become a subjective, unbridled observer of (and participant in) life. Let yourself laugh, cry, be afraid, and so forth, without caring what anyone else thinks.
- Become a subjective, unbridled participant in art and literature. When you read fiction, live in it; when you see a movie, enter the screen; at the art museum, think of yourself as in the canvas. If you have never cried while watching a play, how can you hope to cry when you are in one?
- If it works for you, find a technique class where you work on building to a primal scream. Then when cast in a role requiring such emotional depth, you should have a font of feeling at your disposal, if you can tap it in character. Be careful, though: For some people, not being able to scream can instill insecurity that they will never be actors, when they may simply never be *screaming* actors.

Remember that *holding back generates greater intensity*. The pressure inside a boiling pot increases when you leave the lid on.

Any other technique you come across for filling or tapping your ocean of emotion, whether in-depth or short-cut, go right ahead and try. If it works, keep it in your creative arsenal.

RUDIMENTARY CONNECTION

Just as in playing the piano, a piano keystroke—the transmission of a single sound—is the building block of the pianist's technique, so does the organic transmission of an impulse constitute the basic element of acting. The following exercises build to a continuous series of these impulses; they might be thought of as the keystrokes, scales, and arpeggios of acting.

Do not imagine that these exercises are too rudimentary if you have never done them. All artists, of every discipline, spend a long incubation period on the rudiments, regardless of how painstaking the process might be. If you are in an ensemble or a company, they will even be fun. If you are a working freelance actor, they will be a reminder of what should be going on while you are onstage; you may even want to find a basic technique class where you can practice them.

Odd as they may seem to the uninitiated, if you can do these exercises removed from the context of a role, then connecting within dramatic circumstances should become second nature.

Connecting to the Space

The Hall

Stanislavski recognized how difficult it is to truly connect. His Circles of Concentration exercise (or this version of it) should be done in a theater if possible rather than a rehearsal room so that it helps to alleviate the difficulty intrinsic to achieving naturalness on the stage.

Exercise: Circles of Concentration. Start by choosing any point in the theater. Simply look at it. Stay relaxed, concentrate, and let no expectation of results lurk in the back of your mind. Get to know that point. (No, this is not psycho-babble, but basic acting technique—really.) Spend a few minutes each day with that point. After a few days, expand your concentration to a small circle surrounding it. Then, an ever-increasing circle, until your concentration encompasses the entire theater. Stanislavski's actors engaged in regular exercises over a period of years to eventually connect to every seat in the Moscow Art Theater.[10]

What, did the father of Method Acting and purveyor of the "fourth wall" ask his actors to look out into the audience? Yes, because once you firmly establish connection to the hall, even the imaginary installment of a fourth wall will not short-circuit it. In performance, that connection will conduct your thoughts to the back row, even when you are not looking at the audience. For one, your diaphragm will automatically supply enough vocal power (if you have warmed up beforehand). When you project your inner life, too, you develop what we call *presence*.

The young and those on tour, I have developed a quick version of Circles:

Exercise: Hugging the Back Row. Individually or as a group, literally go and hug each seat in the back row of the theater, and say out loud, "I promise that you will hear everything I say and do not say." You can embellish this with personal statements like "I love you," "you are my friend," or "you are on my side"—whatever works for you. Let this statement be as intimate as you can make it, so your performance will be, too.

Sounds corny, but if you really mean it, it works, especially when accompanied by a vocal warm-up (see appendix 2) and the following exercise.

Exercise: Audience Talk-Back. Get a partner or two—or better yet, ten—to try this corollary to the above exercise, where you fill the hall by projecting impulses that involve text. (The focus of this activity is the projection, not the work on the text.) Half of you sit onstage, while the other half sit or stand in the audience, near the back. Then, quite simply, talk to each other. Make sure you can hear each other without shouting.

Then trade places.

Try this first with house lights on, so that you can see each other, and then turn them off, as during the performance. Work hard to maintain this connection once the house is dark. As always, stay relaxed. Later your rapport with the actual audience should be just as focused, yet easy and relaxed.

To make sure one's connection with the back row is real and specific, I have companies do the following:

Variation. Half the cast (say, of a company of ten or so) stand behind the back row of the house, the other half spread across the stage. Take a line of text treated as nonsense; it can be a line of text from the play you are working on or one of the following:

- **The letters of the alphabet, in order.**
- **The numbers one through ten, in order.**
- **The months of the year, in order.**
- **The days of the week, in order.**

(Keep this list of "nonsense texts" handy for other exercises.) Decide which of these texts you are going to use before continuing. Do not use two at once, because part of the point of using nonsensical text is so that you need not think of what the next "line" is.

The first person, say onstage, connects with a single person behind the back row, realizes he has something he really wants to say to her, and then speaks his nonsensical text to communicate that real something. It is important that he send out a real impulse, albeit on a received text that does not necessarily have anything to do with that impulse. In other words, *three* is not to mean "one more than two," but can only be the set of sounds you use to communicate what you really mean to say, such as "your eyes are very blue" or "your shoelace is untied," or the ever popular "I hate this exercise." A coach—director, teacher, or appointed leader—monitors to ensure that each actor is actually talking about something real.

The person in the back row who thinks she has just been addressed (the addressee) now has the floor, and proceeds to talk, as above, to someone onstage of her choosing. If she is not really the addressee, then the first person (the speaker) interrupts her and repeats his original line, trying to make his connection to the original addressee stronger and clearer. If the actual addressee guesses her identity correctly, she becomes the next speaker and continues by finishing her line of text, this time uninterrupted. As each speaker communicates successfully, he takes a place among that other group until everyone has changed places once or twice.

You are trying to project not just the words, but also the very ray of communication as you fire it, almost like a bullet. So be specific with (1) what you mean, and (2) to whom you direct it.

This exercise is not easy, and at first might take a while. Its effect on actors' performances can be amazing.

The World of the Play

Spend some time alone on the set as your character, and apply a variation of the Circles of Concentration exercise, choosing circles onstage as well as in the audience seats. This is especially valuable when the décor consists of your character's home, or any other location with which he would be very familiar. You want to belong naturally to your surroundings without having to act as if you do. Do more than imagine living in it; actually live in it.

Conversely, you can spend time in a space like that of the play, and then transfer that experience to the stage. Lunt and Fontanne could be found dining together backstage before a performance in much the same fashion they were to dine together onstage. Similarly, when I was rehearsing the role of Biedermann in Max Frisch's *The Firebugs*, "my wife Babette" and I invited our two guests Schmitz and Eisenring (the arsonists) to dinner— served by the actor playing our maid. We addressed each other by character names throughout the evening. Back in rehearsal, we re-created this experience through *sense memory*, which you may have practiced.

Exercise: Sense Memory. Take a small object. Best is an organic one like a piece of fruit that fits in your hand. Each day, sniff, feel, and look at it from all sorts of different angles. Then put it in your hand and leave it there. Feel it and look at it in this one position. Study its sensorial impression on you. Then put it down, and re-create it in your hand in that position. Not just in your mind's eye, but with your senses. Feel its surface, its weight, its temperature; see its color, texture, sheen; smell it. Go back and forth, with the fruit in your hand and out of it, to make sure your memory is accurate.

Note, for example, how your hand adjusts to hold it. When you grasp an apple or orange, most likely your two smaller fingers curve in a bit more than you'd think. Hold your hand the same way without the fruit there as you do with it there.

Do this with the same piece of fruit every day. Put it in your hand, take it out, then magically re-create it in your hand while it is sitting on the table. Because it is organic, it will start to change after a few days—ripen, change color, get softer. Inspect it anew every day. Spend a good two weeks with the same piece of fruit if it lasts that long.

Sense memory is the basic building block of convincing. Once you undergo the above painstaking process and can create an orange that is not there, you will be well on your way to getting your audience to believe you in anything.

The Overall

The best actors apply sense memory to create their entire physical environment, or *overall*, even when it has not been discussed at rehearsal. Many has been the time when a professional actor in rehearsal was not quite believable, and it turned out that he did not even know where he entered from, other than "stage right." Meanwhile, some other actor was incredibly compelling in the same scene. Why? Because, I find out, he had already determined what lay in the wing from which he entered, having established his overall down to the dust on the mantle.

Strive to become the believable and compelling actor. If you are playing the Gentleman Caller, see the Wingfields' faded lavender wallpaper peeling around the edges of dust-covered, yellowing sconces in the living room, even without wallpaper or sconces there. Long before you break a figurine in Laura's *Glass Menagerie*, then, you will automatically sense something strange in the house—and get the spectator to sense it, too.

If on an ocean liner, feel the rocking of the ship, hear the whoosh of the ocean, and smell the salt air to get the spectators as intoxicated as you. Similarly, if you are playing the Rainmaker, breathe the fresh air of the prairie so you can be a breath of fresh air to everyone else in the play, and to the audience.

Connection between Two Actors

Many American actors think that connection means merely making eye contact, but more is involved: you also have to be able to stay connected with something (or someone) at which you are not looking. Yet this is something we do all the time in life. Say you are carrying on a conversation with a group of people who are surrounding you. You stay connected to those on your left even while looking at those on your right, and vice versa—automatically.

With this in mind, let us start with the connection between just two people. If you have not done exercises like this before, it may not be as easy as you think.

Without Text

This exercise can be done one pair at a time while everyone else watches, or, if your area is large enough, with many pairs going at it at once.

Exercise: "Just Looking." Let every actor in the company pair up. Just look at your partner. Just look, and just be. Again, have no results in mind but seeing each other fully. Concentrate, relax, and keep breathing. You will discover how difficult this is as your teeth involuntarily clench, or you hold your breath, or the giggles set in. Get to feel comfortable with this state of just looking at each other. Thoughts will pop up in your mind; at first, try to let them go, rather than entertaining them. Later, try to distinguish the thoughts that are generated by and are about the situation from those that come from nervousness and are unrelated. What, you ask? I want you to monitor your inner life? Yes, because this is not acting, but an exercise—the very one to help you not monitor your connection later when you *are* acting.

Therefore, try to dismiss unrelated, awkward impulses that signal falling out of connection. Do entertain thoughts about what is going on between you. This is the birth of the dynamic connection that is automatic in life but not always in acting.

Variation. Once the above has progressed (over a period of hours, days, or weeks) to the point where you are naturally connected, then try to add a little content by assuming one adjustment at a time. First, assume the mild objective of "trying to find out all you can" about your partner, without words or sounds, and without even necessarily moving (although motion per se is not forbidden if it is spontaneous and organic). It helps if you do not know your partner too well. Wonder specific things about him: what did he have for breakfast? did he sleep enough last night? is he a kind person? Little by little, notice how your partner communicates with every aspect of his physical instrument, down to the hands and toes. Even when one is not trying to use the face, it becomes surprisingly expressive, as does breathing. Eventually you will almost be able to read each other's mind and heart. You may be wrong, but so what? We often misread people, after all. This makes life—and stage life—spicy.

After a while, mere eye contact will no longer be all that's going on; you start to connect from the gut.

Exercise: First Meeting. This is again a two-person exercise, but which two may be left to spontaneity: first one in goes first.

One of your group—say, you—goes into the playing space, or onstage, to explore the environment. The adjustment you assume is that hitherto you have been the only creature in your world onstage. (In a rehearsal space, draw, tape, or indicate a line where this world ends and the rest of the company can situate themselves.) No language has yet been developed. All of a sudden you run across another creature—as the second actor joins you onstage.

You take it from there. Sounds are allowed, but not words. Again, no results are to be forced, and you must have no sense of hurrying. Just see how you would honestly process the addition of a new creature added to your theatrical landscape.

How would you communicate without words? If the people involved in the exercise are naturally interesting, interesting results will ensue. Remember, though, that the results are not the goal—the connection is, this time within a limited scenario.

With Text

Exercise: First Speaking. Go through the same First Meeting exercise, engaging each other with growing interest until one of you gets to the point where he is compelled to speak. Then when you do, your language is one of the nonsense texts. Again, the content of what you are saying must be about what is really going on between you and the other actor, not about what the words suggest. To make sure of this, every now and then the coach may ask you for a verbal translation (in English) of what you really meant when you just said "two-three-four," "February–March" or "Tuesday." Alternately, he may ask your partner what you meant, which you may then either confirm or deny. Your impulses must remain true even though the text is false (or nonsensical). While responding in English, the actors should not look up at the coach but maintain their connection with each other; this requires intense concentration and focus.

Exercise: First Reading. Now use as your nonsense text the actual words of the play—but again, only their sounds, not their meaning. For though you assume the language, do not assume the characters or situation yet.

This exercise is done sitting, with scripts open and at first placed under chairs. You start with the First Meeting/First Speaking exercises until one participant needs to say something. Then, instead of saying "Monday–Tuesday . . ." she reaches down for her script to glance at the next line and uses the words of her character's dialogue. If you get to the point of having to speak and the next line is not yours, then remain silent—with that impulse to speak—until your partner finishes her speech. (The coach may once more intervene to ensure that meaning is unrelated to words.)

The First Reading exercise is not to get you to mean the text, but to get you to the point of really meaning *something,* and having to say it. Having to speak demands more from you than simply knowing the words.

The painstaking parts of this exercise are the long boring periods when participants actually have nothing to say. When you don't arrive at a *must* you are not to speak yet. Pace goes out the window; but you are not working on pace. Those periods help the actors' sense of finding the *must*—the compulsion to speak. If you merely pretend to have to say the next thing, you will look like you are doing just that, or "phoning it in."

Later, rehearsing a play, you will recognize when you have found the right *must* for each line; then you work on finding it quickly. Such a must gives rise to an impulse. *Impulse* can refer to any bit of information, verbal or nonverbal, that is sent out (and received) via a wave of communication; you might even think of it as the wave itself. In terms of electricity, it is the transfer of a charge. It can be as large as the climax of the play or as small as an innuendo betrayed nonverbally by a twitch of the eyebrow, a gasp of breath, or a moistening of the lips. In other words, it is a miniature event for the character sending or receiving it. (We tend to save the word *event,* however, for a moment that changes something or someone a bit more drastically; we talk of the event of a scene, but the *impulse* of a moment.)

Ensemble Connection

An ensemble trading impulses is like a jazz combo jamming. Both actors and musicians, interestingly, are said to play, whether instruments or roles. If the instrumentalists do not really listen and respond to each other when they jam, their solos deteriorate into mere notes, just as in acting.

In the following exercise, there is no text, only the communication of impulses. Each impulse is unpredictable—spontaneously generated rather than scripted or rehearsed—so you simply have to listen and connect in order to communicate, and cannot help but start jamming.

Exercise: Ball Tossing 101. The ensemble forms a wide circle, each actor facing toward the center a good arm's length or more from his neighbor. You might want to start by tossing a real ball. A dodge ball, beach ball, or soccer-sized plastic ball would probably be most effective here, as they can be thrown directly, bounced off a wall, or tossed high overhead, allowing for a few surprises. The ball does not proceed down the line of the circle, but from one person to another at random, generally across the circle. The receiver will be whomever the ball-tosser chooses on the spur of the moment. Each catcher deals with the task of catching the ball without thinking, for if he stops a moment to analyze, he will drop the ball—just as in acting.

Next, put aside the real ball, and toss around an imaginary ball. This requires greater concentration. Here's the catch: Each time someone has possession of the "ball," he changes its size, mass, and substance. It could be transformed into something small and heavy, or big and light and airy, metamorphosing from a Superball® to a Slinky® to a leaden anchor. Everyone stays connected, focused, and prepared for the unexpected in order to catch the continually transforming ball.

Possession of the ball, with the attention of the entire group, corresponds to taking and commanding focus while you deliver a line. The tossing itself is the moment of trying to evoke a response from someone, analogous to transferring or throwing the focus as you give her a cue. Ball Tossing 101 not only helps with connection and spontaneity but also improves the ensemble's focus.

Exercise: Sound and Movement. The Sound and Movement is probably the most comprehensive of all acting exercises. It is like Ball Tossing 101, but now it involves more than just an imaginary ball. As it is highly physical, a warm-up is mandatory. You must be fully stretched and flexed in order to be fully free to react; otherwise you could sprain something in a sudden, highly physical reaction. Ditto with the vocal warm-up. (See appendix 2.)

You can start with just a movement exercise if you wish, and add the sound aspect after everyone in your group has become familiar with the format.

Step 1: After the warm-up, the ensemble stands in a wide circle as in Ball Tossing. First everyone works on getting into the present moment. This is no small order, and can take a few minutes or quite a while. If there is any baggage in your psyche from what happened on the way to rehearsal or from what your boyfriend said last night, now is the time to indulge it and then to let it go. Breathe deeply, jump up and down a few times, and shake it out. Clear your mind and get to neutral, emotionally and physically, so that you can be open and ready to respond to others.

When you arrive at that neutral, start to look at everyone else in the ensemble—that is, connect with them. Finally you are in the moment. Once everyone is, the group is ready to move.

Step 2: The beginner goes into the middle of the circle. How do you choose the beginner? Sometimes one is assigned. I prefer not knowing ahead of time, letting the beginner be whoever first feels some inner impulse so compelling that he has to express it (keeping in mind that this is not a contest). How, you may ask, do you know you are compelled to communicate something until you know what that something is? Ah, this is the very lifelike state that we aspire to attain: not actually thinking our thoughts until the very moment we need to express them. Ideally, then, the beginner does not even decide to begin; as soon as his impulse is born, he starts moving to communicate it. There is no place for shyness among actors, remember.

Once all realize that everyone else is connected and has arrived at neutral, the beginner starts advancing to the center of the circle in a periodic cycle of movement and sound that expresses her inner state with her entire instrument—body, limbs, face, voice. She does not think about her inner state, but just does her gesture, unpremeditated. The period unit should be a few seconds long, perhaps the length of a short sentence. She repeats the sound and corresponding movement over and over without pausing. Perhaps for three or four cycles she develops it, but once it has been established, she sets the exterior gestures into a consistent, repeatable pattern. She also alters the direction she faces with each iteration to give everyone the opportunity to observe, study, and connect with her.

Step 3: While the beginner is in the middle, observers on the ring can be quite active in practicing her gesture, although only one of them will be formally obliged to do so (step 4). Alternatively, they may respond instead of copying, or even do nothing physically, as long as they are connected.

Step 4: Once the beginner has made sure to connect with everyone, she picks someone at random and approaches him, traveling while repeating her cycle. The person picked is no longer a mere observer, but is now obliged to duplicate the beginner's sound and movement precisely. The two repeat the gesture at the same time over and over as the transfer takes place. The trick: you duplicate not just the exterior life (physical, facial, vocal), but the feeling, attitude, and energy as well. Pay careful attention to the precise position of feet, hands, face, and fingers. A sloppy rendition of the exterior life means that inner life is not accurate.

Step 5: When the beginner accepts that the second person's rendition of her sound and movement is exact, she takes his place in the outer circle, and he comes to the center (continuing the cycle as they invert position). On arriving at center, he spontaneously transforms the cycle into a sound and movement of his own. This change is a response to the beginner's gesture, either building on or reacting to it.

Step 6: The second person repeats steps 2–5 above, and so it goes until everyone has been in the circle at least once.

When you first start practicing this exercise, it may take a while to develop your gestures and transfer them accurately. But before long you should be able to respond and duplicate instantly. Eventually you will not need more than three or four repetitions either to establish or to transfer your cycle. The more quickly you get to exchanging the impulses rather than repeating them, the more effective the exercise, the value of which lies in what happens *between*.

The inner life, or *inner gesture*, that accompanies the outer gesture in a repeatable phrase can be capricious and light or deeply personal. Like the outer, it can build on what the previous person was expressing, or it can change it entirely—as long as this change is a response to, not a denial of, the previous person's cycle.

Strive to do this exercise without letting words come into your thoughts as you react. The sensibilities you draw from onstage are not limited to what words can express: so be specific, but not literal or literary. Likewise, avoid programmatic gestures like waving hello, swatting a fly, or doing the twist. The movement and sound should be the abstract expression of your word-free inner state.

The tendency to premeditate and plan what your sound and movement are going to be must be overcome, too (and generally it can be overcome quickly). The point is not that you act well, but *re*-act spontaneously.

Sound and Movement is the ultimate theater exercise, for it summons all the nonanalytical processes you engage in as an actor: connecting honestly, trading impulses dynamically, reacting spontaneously, and expressing with your entire instrument. (Of course it does not involve received circumstances or text, which a script would supply.) It is also a fantastic tool for expanding your range, for as you do it over a period of months or years, you have at your disposal all the sensibilities of your fellow actors which you have duplicated in detail. I believe it was Toscanini who said, "When I was six, I could conduct 'sweetly' in about six ways; now that I am sixty, I can conduct 'sweetly' in six hundred ways." This broadening of means of expression is what growth means to an artist.

Tasks

Stanislavski discussed how difficult it is for an actor simply to walk from one point onstage to another—believably. As soon as we *have* to act naturally, our very purpose becomes artificial. In life, when we fold laundry, scrub pots, or shell peas, we need not try to look like we are, but are free to carry on conversation and look elsewhere. So do we strive onstage.

Exercise: Folding Laundry. Try delivering any memorized speech while you are occupied with some repetitive motor activity, such as folding laundry, setting up chairs, erecting a house of playing cards, or something from a script you are rehearsing. The rote motion aids in relaxation and concentration, and somehow facilitates one's natural connection to the task, the text, and the person addressed. The mechanism is similar to the way chewing tobacco improves baseball pitchers' accuracy. Expressly trying to connect tends to short-circuit the naturalness of the connection; happening to connect while doing something else is far closer to what we do in life all the time.

Substitution Technique

Onstage you will not necessarily be folding laundry. Actors assemble devices they can draw upon, like a bag of tricks, to simulate effects even with no activity to help achieve those effects. For instance, if your posture automatically becomes more regal when you hold a cane or a staff, you can re-create that staff through sense memory when you want to play an emperor; though a real scepter might help, you don't need it.

The task may be a mental one when no prop is involved. On one episode of *Friends,* I am told, the actor shares his secret for how to play a particularly serious moment: simply try to divide 27 into 243 (or something like that; I don't watch the series). Actually engaging in some real task, albeit not the character's task, often comes off more believable than pretending to have the quality you think the character requires. After all, your character is not trying to have that quality; he is trying to do something.

These devices are worth keeping as long as they work. But because what works for you for ten years may eventually become stale, listen to your director when he asks you to find something new.

Conflict

Any cross, gesture, or task actually constitutes a mini-playlet, complete with a local objective and the three components of a phrase: beginning, middle, and end. You cross because you want to attain something. So first, connect to your local objective. Second, execute the action to attain this mini-objective. Third, once you have achieved it, or been thwarted by another character, you assimilate the revised circumstances, which inform your *next* local objective, which leads to the rest of the play. So whenever you light a cigarette, open a window, or lift a box, three impulses are involved—first you want, then you do, and finally you assimilate (to proceed to the next want).

This principle becomes evident when objectives clash.

Exercise: Conflict 101. One person in your group (person A) devises an everyday task-oriented activity with a beginning, middle, and end, like setting up chairs or writing a word on a blackboard or folding laundry. (Having a bunch of props helps.) He does this task once or twice in front of everyone else to crystallize its three components: beginning, middle, and end become want, do, done.

Next, someone else (person B) invents a secret gesture of his own that will just happen to come directly into conflict with person A's. Person B does not demonstrate his task ahead of time.

Then let them both loose at the same time. As A is surprised by B's intervention, the spark of conflict ignites. If person A needs to write on a blackboard, B may need to put away all the chalk. If A needs to set up a row of chairs, B may need to roll out a rug.

As soon as person B acts in opposition, person A, now undone, will tend to connect to his task in a more real way; although the tasks are premeditated, the conflict is not. The hard part lies, first, in devising objectives that happen to conflict, without *trying to interfere* becoming the objective itself. The express objective *to be so-and-so's nemesis* is too simplistic to represent any dramatic scenario. I have found that for person A it is not so important how contrived B's task is, as long as it interferes and surprises. To remedy the inequity between the two participants, I suggest having person B1 act next as person A2, then B2 as A3, and so forth.

Second, both participants should not prolong their conflict unduly, but execute their objectives truly. Your objective was not "I want to have a conflict," so once a resolution is reached, you are done. All you need do to set up your chairs may be to wait a moment for person B's carpet to be laid.

Remember, the first person should not know what the second is about to do, for this kills the drama. *The secret to making conflict believable is for your character not to know how it will turn out.* (See Anticipation and Surprise, pp. 43-44.)

Such a sequence of silent actions appears in Act I, scene 2 of Neil Simon's *The Sunshine Boys*. The two comedians rearrange the furniture in the room to reproduce the set of their old-time vaudeville routine so they can rehearse it. Yet each of them moves chairs by himself, and each recalls the set differently. So after Willie moves a chair to one location, Al places it elsewhere without Willie noticing at first, and vice versa. It is a hilarious scene without words.

To infuse "honesty of purpose" into the blocking, try the following after the play has been staged:

Variation A. During a rehearsal with the entire cast, run through the blocking without the dialogue. Focus on:

- connecting to the local objective of each cross and gesture;
- the beginning, middle, and end of each cross and gesture;
- letting yourself be surprised when someone else's cross interrupts yours; and
- assessing what you have or have not achieved at the end of each phrase: does it lead to the next?

Variation B. Alone, outside of rehearsal, try going through all your blocking onstage. Even Stanislavski assumed actors would do this. The point of both variations is to connect to each component—want, do, done-undone—of all your blocking.

You never cross "anywhere" for "any reason," but somewhere specific for a particular reason.

CONSTANT CURRENT

To be *in the moment* means your senses are hyper-aware, your faculties are sharp, and you are ready to react anew as your character to whatever happens.

Acting in the moment involves:

- *giving up control to the extent that your character lacks it;*
- *surrendering the confidence of what you have rehearsed to the vicissitudes of the present;*
- *remaining open and vulnerable to the possibility of something new and spontaneous that did not occur last time you did the scene.*

This is dangerous, of course, for although you hope that the "something new" will be appropriate to the dramatic situation, it may not be. But this very danger will turn into theatrical excitement as the audience watches you grapple—truly—with all that comes in your way.

Spontaneity

No pre-orchestrated event can recur naturally unless the previous moment generates it. This does not mean that choices should be easy to follow and predictable; they should be logical (at least in retrospect) but not necessarily obvious—"fresh but inevitable."[11] In executing them, the actor strives to make even the most rehearsed contrivance spontaneous.

Spontaneity for its own sake, however, can amount to mere goofiness, invention in place of artistry. Certainly at rehearsal your goal may be to generate ideas, so structured silliness may lead to some inspired bit (see Abandon, pp. 154-155). But to make that bit likely to be appropriate and useable, let your character be the one who acts up, and in the situation, rather than just you the actor cutting up haphazardly.

Dynamic Connection

In performance, the actor strives for a continuous stream of spontaneity, involving unstated anticipations, silent communications, little reactions, tacit suggestions, innuendoes, and thoughts. This constantly varying current, or *dynamic connection,* characterizes daily life, and so makes your stage life believable. But no rehearsal period is comprehensive enough to orchestrate these myriad nonverbal impulses; and no actor's mind could consciously reconstruct such a complex series. Through practice, though, we strive to make dynamic connection automatic.

"RARE"

Exchanging one of these impulses involves a cycle of activity similar to that of the Conflict 101 exercise. It may be described by the acronym:

RARE
1. Receive
2. Assimilate
3. React
4. Evoke

1. *Receive* the impulse; absorb new and changing circumstances. This essentially means to listen—totally. Again, when you listen onstage, do it for the first and only time, as if without knowing the other character's lines or designs. Pay attention to everything that is both said and unsaid, not just with your ears but with all your senses, including the sixth one: Listen through your very pores.

2. *Assimilate* the impulse you receive; factor in the new information to reassess your thwarted objective. For the most part, your objectives will be thwarted again and again, because this makes a play interesting. (An objective not under constant challenge may not be the right objective: search for another.)

3. *React* by revising your local objective to the new circumstances, and putting this new objective in action. Cope with being thwarted so as to achieve your objective, or your super-objective, later. In other words, manipulate the other characters in a fresh way to suit your revised purpose. Think of the word *react* as "act anew," so you remember to find new actions all the time: repeating a previous intent does not move the plot forward.

4. *Evoke* the next reaction with the impulse you emit. This will require the other character, who has been receiving and assimilating, to adjust his own objective—react—to the new circumstances you have given him. Invariably, the other character's reaction will not be what you expected, so it will in turn evoke a new one from you. (See Anticipation and Surprise, pp. 43-44.) Like gears interlinked, one actor generates another's next line and action—just as in life.

These activities do not necessarily happen in order. In theory: you receive and assimilate while the other characters are talking; you react (roughly) the very moment you are about to start speaking, and you evoke in the very moment you end your speech (particularly if your last sentence asks a question). In practice, though, you will find that you are always doing all four steps, for while you are speaking you also survey the reactions of others—who are undergoing the same cycle during your lines. Even silence evokes.

These phases are the actual components of live acting. By making each moment of the play lead newly to the next, the characters seem to be driving the action with a will of their own. You keep the audience in suspense as to whether the play is even going to end up tonight as it is supposed to.

The constant current of dynamic connection is like a natural stream. Though you return to swim at the same point you swam yesterday, you cannot actually swim in the same water. Analogously, your blocking to "rise and cross to window" may occur in Act I, scene 2 every night, but the motivation for doing so must rise from each particular evening's current. So you do not merely repeat the blocking; you re-create the inner life (the source) and the impulse (the wave of communication) that will regenerate it. *You connect the moments of a performance only when those moments occur in the actual performance.* And on some level, you don't really know ahead of time that they will connect. Herein lie the danger and the thrill. But without this danger, gesture becomes semaphore. From it emerges dramatic momentum that is true. Your performance comes alive. And it is born anew every night.

Perfectionists beware: acting is never about perfec*tion*, but perfect*ing*.

Repeat the form, not the performance.

Of course, you want your next impulse to be the one that just happens to generate the next bit of blocking.

In delivering lines, this means that you should *talk not fast, but relentlessly.* Listen and formulate the next speech while the other character talks, so that you almost have to interrupt. In other words, pick up your cue, but not just technically: do it psychologically, so that your character must pick up her cue because of the urgency of her drive. The point when your character has to speak is usually a few words before the other person has finished talking, anyway; unless someone is asking you a question and waiting for your reply, the very act of speaking also involves the action of stopping others from speaking. Therefore, incipient adverbs and interjections like "well," "indeed," and "O" (scripted ones, that is) should generally propel you into the rest of the sentence. For one, why would your character start speaking without something substantial to say? For another, if you pause before saying anything, why wouldn't the other guy resume his speech?

Your point of departure in performance is to pick up your cues, which means reacting while listening, not after the previous speaker's line.

During a long speech of your own, picking up your interior cues requires a lot of mental energy, since you have to formulate what you say next while you are speaking. Saying one thing while thinking of the next may sound odd, yet we do it in life all the time: your mental processes flow as continuously and relentlessly as a waterfall.

The living character is playing a continuous game of Ball Tossing 101, always throwing, catching, or transforming the ball, always engaged in the RARE cycle. The ball becomes the actual substance of the play—text, meaning, stakes, emotions, events, and so on. Interrupting the cycle means letting the ball drop and losing the audience. But if you remain engaged in RARE as relentlessly as you breathe, you keep the audience engaged: much as the heart processes blood, the RARE cycle restores fresh oxygen to your will and then circulates it throughout the hall. This process, in other words, involves the audience—in you.

CONNECTING TO THE SPECIFIC AUDIENCE

Recall Hamlet's advice: "suit the action to the word, the word to the action." Today we also suit the inner life, the style, and the audience venue.

A small, subtle reaction—often perfectly fine for camera work—may only reach the front rows of a theater. How many times have you watched a play from the rear of a hall and noticed that the front rows laughed at something you could not quite see? With just a little bit of craft, though, the actor can include the whole audience.

The smaller the audience, the less you need to project. Playing to a balcony that is not there is as dishonest as playing to just the front row when there is in fact a balcony.

Adjust your performance to the shape as well as the size of the hall. Theater-in-the-round, three-quarters, and a proscenium hall all require different behavior. I heard tell of an ornery producer's response when asked about comedy in the round: "What's the point? It's gotta be not funny to *someone.*" You will always have your back to some part of the audience, and each spectator visually misses half the play; but your goal is to make sure they do not even realize it.

As in any hall, your devices for reaching everyone include:

1. creative stage business;
2. augmented physical and vocal activity;
3. deeper breathing;

4.   heightened stakes;
5.   hotter passion.

The list goes on.

To stay connected with spectators behind you, engage your back and voice all the more. Try not to keep your back to any one part of the audience for too long, lest those spectators lose interest.

Staging in the round, then, involves more crosses than full front staging. A *translational* cross is traveling from one location to another; a *rotational* one is changing the direction you face. The most believable crosses comprise a little of both, because when we displace ourselves in life we also alter our axis a little, and vice versa. Fortunately we can exploit this principle of axis adjustment to stay opened up to the various sections of the audience. For a naturalistic play in the round, the task is to generate those extra crosses naturally, especially rotational ones. You may assume 101 tiny tasks, each with a local objective that has nothing to do with the script per se. This is why characters in a parlor drama are always lighting a cigarette, turning on a lamp, sipping a cocktail. These activities not only betray character but also connect inner life to the entire house.

TOTAL ACTING

The natural connection to the entire audience with your entire instrument is *total acting*. To get an idea of what I mean, try looking at movies from the 1930s that featured the great stage stars of the day, before actors were expressly trained for film. In *Fire over England* (1937) you can see how Laurence Olivier used his whole body to communicate. In a theater, his craft must have come across as full and very exciting. But contained in the camera frame, he looks dangerously close to overacting. With William Wyler (the "actor's director") in *Wuthering Heights* (1939), he started to tailor his performance for the camera instead of the balcony. Note, though, that even in later films like *The Boys from Brazil* (1978), he keeps his hands moving more than most American actors do—not to distract, but to be thoroughly expressive of his character. His highly physical *King Lear*, available on videotape, is about as perfect as an actor can get. Yes, I am recommending you track down this video, but not that you necessarily move your hands as much as Olivier did (especially in a small theater) unless you are Olivier.

In Wyler's 1936 movie *Dodsworth*, stage veteran Walter Huston plays the title role, a workaholic always antsy to start another project even after his premature retirement, during which he is supposed to enjoy himself with his supposedly loving wife. Huston never stops moving throughout the picture—pacing, stroking, fidgeting. Yet since every gesture is expressive of his inner life, you might not notice how busy he is. Late in the picture, he sits down to talk to his wife. For the first time, his arms are at rest, and his face is not moving. The contrasting stillness made me bubble in anticipation of what he was about to do. While I will not reveal what happens, I will tell you that the next moment is the film's climax.

Walter Huston and Laurence Olivier did not merely find the subconscious through-line that is the province of the film actor; each was constantly expressing it through his limbs, his breath, his face, his voice, his eyes, his creative choices, and his soul—total gesture.

To act by jiggling your knee, stroking your nose, tapping your fingers, and flexing your toes, get your character to the point where he *has* to do so. Each activity should be complete and believable in its own right (and not take focus unduly): otherwise, the fidgeting starts to look like trying too hard. Let the audience see a living, breathing character who just happens to be so alive and expressive as to be continually revelatory.

Voice and Body

To connect with your entire instrument, start engaging its various facets. A simple vocal adjustment might suit your character at the same time it reveals him to you. Try talking with only the upper part or only the lower part of your register; or hardening your consonants; or lengthening your vowels; or singing your lines. Figaro in Beaumarchais's *The Barber of Seville* might be a jolly character for whom almost singing his text would work in performance. Yet any character might benefit from trying this, especially one whose speech is lengthy, festive, or silly. Recall Lou Costello wailing, "Hey, Abbott!"or "I'm a bad boy"; he virtually did sing. Subtler vocal adjustments you might try include speaking with more acerbity or with more sweetness, or with a heightened nasal quality, or more from the diaphragm.

Then focus on your character's physical life, including body position. Try altering your center of gravity, or the way you walk, hold your head, sit, or stand. Maybe your character's weight is always on the balls of his feet, as if he is ready to pounce; maybe you always sit back or stand on your heels, and are notoriously hard to get moving. When you walk, with what part of your body do you lead? Some people lead with their noses, others with their chests, knees, or genitalia. Experiment with any of these and numerous other options, and suddenly the character's inner life changes, too. Which choice is right for the role, and which is best? You decide.

Exercise: Dance-through. The cast runs through the play—every single line—without speaking the words out loud, but using physical and facial gestures to convey the unstated text. To be understood, the actors must be especially clear, making every gesture specific to each line. Virtually no two movements can be the same, or it will look like you are repeating yourself. The gestures may be exaggerated as long as they make the text (and action) clear. Your palette of expressiveness cannot help but expand as a result.

When you put the performance back together after this exercise, the text will be a welcome friend to make clarity easier. You need not *try* to apply the exercise: simply *let* your physicality be fluid and expressive, and it should be.

We tried such a terpsichorean silent run-through while rehearsing *Romeo and Juliet.* When I explained the ground rules, the cast was daunted. Once we got under way, however, they were surprised to find that they and the prompter were able to stay together throughout Act I. By Act II one actor finally called for a line. The prompter confessed, "I lost you at the top of the page; let's go back to . . ." and the Nurse and Juliet realized that they had jumped a couplet a few lines earlier. But everything else had been thoroughly clear, communicated exclusively through physical work. What had been thought impossible became invaluable.

Exercise: Sing-through or Bounce-through. To explore vocal variety, try a corresponding company exercise where you alter the pitch or color of your voice with every word, or make yourself speak/sing from the top and bottom of your range with every sentence. Investigate the full potential of varying timbre, color, rhythm, and volume. Try making yourself bounce from one color to the next with each word, yet still making the meaning clear, which is the hard part. In other words, don't bounce around vocally instead of communicating your thoughts and feelings, but in order to communicate them more expressively; otherwise it's just a game.

As with the dance-through, you then discard the exercise and see what natural effect remains on your performance. Suddenly line readings free up and fresh colors emerge.

Passion and Breath

Every actor is familiar with the *speed-through,* which tests that he knows his lines and cues—and thoughts. To heighten the text, I have also found great value from the *slow-through,* or *climax-through:*

Exercise: Slow-through or Climax-through. Treat each line as if it were the climax of its own melodramatic play. Overdo for the purpose of this exercise. In addition to speaking in slow motion: (1) raise the stakes, attitude, and emotion on each line so that you *have* to broaden the words; (2) breathe deeper to support this augmentation; and (3) distinguish every line from every other one. Stretch vowels to their limit; remember that they convey the emotion. (See Musical Language, pp. 192-194)

Someone monitors to ensure that the actors keep breathing, since in life it is our tendency, at sudden bursts of emotion, to skip a breath. Onstage, try to do precisely the opposite—breathe deeper—so that the emotion is not bottled up but released. Make the audience breathless instead of yourself.

Danger: Do not let the exercise deaden the pace in performance; it should simply deepen the substance. Restore the scene to performance tempo afterwards.

Exercise: Keeping Focus. This exercise is particularly valuable for actors who are too generous in giving the ball away before the end of their speech.

Let everyone choose a bite of text from the play you are rehearsing—a sentence or two consisting of five to twenty-five words. As in the above exercise, deliver the line to the audience like a climax, full of inner life. While you speak, connect with every seat in the house, commanding the focus of the entire hall with your intent. After you finish talking, keep the focus, maintaining that heightened inner state to do so. Three to ten seconds later (you do not know ahead of time exactly when), someone else claps her hands, taking the focus from you for her own delivery.

In all this work, it is the exercise requiring more work that paves the way for the effortless yet electric performance. Since you engage every muscle of your face and body, every nuance of your speaking voice, the deepest breath to support the highest passion, and the most personal stakes, your inner life now reads to the back row of even the largest amphitheater without your having to mug, or work, at all. All you do is invite the audience to participate.

Substance + Connection + Invitation = Projection

THE INNER ARBITER

The curse of any artist or writer is that he can never merely cry or laugh—he has to notice it. Stanislavski said it was the actor's obligation to be so callous as to observe the details of his emotional state even at tragic events like a father's funeral. It is obviously important to study the emotions of life: but when acting, avoid even thinking about them. Staying *in charac-ter* means that you experience each event from within your character's shoes rather than stepping out of them to think about what your character would do or feel.

An exercise is not acting, though, and so may have emotional content as its expressed goal. But while you may be able to work on intensity of feel-ing, you cannot evaluate its honesty through introspection. After all, when in life do we ever monitor how truthful our thoughts and feelings are? A dramatic character certainly does not want this extra burden. Far more important than whether your emotions are true is what they do: evoke appropriate responses. In other words, the moment you notice you are acting honestly or organically—connecting—you are no longer doing so.

You can't notice your connection and have it, too.

What about *subconscious* awareness of being connected? Ah, this inner sense is instinct, the gut feeling that lets you know you are soaring, with-out your actually having to watch yourself soar. How do you develop this instinct?

In class or ensemble work, the eye of the coach, instructor, or director may tell you when someone is falling out of a scene, phoning in a response, or forcing an emotion. Over time, her gentle remonstrations of "listen" and "stay connected" contribute to your own sense of discrimination regarding what is true and honest. This process of constantly being corrected by a coach may seem like creative constipation, but the point is actually to cure you of self-induced constipation onstage.

Take advantage of the time you spend in acting class, or in rehearsal when you are off stage, to pay attention. Instead of tuning out, concentrate on what the active performers are doing. In this way you build up your own stamina for concentration, and soon you are able to tell instantly when someone is disconnected, self-conscious, forcing, or lying. You are develop-ing your own arbiter of honesty.

This arbiter is a third eye, one that is inner, not outer; instinctual, not analytic; organic, not self-conscious; and like all technique, it cannot serve you if you are still serving it.

Acting is like surfing. To ride the wave you juggle the external variables: the other surfer coming at you on your right, the wind from your left, and the shark up ahead. If instead you look beneath the surfboard to see what is holding you up, you lose your balance and fall off, and the shark will get you.

The inner arbiter is the sense of balance, one's skill at staying on the wave, or in the scene.

Listen—not just with ears, remember—to everything around you: to fellow actors and audience, and also lighting, sets, costumes, technical effects, and music. These stimuli make acting easier, taking you from moment to moment.

To list-en fully is to en-list everything you can.

If you truly listen—connect—to what is different and new each perform-ance, you cannot help but to do it the same, yet not the same; to be in control, yet out of control; and to do it again—for the first time.

So concentrate on executing your actions and on listening, not on monitoring. Let your inner arbiter serve as Connection's pilot. Then you imbue your performance with the breath of life, and your craft becomes invisible, your work seamless, your reactions inevitable, and you just might release the same potential that Olivier unleashed when he performed on that day of magic. And you won't know how you did it.

CHAPTER 5
SHAPE

THE ACTOR AS STORYTELLER

Shape means Story; good Shape means good storytelling. To a certain extent, it is the director's and writer's province, but it is the actors who eventually give the play, so in performance, script and staging must become their own; to recreate the play, they effectively become its authors for the evening, each actor with his own part. Shape is even more important than analysis, which is after all a tool for telling that story. Analysis is a means; Story is *it*.

Another way of looking at the theatrical circumstances (see p. 10) is that onstage you actually play at least three roles:

1. *Yourself*
2. *the Character*
3. *the Storyteller*

The Storyteller's objective is to tell the whole story, not just his own, clearly and compellingly.

Say you are playing Nicholas Nickleby, who has the following dialogue:

Nicholas: Nicholas rose up, and wrote a few lines in pen-
                      cil to say goodbye, and resolved that, come
                      what may, he would bear whatever might be in
                      store for him, for the sake of his mother and
                      his sister, and giving his uncle no excuse to
                      desert them in their need. (1.6)

It certainly does not help you attain your character's objective to introduce the next scene. These lines are spoken by Nicholas the Storyteller, not Nicholas the Character. To say them you might step outside one character to become the Narrator, or you can remain in character as much as you can. Either way, *the objective of the storyteller ultimately supersedes all others.* It is the storyteller, after all, who yields focus to another actor, takes focus when your character would rather hide, or removes a chair from the stage while exiting up-left to assist in the next scene change.

THE DYNAMIC THROUGH-LINE

Shape starts with the notion of "beginning, middle, and end," but entails much more: recognizing when events occur and what kind of events they are; how to execute them; and orchestrating them over the course of the evening into what we call a *through-line*. To be compelling, make your through-line as dynamic as possible—ever changing, moving forward, and building to a finish. Your character is never at the same dramatic point at two different moments of the play, since circumstances keep changing; so keep growing physically and/or psychologically, if only a little bit. In other words, suit your physical, vocal, facial, and inner life to each precise moment—and never revisit the same moment twice.

In life you subtly transform from moment to moment like this all the time, depending, for starters, on whom you are with. Onstage, too, once another character enters or exits, something is different. Christopher Plummer's Iago changed body position and voice from the upright ensign to the slithering snake, depending on whether he was serving Othello or manipulating Cassio. Richard III will certainly woo Lady Anne differently from the way he will win over gentlemen. Of course you cannot consciously play all the minutiae of this journey, but you can define ample guideposts.

These guideposts are events—when something in the dramatic circumstances changes.

Event means change—so change!

The change may be subtle, of course, and may not even read to the audience.

Perhaps you have been in a show where one actor yelled—all the time; or where a supercilious character spoke superciliously, but with no nuance distinguishing line from line. A vocal style might be your attack, or approach to the role: but an approach is not a solution, only a point of departure—so depart. Find a unique declamation for each line. If your character is always supercilious and you have 283 lines, find 283 varieties of superciliousness. And if you yell at someone at one moment, and she doesn't do what you say, why yell again? It didn't work the first time. And if she does do what you say, you needn't yell again.

So we change not just from scene to scene and from event to event, but from line to line and moment to moment, too. Differentiate your character from one moment to the next based on:

- *where you are;*
- *whom you are with;*
- *what precisely you are saying, hearing, and doing (that you did not say, hear or do a moment ago); and*
- *what has happened so far.*

Thus you start to orchestrate your character's through-line.

French Scenes

When we talk of the "event of the scene," we are talking about *French scenes,* determined by the entrance or exit of a character. Whenever a character exits or enters, though the action continues, a new French scene starts. So a French scene is the period of time during which a particular assortment of characters is onstage. (Note that each entrance or exit marks a little event of its own.)

Delineation by French scenes is still honored in published editions of many classical plays. At every exit or entrance (with minor exceptions), a new scene number is assigned. You can almost count the French scenes by the scene numbers.

Even in other plays, though, each French scene delimits an event. To locate the play's events, mark your script at every entrance and exit; between every two consecutive marks, there will be an event (usually near the end of the scene). A simple yet invaluable exercise too often neglected: *mark your events in your script.*

More than one character may change before the next entrance or exit. Let us say that each event corresponds to a *sub-scene.* (French scenes can contain several sub-scenes.)

Identifying French scenes will help greatly when the event is not too clear, say in a very talky play. It might seem as if there are more words than action, but you know that before any character enters or exits, something will have happened to alter the circumstances for someone to move the plot forward. Until that event comes, find a way to keep the audience in a state of anticipation. Let one shoe drop and keep threatening to drop the other until the playwright finally lets you. Eventually you attain your objective—or not; along the way, pray remember that there is an event in the word *event*ually.

Example. Act II, scene 9 of Molière's *Learned Ladies* is awfully long, and at first glance nothing seems to be happening for all those words. Chrysale is effectively the Henpecked Husband. His brother Ariste berates him for his pusillanimous deference to his wife in what may at first appear to be a repetitive scene, merely rehashing the status quo.

The present circumstance concerns his daughter's marriage to his wife's choice, the fop Trissotin, versus the man she loves, Clitandre. In this short scene, the brothers start out trading short lines:

Ariste: What did you say, then?
Chrysale: Nothing; and what I did
            Was wise, I think, for it left me uncommitted.
Ariste: I see! What strategy! How nimble-witted!
            Did you at least suggest Clitandre, Brother?
Chrysale: No. When I found her partial toward another,
            It seemed best not to push things then and there.[12]

Nothing has changed so far except that Ariste has been apprised of Chrysale's actions.

Next, each brother goes off on a long harangue of his own. The husband bewails the situation, and then his brother decries his "cowardice." Can the event of the scene be merely talking? No, it cannot. They are only revving up for the scene's climax. After quite a bit more repartée, Chrysale finally resolves:

Too long my will's been crossed;
Henceforth I'll be a man, whatever the cost.

End of the act.

The event not only of the scene but of the *act* should be conveyed in this last line, with an arrow to the future that coaxes the audience to stay for Act III.

How do you keep the modern American audience engaged when the characters talk for such a long time before anything happens? Devise as many mini-conflicts as you can think of until the big event. In my production, the brothers played billiards, smoked cigars, and drank brandy, all totems of the bourgeoisie that Molière was so fond of sending up. Chrysale would take out his marital frustration by hitting the billiard balls violently with his six-foot cue stick. The audience, understanding his passive-aggressiveness more than he did, howled. (Analogously, the preceding ladies' act took place in the family's observatory, so that the sisters' discussions of male suitors could be accompanied by passionate grabbing of a swinging six-foot telescope mounted on a tripod. It was a really nice telescope.)

Ariste does not always play his objective—to provoke his brother to action—aggressively. In fact, he keeps trying different tactics; for example, belittling his brother with faint praise, "What strategy! How nimble witted!" He may even pretend to Chrysale that he is giving up; but he need never mislead the audience that he is. Rather, he should keep trying to involve them in his continued frustrations.

To keep a long speech or long scene growing:

Try different tactics.

A conversation that seems to be prolonging the status quo really involves a continual jockeying for status, if for nothing else. There is a mini-conflict inherent in the sheer act of speaking: that of *seizing or ceding the floor*. Every speech's beginning and end constitute events, if only small ones.

A character seizing the floor provides one of the big events of *Once Upon a Mattress*. In the last scene, King Sextimus, a henpecked husband rendered mute for years by his wife, Queen Agravain, finally speaks aloud for the first time—shutting her up.

Quick French Scenes

What about when a character is left alone onstage for a couplet or two? Yes, that couplet or two constitutes a French scene that contains an event that furthers the action. Just knowing that there has to be an event may provide the clue to making those few words active.

Example. In the opening of *As You Like It*, Oliver squabbles with his younger brother and ward, Orlando. Their late father, Sir Rowland de Boys, left Oliver the family estate and the responsibility for Orlando's education: he willed Orlando a thousand crowns for which Oliver is the miserly trustee. Since Oliver has been lax in his responsibility, Orlando's frustration has grown to outrage; hence the quarrel. Orlando goes so far as to attack Oliver and is clearly the physical superior of the two; but he stops himself from actually hurting him because Orlando is, after all, good. After the aborted fisticuffs, Oliver agrees to give Orlando "some part of [his] will" so that Orlando can educate himself.

Once Orlando exits—which delineates a new French scene—Oliver is alone:

> Is it even so? begin you to grow upon me? I will physic
> your rankness; and yet give no thousand crowns neither.
> Holla, Dennis! (1)

Enter the servant Dennis, marking the end of the French scene.

What was the event of that short scene? Well, Oliver seems to be changing his mind: he will not give up the thousand crowns after all. Rather, he will "physic" Orlando's "rankness" (treat his foulness)—*how* is precisely what you want to get the audience to wonder.

After a short scene with Dennis, who confirms that the court wrestler awaits, Oliver, alone again, says:

> 'Twill be a good way; and to-morrow the wrestling is. (2)

Enter Charles the wrestler, and the French scene is over.

What happens during this single line (2) that constitutes a change in some character's situation? Well, Shakespeare wants to keep us in suspense, so he does not tell us right away. But about fifty lines later Oliver confides to Charles:

> I had as lief thou didst break his neck as his finger. (3)

("I'd just as soon you kill him as maim him.") He had been planning to get the court strongman to accidentally kill his brother. The villain is unveiled. Line 3 suggests how to play the earlier one-sentence, seemingly bland French scene (2): actively plot Orlando's doom, infusing that line with a huge arrow to what follows. This arrow should get the audience to think "What wrestling? What does he mean by that?" It's almost like twirling your moustache; without a moustache, use your mind, your face, and your voice to betray intent.

Note Shakespeare's dramatic rhythm: the pace and pattern with which events occur, much like the chord changes in a song. With several quick French scenes in a row, he thrusts the plot into dire circumstances quickly.

When a French scene has no dialogue whatsoever, now you know it still needs an event. Think of the chase scene in a farce. A dozen doors may open and close within a single minute, comprising as many French scenes. If you do not have something happening between each entrance and exit, it's only blocking; if you do, it's a hoot.

THE AUDIENCE'S THROUGH-LINE

Besides constructing your character's through-line, you also construct the audience's. If your route for the audience is flat, straight, and smooth, it will hardly be an attraction at all. It is much more inviting to offer the passenger an adventure of thrills and, yes, even terror: a roller coaster.

Through the *fundamental actor question* you erect the scaffolding of that roller coaster. It is in two parts.

> *To be clear and engaging, ask yourself:*
> *"Where must I take the audience now—*
> *and what do I have to do to take them there?"*

> *To be compelling, add the following corollary:*
> *"Where might I take the audience now—*
> *and can I get away with it?"*

These two questions lie at the root of almost all acting choices. Keep in mind that if a choice interferes with clarity, then you have failed to "get away with it": either do it better, or do something else.

The Building Blocks:
AND SO . . . ?, AH!, WHAT?

What Oliver did in the above short scenes was to generate a post-beat *for the audience* (see Pre-Beat and Post-Beat, pp. 55-57). To do this, ask yourself, "AND SO . . . ?"

> *The principle of "And So . . . ?":*
> *Everything you do or say onstage*
> *begets a consequence—*
> *for your own character, for another character,*
> *or for the audience.*

Put a whole lot of AND SO . . . ?'s together, and eventually you lay the rail of the audience's roller coaster.

On the one hand, AND SO . . . ? is what we ask at rehearsal to shape the play. On the other, it is what we hope to make the audience ponder during a performance. The audience's response can be subliminal or conscious, but to compel them to make it we find the *must* for our audience as well as for our character. In fact, *respond* comes from "to promise in return"; we want the audience to give us something back.

There are two basic types of response, with endless variations, that we hope to elicit: "WHAT?" and "AH!" The former is anticipation; the latter, arrival. Each constitutes an audience event.

The WHAT? (including "Uh-oh!", "Whoa!" and the like) is a moment we get the audience to wonder about something to come, such as "what does that mean?", or "what is she going to do?" The AH! ("Wow!", "Whew!") answers an earlier WHAT? and reassures, in retrospect, that their engagement has been warranted: "ah, that's what it meant," "ah, that's what she decided to do after all!" By eventually rewarding each WHAT? with an AH!, we inveigle the audience to stay on the ride and engage in subsequent WHAT?'s as the plot develops. WHAT? puts our audience in suspense; AH! helps keep them there.

So you want to take the audience on a roller-coaster ride like the following: "AND SO the audience suspects now that Lizzie is carrying Reg's child—Uh-oh!—and then later realizes—AH!—it's not his child after all—Whew! But," we hope they will wonder, "WHAT is going to happen next?" You would tailor your acting choices, then, to this audience through-line.

The time from each WHAT? to its corresponding AH! constitutes an *arc of suspense,* a bump or loop-de-loop on the roller coaster. The *arch of the play* might be thought of as the aggregate of all the arcs of suspense, some overlapping or nested within others. Live acting means regenerating the entire arch of the play *with the audience* night after night.

This arch might be thought of as comprising two components, dramatic and thematic. A synonym for *dramatic arch* is *plot.* The *thematic arch* is everything else.

PLAYING THE PLOT

Story refers to what happens: just the facts. But *plot* suggests the pattern of "this happens and therefore that happens, which then leads to that other thing happening." Plot incorporates causality and inevitability: a sense that once the ride has started, there is no stopping till the end.

Plot can be likened to the downward course of a slalom skier.[13] Its overall shape requires a beginning, middle, and end: the starting gate, the hill, and the arrival at bottom. Along the way the flagpoles outline the zigzag pattern of plot complications. Every time you turn the audience around one pole, you steer them downward to another. Say each slalom pole marks an audience event, a WHAT? or an AH! There are large events and small ones, depending on the magnitude of the resulting change: the event of the play, of the act, of the scene, of a speech, even of a cross to downstage left.

To keep proceeding downhill, act in phrases, from event to event, taking the audience through their progress as well as your own. This keeps them suspended in a continuous series of WHAT?'s and AH!'s. To that end, dramatists overlap their arcs, planting the next WHAT? even before the prior one's AH!; otherwise there would be a break in the action, which can read like a gap as wide as a Mack® truck.

Rhythm, clarity, focus, physicality, inner life, aesthetic choices, and so forth will all be affected by whether a moment is a WHAT? or an AH!, and what part of the play's structure it constitutes. For example, during the exposition, avoid talking too fast, because the audience needs to process the information. Conversely, you generally want to keep up the pace after the *climax and dénouement;* the audience probably needs you to "get on with it." At the moment right before the end of Act I, the last WHAT?—the "Big WHAT?" of the act—should be so juicy so as to provide an *arrow to Act II:* a compelling reason for the audience to return after intermission (you can't let 'em go till they gotta come back).

At the *point of no return,* an event that renders the hero no longer able to reverse his course, the spectator may scream silently: "Do it do it do it!" while a voice inside our hero screams: "Don't do it don't do it don't do it!"—or vice versa. At one preview performance of *Othello* (with James Earl Jones) someone in the audience actually bleated "Don't do it!" the moment before Othello killed his wife Desdemona. (All theater *is* children's theater, remember, when it comes to involving the audience.) If your audience ever talks back like that to you, congratulations!

Example. In *Hamlet,* the point of no return occurs at the exact moment "the king rises" in III.2, for only then does Claudius discover that Hamlet knows he killed King Hamlet Senior. Once Claudius knows that Hamlet knows, and Hamlet knows that Claudius knows that Hamlet knows, they can never be the same as they were before. From that point on, neither is safe from the other, even though this is never stated in their dialogue with each other. Notice, by the way, that structurally III.2 arrives at the exact midpoint of *Hamlet.* This particular point of no return should also be a big WHAT?, and in many productions of the play serves as the arrow through intermission.

As a matter of fact, if you don't charge the rest of the play with these new circumstances *sub rosa*, it will look as if nothing's changed between them. Yet their mutual machinations as they try to do each other in constitute the major conflict of the second half of the play.

The word *dénouement* suggests a knot being untied. So you may want to fashion the core of your character somewhat like the tightly bound center of a golf ball, which consists of elastic strips wrapped tightly around each other in a highly compact nucleus of potential energy waiting to burst. This core gets wound tighter and tighter, building the tension, until the knot unravels—or explodes—and the nucleus is exposed at last. Because of the rising crisis, the actor's tendency might be to play the climax with a lot of energy, and hence too fast. But by remembering the audience, you will play powerfully, yes, but not so that the audience cannot follow the accelerated sequence of events from the precipitous rising action ("What? What? What? What? What?") through the climax ("WHAAAT?!") to the dénouement ("Ah! Ah! Ah! Ah! Ah! Ahhhhh!").

Your sense of structure should ensure that you send the audience's focus to the right place at the right time so they do not miss an important event. Hence, you would never jump on or distract from a fellow actor's line (or business), especially when it conveys essential information. And to involve your audience in your character's moment of crisis, you might silently face the balcony.

So you see, there is hardly a difference between process-oriented and result-oriented acting once you consider the *audience's* process.

PLAYING THE THEME

While the dramatic arch provides the scaffolding of the roller coaster, it is not what inspires a playwright to write a play; this inspiration comes from the theme. The point of the play may really only be what the audience retains after they have forgotten the plot.

At the end of the futuristic movie *Planet of the Apes*, when Charlton Heston sees the ruins of the Statue of Liberty, he and we realize that the planet is Earth, and that mankind blew it. Science-fiction thriller turns into morality screenplay. The thematic arch of a stage play, too, becomes particularly evident in its last moments: once the plot is resolved, it is time for the theme to be fully realized—the *"AHH!"* An anacrusis (technically, an "upbeat") will add a final "WHAT?" before the audience leaves the theater. This can be (1) a mandate to the audience to live better; (2) the introduction of a complication that tonight's play will not resolve; or even (3) the beginning of a new play, like a sequel. (The anacrusis of *Planet of the Apes* involves all three.) Actors playing these last moments can try, for example, facing the audience. Inner dialogue: "You will take this lesson to heart, won't you, audience?"

Or a production can try something more boisterous.

Example. In *Taming of the Shrew,* my Lucentio could not understand why the play did not end with Petruchio's last couplet as he and his wife leave, perhaps to consummate their weeks-old marriage:

Petruchio: 'Twas I won the wager, though you hit the white;
    And, being a winner, God give you good night!
      [Exeunt Petruchio and Katharina]
Hortensio: Now, go thy ways; thou hast tamed a curst shrew.
Lucentio: 'Tis a wonder, by your leave, she will be tamed so.

Many productions indeed cut these last two lines (as did the Zeffirelli film with Richard Burton and Elizabeth Taylor). But you cannot cut a Shakespeare play without diminishing it in some way. The anacrusis Shakespeare wants us to consider is Lucentio's state of "wonder." How do we make this active?

Well, there's a clue: the last three lines are spoken by the three new husbands. Perhaps Lucentio is wondering about how now to tame his own shrew of a bride. Inspired by the actor's quandary, I had him grab Petruchio's leather riding crop while Hortensio borrowed handcuffs from the Officer (now a guest at the wedding feast). Then they approached their respective brides—with portent—as the other guests cleared the way and the lights faded to black.

A play, then, does not end with the last moment onstage; the most important act of a five-act play may very well be the sixth.

Occasionally, an author stops the plot before the end—HOLD EVERY-THING—in order to articulate themes more expressly, by waxing nostalgic, poetic, comedic, or philosophical.

The Principle of Thematic Application: Any part of the play that has no bearing on plot *must* have everything to do with theme.

Put all these moments together, and you get the thematic arch, the audience's journey toward some realization. The thematic arch can almost be thought of as its own roller coaster ride, sometimes intersecting the dramatic arch, at other times parallel to it. Part of our job is to fuse the two roller coasters into one.

During a *thematic event,* instead of one of the character's circumstances changing, it may be only the audience that changes. Dramatic events change characters to forward the plot. Thematic events change the audience to advance understanding. (Some events are both dramatic and thematic, of course.) Blatant expressions of theme might involve prolonged passages of philosophy, politics, poetry, biography, nostalgia, allegory—the essay of the play. To keep the audience engaged, find a way to deliver essay as entertainment and intrigue, with bright and varied colors or compelling depth (*entertain:* from French, *entre* + *tenir* = "to hold between," or "interhold"). Fortunately, playwrights tend to render many of their thematic scenes as delightful diversions anyway, with song, dance, wit, or zaniness. And even when serious and direct, say during a thematic climax, an author often paints a bold splash of the most delicious color. In the last speech of Garson Kanin's *Born Yesterday*, corrupt lawyer Ed Devery toasts a corrupt client and senator:

> To all the dumb chumps and all the crazy broads, past, present, and future—who thirst for knowledge—and search for truth—who fight for justice—and civilize each other—and make it so tough for sons-of-bitches like you—and you—and me.

You get the idea.

It is harder for actors when the playwright stretches out thematic events over longer periods. In *Man and Superman*, George Bernard Shaw interrupts the main story with the entire second act, a playlet entitled *Don Juan in Hell*. The characters in Hell are played by the same actors who play the living personages of Acts I and III, and so the detour functions as an analogy of the play's issues. Not only is *Man and Superman* performed without this middle act as often as with, but *Don Juan in Hell* is frequently performed on its own.

Identifying a thematic scene can often be tricky, though, for it may read just like—conversation. French-scene analysis can help you locate these hidden thematic scenes: since there must be an event between any entrance or exit and the next, when nothing happens dramatically, something thematic must be going on.

It is therefore never the case that *nothing* happens. Sometimes you may think you are forcing the event; but when you do, a once passive scene can start to scintillate, which is probably how the playwright originally conceived it.

In other words, scenes that defer the plot are the very ones that must make the play—so play!

Example. The opening French scene of Arthur Miller's *All My Sons* differs in various published versions, but it boils down to the following. Joe Keller, "nearing sixty," is "a man among men." Dr. Jim Bayliss, "nearly forty," is the next door neighbor; he is "wry," with "self-effacing humor." We are in "the back yard of the Keller home in the outskirts of an American town." The upper trunk of a small apple tree

(. . . *lies toppled* . . . , *fruit still clinging to its branches. At curtain, Jim is standing, staring at the broken tree. He taps a pipe on it, blows through the pipe, feels in his pocket for tobacco, then speaks*)

Jim: Where's your tobacco?
Keller: I think I left it on the table. . . . Gonna rain tonight.
Jim: Paper say so?
Keller: Yeah, right here.
Jim: Then it can't rain.

(*Frank Lubey enters* . . .)

End of French scene: And we're off.

OK, so what constituted an event? Well, eventually the play reveals that Joe Keller sold faulty parts to the Army Air Corps that caused the death of some American pilots during World War II. He duped his business partner into taking the rap, and came out smelling like a rose himself. Or so the record would report.

Cryptically, the opening sequence suggests, "Don't believe everything you read." So Dr. Bayliss can let the audience suspect—in the first beat of the play—that he at least is not convinced of the truth of events by their record. At first, the discussion concerns only the weather, but we subsequently find out that even though Keller got off scot-free, everyone in town knew he was the guilty one. Later, additional layers of façade will be stripped away to reveal more of the truth: Keller's older son Larry not only died in World War II, but volunteered for a suicide mission once he found out what his father had done. In effect, Joe killed his son.

This opening scene is not just about tobacco and the weather.

So how do the actors play this? Any number of ways. Dr. Bayliss could look up at the sky (that is, at the audience) with a wry, all-knowing smile— just on the verge of a smirk. Joe Keller, absorbed in his newspaper, may react a second later to Jim's surliness, as if to say, "What do you mean by that?"

or more specifically, "Well, if you can't believe what you read in the paper, what can you believe?" Either character could chuckle cryptically: Keller hiding a secret, the doctor already knowing it. On a good day, this five-line opening French scene will generate that first WHAT? in the audience.

This scene also introduces the metaphor of the broken apple tree. Soon we find out the tree is Larry's tree, therefore a symbol for the dead son. Since Dr. Bayliss is discovered pondering the tree, perhaps he expects something to happen concerning Larry. The actor could convey this by, say, nodding as he taps his pipe on the trunk.

This opening salvo pays off down the road, at the thematic climax. Joe's remaining son, Chris Keller, thinks the world of his father in Act I. By the end of the play, though, Chris has discovered the truth and gets his father to agree to turn himself in to the authorities and serve a prison sentence. As Joe gets his things, Chris answers his mother's "What more can we be?" with:

> You can be better! Once and for all you can know there's a universe
> of people outside and you're responsible to it. . . .

Playwright unmasks pamphleteer: if this is not a direct mandate to the audience, I do not know what is.

A moment later, Joe shoots himself. Here, as in any integrated structure, the thematic climax has actually served the dramatic action, pushing Joe Keller to his self-inflicted doom.

The thematic arch started in the first five lines of the play. The curtain rises on Keller's world, not a cloud in the sky, a perfect Sunday morning. Though nothing dramatic happens in this first French scene, all is put in place thematically for what follows: balmy day, fallen tree, and a newspaper that neighbor Jim does not believe.

Note that the "essay of the play" here is conveyed not just in polemics, but also through plot: *Plot itself is a vessel of theme.*

When a play consists largely of thematic scenes, then they, not the dramatic events, may constitute the structural skeleton. Perhaps the play makes its points in little units, like *Spoon River Anthology*, an album of narrative poems. Or it may visit the same point over and over, like *Waiting for Godot*. The slate of built-up suspense gets wiped clean, starting the audience at zero, again and again. The ride is more a Ferris wheel than a roller coaster. (Most use the terms *cyclical* and *linear*, but I recommend thinking in terms of carnival rides: we are, after all, purveying thrills.) Instead of generating a plot, which is *stuff happening*, such a play may be *about* stuff: celebrating it, exposing it, remembering it, lampooning it, convincing with it, understanding it, or giving it a new treatment. This may be more difficult to render compelling, for plot manipulates the audience automatically, increasing suspense as it builds to a single big bang. Theme, for the most part, must be manipulated by actors in order for it to manipulate the audience.

To help you keep that ride dynamic and not repetitive, think of a Ferris wheel that spirals farther out and up with each revolution. Then, when you get to the top of the Ferris wheel for that last time—AHH!—it should be as if the clouds in the sky are swept aside for the first time.

Example. *A Chorus Line* tells the audience right away WHY they are watching: to see WHO is going to get a job in the chorus line. At the end of the first scene they also realize that they are going to hear biographies of the various auditionees. HOW?—Through song and dance. The auditionees' scene-songs could be presented in almost any order, and any one of them could be deleted without affecting the overall story; so the piece is cyclical. But the ever-expanding Ferris wheel of its structure keeps the audience interested and brings them to their final AHH!

Once you are able to identify thematic events your next step is to give them their due, investing them with wonder, rapture, exhilaration, and awe.

Example. In the seventh and final scene of Stoppard's *Arcadia* (which encompasses both cyclical and linear features), Chloë debunks the mystery that has been plaguing Valentine, the amateur scientist, since we first saw him.

Chloë: . . . it's all because of sex.
Valentine: Really?
Chloë: That's what I think. The universe is deterministic all right, just like Newton said, I mean it's trying to be, but the only thing going wrong is people fancying people who aren't supposed to be in that part of the plan.
Valentine: Ah. The attraction that Newton left out. All the way back to the apple in the garden. Yes. (*Pause*) Yes, I think you're the first person to think of this.

Note Valentine's line, "Ah." This constitutes one of the audience's AH!'s as well. His subsequent "pause" (a word you are quick to recognize by now as a clue) probably involves a huge unsaid thing—one the playwright wants to be sure the audience does not miss.

In the last beats of the play, during the plot that takes place 180 years earlier, two young people make a parallel discovery:

> Septimus: When we have found all the mysteries and lost all
>   the meaning, we will be alone, on an empty shore.
> Thomasina: Then we will dance.

Septimus and Thomasina, tutor and student, proceed to waltz for the remainder of the play in a theatrical rendition of the same theme, finally making sense of the play's very first line,

> Thomasina: Septimus, what is carnal embrace?

The audience has been on a thematic journey all along—about love, and so much more—that finally climaxes in dance.

Any play, then, contrives to keep the audience in a perpetual state of what, why, who, where, and/or how. Its ultimate mystery might be thought of as *why* the play was written in the first place, or why we are sharing it with the audience now. This mystery should hold the audience until that last drop of the curtain before bows.

> **Every play is, in some way, a mystery play:**
> **if not a whodunit, certainly a what's doing?**

Foils & Other Rhetorical Characters

Some characters are actually born to purvey theme, notably those that parallel and contrast with others in key ways. These roles, known as *foils*, are distorted mirror images. With one character, the playwright reflects (or even satirizes) another.

Example. In the *Henry IV* plays, Pistol, Bardolph, and Nym appear as cronies of Prince Hal. When the prince becomes king in Henry V he severs his social ties with them. Now they become satirical characters, the embodiment of everything you do not want in a soldier: almost the *Saturday Night Live* version of king and company.

Lest the actors miss this relationship, Henry starts III.1 with:

> Once more unto the breach, dear friends, once more;
> Or close the wall up with our English dead.

The very next scene echoes the "breach" line with:

Bardolph:	On, on, on, on, on! to the breach, to the breach!
Nym:	Pray thee, corporal, stay: the knocks are too hot . . .
Boy:	Would I were in an alehouse in London! I would give all my fame for a pot of ale and safety.
Pistol:	And I. . . .

Then they sing awhile, instead of fighting: the mirror image, distorted. They are cowards—anti-soldiers.

Since you, as Bardolph or Pistol, have nothing to do with the (main) plot, you have everything to do with this theme. So you know you can go all out in lampooning the king and the soldiers. (The word *lampoon* comes from the Italian word for *raspberry*—both the fruit and the Bronx cheer. This suggests a far more aggressive, vulgar, and actable activity than merely mocking.) Satirize Henry V's mannerisms overtly. Bardolph's "breach" line might mirror Henry's in gesture and staging, with one specially selected distortion—say, drunkenness. Let these distortions grow over the course of the play so that the audience will look forward to your next entrance, just as we look forward to Steve Martin or Eddie Murphy hosting next week's *Saturday Night Live.*

A foil serves as a living metaphor for another character in a parallel or inverted plot; the commentary is purveyed through the comparison and contrast. So interpret aggressively: give your character a brazen *attack* to enhance that contrast. Make your Mrs. Lovett or Sweeney Todd grotesques: let Johanna and Anthony be the "straight couple."

Foils are one type of *rhetorical character,* which advances the play's essay more than its main plot. Rhetoric gets a bad rap today. Sometimes the word is meant pejoratively to refer to affectation, exaggeration, or bombastic, inflated speech. But think of it rather as "the art of oratory, . . . especially the persuasive use of language to influence the thoughts and actions of listeners."[14] Note that it involves taking action on others: in fact, Rhetoric is the mother of Drama.

Rhetoric *is* active.

While in life a rhetorical question expects no response, onstage rhetoric always demands one, usually one that must remain unstated. All language is rhetoric: every time a person speaks (in life or in a play), she chooses the most persuasive words she can.

Fortunately, playwrights tend to fashion their rhetorical characters into fools, comics, clowns, wits, singers, poets, satirical foils like Pistol and company, or the zany mechanicals in *A Midsummer Night's Dream.* Their sense of humor might not only help them get away with caustic comments, but also shine a light on what makes them human—and compelling.

Wit is like a distress signal, a flare shot up from a shipwreck. In William Inge's *Picnic,* the wise-cracking spinster Rosemary keeps her head high with humor. "Shoot, Mrs. Potts, I'm just a tease," she explains in Act I. In Act III she bares the despair beneath: "Oh, God! Please marry me, Howard. Please . . . (*She sinks to her knees.*) Please . . . please . . . " So humor palliates horror. Or, as Brecht said, a situation needs to be sufficiently tragic to be comic.

When playing a role that is not written particularly funny, you may have to be more inventive to hold your audience. You can (1) apply the force of your personality to make it funny or empathetic, or intoxicate by being charming, adorable, sexy, poignant, warm, self-effacing, or all of the above; and/or (2) shape your speech with a shot of momentum, which, though it may not further the plot, will grip the audience. Think of inner dialogue that will make them wonder what you are going to say next, or what might happen next to them. Consider the Emcee in *Cabaret,* who does not further the plot one bit, but gets us to look forward to his next appearance. Here outrageousness helps, which songwriters Kander and Ebb enhance.

In spoken text, try treating your long speech as a song or aria, and you are halfway to charging it with the same razzle-dazzle as the Emcee. Find the rhythm, build to a climax, and sell it, and you will grab the audience.

Use the same principles when playing a captious cynic or melancholy curmudgeon. Then, to give your character a dose of poignancy, investigate why you have removed yourself from the others in the play. Jaques in *As You Like It* is not simply a social recluse, but an emotional barometer. Our introduction to him is through a report of his weeping over a wounded stag as he rails against the herd's cruel indifference—and Man's. Later he saves the country wench Audrey from a sham marriage to Touchstone, who was planning to use and then abandon her. So upon closer examination, melancholy Jaques is not merely sad, but sensitive. More, he adores the Fool and champions the downtrodden: these constitute action, through which you can get your audience to root for you. This curmudgeon, like *Picnic's* comedian Rosemary, suffers from a capacity for hurt so great that the heart has enlisted the personality for protection.

So if you are playing a fool, a wit, a clown, a curmudgeon, or the most humorless cynic ever born, find the incredibly human thing about him that will get the audience to hear your wisdom. When the playwright exposes or lampoons, you expose or lampoon, too, in the most active, entertaining, involving way possible—theatrically.

STORYTELLING TECHNIQUES

In shaping an entire play, each script presents unique demands. There are, however, several exercises that can help sharpen your sense of shape—first in general, and then with regard to a particular script you are working on.

Beginning, Middle, and End

This set of exercises helps give your acting a sense of beginning, middle, and end. First, the beginning.

Exercise: Aborted Speech. Choose a sentence to say aloud. It can be either your own words or a line of dialogue, but do have it in your mind ahead of time. Then take in enough breath to say it—but do not say it. Have a real reason for aborting your speech (other than the rules of this exercise). Now adjust what you want to say, and inhale again to say it—and again, find a reason not to say it. See how long you can sustain this in front of an audience. Remember that the secret to suspense is not what you do, but what you are about to do. The trick to making this exercise work is to be specific and real at each moment with what you are about to say, and with what aborts your impulse to say it. If you fake it, it starts to look like—acting.

Exercise: Phrases Clashing. Expand the exercise to include two people: interrupt each other, not necessarily verbally, but with an action. Person A starts to speak (again, don't pretend—really have something to say). But person B lifts a finger or grunts as if to say, "Wait a minute," after which he then either brushes off A's clothes, or sets up a chair, or closes the window, or turns on a stereo. When B is done, person A can continue—or so it seems. Except that this time person B will interrupt to sweep the floor. And so on. It starts to sound like a Laurel and Hardy or Charlie Chaplin routine, but remember that these clowns' silent bits were brilliant: all they had was Shape. If you can shape a scene without text, imagine what you can do with it.

Taking the Audience with You Nonverbally

Many of the following exercises (and much of this book) treat the nonverbal aspects of acting. Here, think of nonverbal not as silent, but as that which is other than the word itself: vocal life, proximity, body language, breath, the subconscious, and so forth.

Exercise: Conducting. To work on taking the audience with you on your through-line, try conducting the other actors of your company. Use a baton of some kind, but not a score. Let the group gather makeshift percussion instruments and practice several different meters together: 2/4, 3/4, 4/4, and even 5/4. Try having a bass drum beat on the first beat, and the others on subsequent beats.

Then try to lead the group through unexpected surprises. Start off in 4/4, and without letting them know ahead of time, change the meter to 3/4. Without speaking, keep everyone together as you change it. To do this successfully, you not only anticipate what's to come, but set it up so your percussionists can anticipate along with you.

This is exactly the rapport you want to generate with your audience (and your fellow actors, for that matter)—involvement, anticipation, inner dialogue, and mutual complicity.

The Take and Related Bits

We've discussed the shape of a cross or gesture (see Tasks, p. 96). Now let's work on boosting the dramatic event implicit in that gesture, through a device known as the *take* (short for "take focus").

Exercise: Entrance Take. You can use a scene you are working on, but any scenario will do. Instead of just entering and talking, stop at the place you enter, take focus for a second, and then continue onto the stage. During that moment you stop, silently betray to the audience why you entered, as well as what is going on in your mind as you size up the situation onstage. For example, Reginald enters to talk to Miss Elizabeth, his fiancée, about something very important, but suddenly sees Sir Dashwell still here. "Hmmm, that Dashwell character never leaves her alone for a minute; how can I get a moment to talk to her privately?" Then you propel yourself the rest of the way into the room, your plans slightly adjusted. Then, cover up your discombobulation so that the audience will know something rich is going on, but Sir Dashwell will not.

Exercise: Exit Take. Instead of just walking off stage, pause for a moment at the door (or whatever the exit is), take focus as you crystallize what you are plotting, and then head off. The characters onstage may even give you focus for a moment by noticing you stop. You sort of thrust your inner life onto the audience, just about forcing them to conjecture, "Oh, my, what's he going to do?" In other words, you make your post-beat active and clear. (See Pre-Beat and Post-Beat in chapter 2, pp. 55-57.)

Exercise: Take Mid-Task. Instead of just going to open the door, let your hand pause for a millisecond a few inches from the door knob as you are about to grab it. Or as the butler hands you the mail, let yourself stop for a beat as you reach for the envelope on the salver; then the audience suspects that receiving the letter may have life-changing consequences for you.

This does not mean that you should open the door or receive the mail slowly, though *slow motion* is another way you might take focus. Technically, a *take* is like a "soft freeze," and implies that you are still for a beat, though maybe not completely frozen.

Exercise: Double Take. The common double take does not work if you keep your head bouncing back and forth between two focus points. Rather, let it take you a few seconds to realize what the other character has just said or what you have just seen. Then look up—toward the audience, most likely— as you realize it (or right before). Then turn to her again, holding up the dialogue a moment, since the audience will probably laugh as they realize what you are thinking. Now try it again, smoother and clearer. Essentially you invite the audience to read your mind between the first glance and the second. Usually they are a second or two ahead of you.

Do not be afraid of overacting in these take exercises, even if you look clumsy once or twice. The point of the practice is clarity, not subtlety, which you will work on later. In front of an audience, if you render these takes in character, with inner life and conviction, they will seem surprisingly natural: all you are doing is inviting the spectators to see what you are not saying.

In the old days an overt take would often fit the style of the production; today, you can find a way to execute a take without anyone knowing you are doing it.

Keep in mind that you tend to take focus when you are suddenly still after a period of motion, you move differently from everyone else onstage, or others give you emphasis in another way. Make sure that when you take focus technically, you also earn it dramatically: merit that focus.

As an adjunct to the take exercises, try:

Exercise: Reaction to Task. After you down that shot of whiskey, let us know that it's good. Or if someone interrupts your drinking of it, react with a tacit version of Homer Simpson's "d'Oh!"

As in the Folding Laundry exercise, choose a repetitive, sequential task (setting up chairs, opening or closing windows, erecting a house of playing cards) but now try executing it *with* your audience. I don't mean have them get up to help you, but take them along. Differentiate your reactions to each element of your task: certainly the twenty-third card placed in that house would be a far greater achievement than the third. Find twenty-three different takes, in other words.

Feel free to let these reactions emerge with *vocal life:* sounds that are not quite text, not quite spellable interjections, but grunts, sighs, breaths, groans, hums, coughs, moans, and so forth. Rather than manufacture the vocal life artificially, let it emerge naturally out of each moment. The point is to develop a broad agenda of ways to communicate your genuine little ecstasies and frustrations. When your character has no lines, vocalizing will become one of your most valuable shaping tools.

Shaping Speeches and Scenes

Every gesture you make can be as full of meaning as the take and help the audience follow the flow of your inner life. Cigarette smoking, for example, affords you a series of occasions for revelation. Every time you light one, or puff, or flick an ash in an ashtray, you are given a sublime opportunity to betray what is going on inside you, even when your inner life has nothing to do with smoking per se. This is why cigarettes became so popular in movies in the 1930s and '40s (in addition to giving actors something to do with their hands). It is not so much that smoking has character, but that it *betrays* character. (See discussion of tactile connection in Gesture, p. 9.) Through such tactile activities, you can orchestrate meaning.

Exercise: Smoking, Sipping, Snacking. Choose a scene or speech. Then play it while letting each action with a cigarette reveal a huge unsaid moment. If you don't smoke, you don't have to light the cigarette; the exercise will be nonetheless valuable.

The same principle could be applied to activities like sipping tea or eating bonbons or crackers. Say the conversation suddenly turns to the person of your dreams. A carefully timed sip, or the plopping of a chocolate in your mouth—keeping your eyes up—might just betray all your pent-up desire, disdain, or both. Chomp a cucumber as you talk about the emptiness of life, and the juxtaposition turns hilarious. Chekhov's governess, Charlotta, uses just this idea in the beginning of Act II of *The Cherry Orchard*. Look at this and his other plays for more ideas on orchestrating inner life with tactile activities like card-playing (*The Seagull, Three Sisters*) and taking snuff.

Example. In the opening of *The Seagull*, the comically miserable Masha (dressed in black, in mourning for her life) deflects a marriage proposal while taking snuff:

| Medevenko: | Who would care to marry a man who hasn't a penny to bless himself with? |
| Masha: | Oh, nonsense! (*Takes a pinch of snuff*) Your love touches me, but I can't reciprocate it—that's all (*Holding out the snuff-box to him*) Help yourself. |

She is far more interested in snuff than in love—his love, at any rate. The insensitive juxtaposition of the two makes her pathetic circumstances—and his—laughable.

Absent tobacco and comestibles, sound, lighting, and scene changes help take the audience from event to event. Think of the trilled diminished seventh chord that accompanies the moment in a melodrama (or a silent movie) when Nell's life is threatened by the villain. Usually you want to convey dramatic portent without that diminished seventh chord, of course—but do convey it.

Exercise: Nonverbal Scoring. The next exercise builds on the dance-through and sing-through (see p. 105) and is evocative of Stanislavski's tempo-rhythms (see p. 154). It will work most efficiently when you have already identified the events, but can also be used to help locate them. "Events" here, though, include big ones and small ones, like changes in tactics, speaker, and topic.

Let each actor, in addition to or instead of saying the text, find some other means to communicate: banging a drum or a table, emitting vocal sounds, playing an instrument, performing continuous movement, singing, or all of these alternately. The actors work through the scene by performing an abstract expression of each line, heightening emotion, tone, mood, actions, and so forth. At each event, they change something—timbre, tempo, pitch, or whatever—so as to convey the event. It is as if there were a musical score rolling that diminished seventh chord, but it is the actors playing the score. The director or coach should make sure that some change indeed accompanies each event, and have the actors go back to repeat any event that is missed.

Tailor the exercise to the proclivities of your particular company: the abstract expression could replace the text, as in a silent dance-through, or provide a means to deliver the words, as in a sing-through, or a mixture of both, if it works for your group. Have someone on book to help everyone keep their place.

Some of what you come up with may be applicable to your perform-ance, such as percussive line delivery. An invisible result will be simply to infuse your work with a bold psychological texture that clarifies the shape of the scene; you might intrigue your audience with a case of the willies for no identifiable reason.

You will also find Nonverbal Scoring an effective tool for working a monologue.

Here is an exercise to help you put words into phrases by instilling a sense of the end of a line at the beginning, which is the way we talk in life, after all. It is also useful in nailing down the effortless musicality of a British, Southern, or aristocratic dialect.

Exercise: Goal Words. Take a speech and circle roughly one important word per sentence. Let these words serve as keys to your larger phrases, convey-ing most of your meaning; let all the rest of the words serve as function words to get you to each of your key words.

In saying the text aloud, trip along as quickly as you can on the function words; and land on, or ride, the goal words with the meaning with which you have charged them. Avoid (1) speaking too quickly on the incidental passages (or you will indeed trip); or conversely, (2) merely accentuating the key words too hard, or too technically, without meaning or variety.

Next try choosing a different goal word for each sentence. This will require adjusting your inner monologue of innuendoes and such.

Here is a sample of two options from Gwendolyn's speech to Cecily in Act II of *The Importance of Being Earnest*:

Oh! It is strange he never men-tioned to me that he *had* a ward.	Oh! It is strange he never men-tioned to *me* that he had a ward.
How *secretive* of him!	*How* secretive of him!

He grows *more* interesting hourly.	He grows more interesting *hourly*.
I am not sure, however, that the news inspires me with feelings of *unmixed* delight.	I am not sure, however, that the news inspires me with feelings of unmixed *delight*.
I *am* very fond of you, Cecily; I have liked you ever since I *met* you!	I am *very* fond of you, Cecily; I have liked you *ever* since I met you!
But I am *bound* to state that now that I *know* that you are Mr. Worthing's ward, I cannot help expressing a wish you were—well, just a little *older* than you seem to be—and not quite so *very* alluring in appearance.	But I *am* bound to state that now that I know that you *are* Mr. Worthing's ward, I cannot help expressing a wish you were—well, *just* a little older than you seem to be—and not quite so very *alluring* in appearance.
In fact, *if* I may speak candidly—	In fact, if I may speak *candidly*—

Try either of these solutions, or others of your own. This is a way of kneading the text, not unlike how a potter shapes clay or a baker, dough. Remember, though, that this is an exercise, not acting. Do not let anyone catch you working on this during a performance; you can't knead the clay after you've fired the pot.

Exercise: Titling Subsections. When you put the whole speech or scene together, you want to take the listener from point A to B to C to D. Try first to identify A, B, C, and D; then assign a title to each of these subsections corresponding to your sequence of tactics, topics, images, or whatever. For example: A. scold; B. apologize; C. heal; D. embrace.

Shaping a Play

To cast the illusion that the audience is glimpsing life rather than watching a performance, Ibsen, Chekhov, and any number of other playwrights start out with characters undergoing simple daily rituals of taking tea, buttering bread, setting the table. Hence the monikers *bread-and-butter naturalism, kitchen-sink realism,* and *cup-and-saucer plays.* Once an ordinary atmosphere is established, the playwright then sneaks in a dramatic event, sometimes as late as the end of Act I, which, for the MTV-generation audience, is too late. A company must figure out how to render the most casual dialogue compelling. To do this, dig deep down to find events. Then charge your dialogue with electricity at those events to grab that audience.

We can broaden the titling exercise to help articulate those events, grab the audience sooner, and shape an entire play.

Exercise: Titling the French Scenes. The ensemble suggests a few words of text (usually from the dialogue) that correlate with the event of each French scene and serve as the scene's title. Naturally, actors will come up with different titles to correspond to their own events. So the group as a whole chooses titles based on the events for the audience, while privately each actor may also assign alternate titles for his own character.

Example. Federico García Lorca based *The House of Bernarda Alba* on a real household he knew of, where the martinet of a mother kept her daughters locked indoors, apparently to protect them from the attentions of men. Lorca starts by offering a sneak peek into what at first seems like an ordinary day in the life of an oppressed household of women bored out of their skin—and out of all sympathy as well. They talk, they embroider, they fight, they wallow. AND SO . . . ?

What makes the play gripping does not occur until later, when the herd of male laborers passes by the house, and the sexual tension begins. I realized during rehearsals that the first half or so of the play might be no more interesting to today's American audience than a documentary on Spanish domestic life. So we spent a rehearsal naming the French scenes, posted the list on the call board and thereafter used these titles to refer to each scene. Within a few days, sparks started to fly. The audience may not have been sure what was bubbling beneath the dialogue, but they could tell something was. It was like a symphony where the ostinato in the bass builds to the clashing entrance of the horn section. How was this achieved? Through identifying the structure of the story and making sure each scene told its part of that story.

Here is a sample of our working French scene and sub-scene titles for *Bernarda Alba*, all of which come from the script's text (dialogue or stage directions). I have included Act II here instead of Act I, because it's a little clearer to those unfamiliar with the play. Note how the dramatic structure jumps out of the list:

French Scene (and Sub-Scene) Titles
The House of Bernarda Alba (Act II)

scene
a.	Something's wrong with Adela
b.	She hardly sleeps
c.	Leave me alone!
d.	Laces here!
e.	Don't defy me
f.	Always arguing
g.	And be quiet
h.	Laces
i.	40–50 handsome young men
j.	What's wrong with Martirio?
k.	Where's that picture?
l.	Don't joke with me
m.	What scandal!
n.	Search
o.	Can't I play a joke?
p.	Something very grave is happening here
q.	That's a lie!
r.	I heard him leave at four, too.
s.	Mother, don't listen
t.	A big crowd
u.	I'll see you dead first
v.	She killed it
w.	Kill her!

These titles also happen to provide a convenient way to call rehearsals or give notes; as soon as you mention the French scene "40–50 handsome young men," cast and crew know exactly to which scene you are referring, and which characters are involved. Meanwhile, the dramatic structure becomes ingrained in the company's subconscious.

Titling is helpful not only in bread-and-butter naturalism with camouflaged structure, but also when the structure is opaque, such as erudite Theater of Ideas, or scripts that are just plain weird. It gets you to crystallize what is going on when it's hard to tell what is. For if you can't tell what's going on, you can't bring the audience along.

Objective Correlatives

Objective correlatives are objects that call to mind, through comparison or association, something else that is not there (the category encompasses symbols and metaphors). These objects may be things or activities, sounds or songs, even smells. The very phonemes of speech are correlatives of intrinsic meaning: "mah" stands for things maternal in any language.

Technically, a metaphor refers to a comparison between two entities that have at least one trait in common (the comparison) and one not in common (otherwise it would be an identity). "Ravenal is a dog with women" compares distinct living beings with appetites that are similar. With objective correlative, however, the two entities can even have nothing in common; yet through the one, the other is expressed.

Metaphor, the key ingredient of poetry, is static; objective correlative tends to be dynamic, advancing dramatic action and suspense.

Example. In Emlyn Williams's play *Night Must Fall,* a newspaper story identifies the murderer with a certain song:

> A keeper in the Shepperley woods was closely questioned last night, but he had heard nothing, beyond a woman's voice in the woods on the afternoon in question, and a man's voice, probably with her, singing "Mighty Lak a Rose."

When a stranger walks in whistling that very song, the audience wants to jump out of their seats to prevent another murder.

Repetition of an objective correlative renders it a *motif.* Our responses to it become like those of Pavlov's dog, whose mealtimes were always signaled by the ringing of a bell until finally the sound of the bell itself made him salivate. The *Jaws* theme signals the shark nearby, while in *Psycho* we fear when another murder is imminent because—well, watch the movie.

A well-executed objective correlative gets the audience to put two and two together; indeed, it brings them to the point where they *can't not* do so. This constitutes the best sort of audience participation. In *The Caine Mutiny Court Martial,* Captain Queeg's fondling of those two steel balls is more than a metaphor of impotence; it signals neurosis and lost control, provoking great anticipation of what is going to happen next.

CHAPTER 6
HEIGHTENED
THEATRICALITY

Today, how can the theater hope to offer thrills to compete with the technical effects possible in the cinema? Some long-running Broadway shows have featured helicopters landing, chandeliers falling, and kitties ascending to heaven. Absent this technology, it may not be enough for the actor merely to involve the audience; you need a magazine of theatrical techniques at your disposal that can captivate, intoxicate, and thrill them in as many different ways as possible. With this in mind, let's expand chapter 1's introduction to theatricality with some ideas for blowing the roof off the audience.

Pyrotechnics and spectacle are perfectly legitimate means for giving the audience a good show. But another sort of excitement comes from human thrills, which are the actor's domain. These are thrills of the soul. With a hefty dose of craft and courage, the actor's work can be as exciting and wonderful as the biggest-budgeted blockbuster on Broadway.

THE SHOW OF THE SHOW

When we think back to the Christmas mornings of childhood, we think of traipsing downstairs and catching that first glimpse of stockings overstuffed and the assortment of shiny boxes under the illuminated tree. We'd forget about the toys by about noon, but the memory of their anticipation would haunt us until next year.

A performance is also a gift, which we want to wrap up in a bright bow and make our audience, like the child on Christmas morning, wonder about what's inside. We do this through imagination, bravura, spectacle, and celebration—the *show* of putting on a show.

Often a merely competent staging of the story is not enough:

Tell it and sell it.

Do not confuse this with "showing off" in the negative sense. What I am talking about is intrinsic to the theater, which, like Oliver Twist, asks for more: Every time actor or audience enters through its portals, the theater invites more, demands more, expects more, and therefore must offer more than any alternative.

There is nothing wrong with those helicopters and chandeliers if they get people into the theater and suit the dramatic action. Even nudity may set the audience a-tingle: the challenge is for it to emerge naturally, because of the intimacy of the moment. So do you need to take your clothes off onstage? Well, literally, no; but figuratively—yes! Strip off the outer layers and bare your character's soul, or even your own. That's why you are there: to make the theater a wonderful place where jaws drop, eyes get misty, and hearts skip a beat every once in a while.

To start evoking wonder in those who are watching, first, have a whole lot going on inside in addition to the text itself; second, don't necessarily let anyone know. "Anyone" will certainly be the audience, but may very well include the other actors and the director. They will certainly notice subliminally, the other actors wondering what's going on as they play off you, and the director shaping not just the script, but what you don't say, too, into a wonder-ful production.

Such an intrepid approach requires courage. The first step takes the courage to offer all of yourself, and more. The second step takes the courage to trust that what your character is concealing will actually be revealed: the courage to let it happen instead of making it happen. And as always, when you make your choices, remember the audience.

To evoke wonder:
1. *Amplify: Have lots going on besides what's in the script.*
2. *Don't tell what you have going on.*
3. *Be brave, or at least act brave.*
4. *Remember the audience.*

In acting terms, consider what will make a moment more exciting—or most exciting—yet still work from the audience's point of view. Other actors settle for the casual rather than the extraordinary; then, if "it ain't broke," they "don't fix it." I invite you to strive beyond what is merely believable, or what merely works:

If it ain't broke—break it!

This is a fundamental principle of brilliance in all the arts: if you settle for mere competence, then mediocrity is just around the corner.

Fight, then, to convert insecurity into a captivating sort of vulnerability, and not to let it lead to a lack of daring for fear of making—shudder—a fool of yourself. When your role calls for it, make the best darned fool of yourself possible. Of course, it helps to have an adventurous rehearsal environment with enough time for experimentation, knowing that you can distill later. Once you have the trust and the time, though, the rest is up to you. So take risks, dig deeper, go further, act sillier, and don't let anyone stop you. It's your job.

INVISIBLE THEATRICALITY: THE ACTOR AT PLAY

Some roles are naturally outrageous; usually, though, a character wants to cope with crisis and hide vulnerability. Either way, you want to be able to play at the brink.

If you're not on the edge, you're not in the drama.

Of course, you needn't let anyone know that the edge is where you are.

Inner-to-Outer Techniques

When the play is naturalistic and your role lies close to your own type, you can achieve a rather eerie sense of wonder if you start simple: Assume the character includes all of yourself, and then make as few adjustments as necessary to bridge the gap between you and the role. (See Adjustments and Secrets, pp. 37-39.) Too often actors draw from less than themselves, instead of all of themselves plus something else that transforms them into the character. Instead, try let your personal experience make up the bulk of the character's. Remember, the director cast you for a reason. Why use more adjustments than necessary? This approach will be particularly effective when time is limited and casting is to type.

Maybe one adjustment will suffice, and provide enough of a psychological buffer to free you to risk playing very close to yourself. An adjustment furnishes a kind of mask—not that you hide behind, but that protects you as you reveal through it. This masking effect is the *defense of fiction*.

A little artifice can set you free.

(*Artifice* suggests "crafted with artistry," not "phony.") Once you say "I am now someone else" you can bare your heights of joy and depths of sorrow without the audience's knowing it is *you,* who are, after all, just acting.

Augmenting the Method

Perhaps the ultimate process-oriented rehearsal period would start with the First Meeting and First Reading exercises (see pp. 91-92), and then generate the play gradually by layering on details one at a time—circumstances, environment, physical adjustments, text—all the while maintaining honest connection. Never forcing an emotion, you never have a false one.

This slow rehearsal method is like building a statue out of grains of sand. Nevertheless, it has much to recommend it if it works. You stay firmly rooted in the organic while gently expanding to the extraordinary. How would you reach a high level of excitement? Slowly, but surely. Slowly alone, though, might result in something dangerously close to boredom. But surely, a Method actor can apply some theatrical instinct and "go a little further" with each repetition of a scene—never forcing, just growing. Infuse your performance with three percent more energy, sadness, or goofiness each rehearsal, and after a few weeks you will have doubled your energy, sadness, or goofiness. (Of course, this process will involve directives more actable than "act goofier.") With brilliant actors, this method has produced brilliant performances.

Since you would start with "nothing" and only gradually fill your creative tank, this would require a long rehearsal period, a rare luxury in our professional theater. In Europe, actors may still rehearse a play from two to eight months; in the United States, we get one to four weeks (a fifth week or a preview period is an extravagance). Alas, you will probably never be at a rehearsal where the director says, "Today we are going to work on our organic connection," which Stanislavski might have said to his company. Yet it would indeed be advantageous for every actor to have this experience at least once, if only in a one-act, to root your work in a solid foundation of organic connection.

With the typical time constraint, however, it is more practical to craft a statue from a huge block of marble than to assemble one from grains of sand. Still, you can augment your foundation, which is rooted in the

Method, by simply remembering that the audience needs your creative juice. In this way you jump-start the process of going a little further.

How? By stoking your creative furnace with volatile fuel, and lots of it.

Images

For one, you can assemble images and secrets that make you more interesting. To the actor, the word *image* refers to far more than just some picture in your mind to specify your thoughts and color your speech (though it is that, too). An actor's image can be a person, a place, an emotion, an experience, an abstract concept, an attitude, all sorts of things.

Be careful not to let the audience catch you creating an image, however. They came to see the play, not the work. A *workable* image should do three things: (1) charge the text and the moment, rendering stage life clear, personal, colorful, exciting, enchanting; (2) evoke a response in the other actors (and in the audience), so that one moment leads to the next; and (3) affect you automatically without your having to work at all.

If you have to work your image, it won't work for you.

So tax your imagination to the limit. Let the raciest, funniest burlesque show be only a tenth as interesting as your hidden, even pornographic thoughts. Aren't we all pretty racy anyway, deep down? It is part of what will make your character breathe like a living being.

If your images are strong and colorful, the audience should get *some* imagery; if you choose tame images, the audience may get the *text;* if you say the text *without* imagery, the audience will fall asleep.

Again, try to keep these images secret so you get everyone to wonder . . .

Exercise: Filling the Tank. When rehearsing a play or audition monologue, try this exercise to help you come up with images. You must already have a speech well memorized.

First, a warm-up is in order—both physical and for relaxation (see appendix 2).

Second, you need a private space to rehearse where no one will interrupt you. Take the phone off the hook if you are at home.

Then, find some way to make your space special to you. Light a candle, turn the lights down, burn incense, whatever works for you.

When you are ready, lie down on your back on the floor or some other hard surface with enough room for you. A pillow under your neck will help your back sink into the floor. As you are going to be filling your creative viscera with images, you want your literal viscera also to fill with air—and inspiration. Therefore, breathe easily throughout your work. Feel your midsection expand and your back sink into the floor as you inhale.

You may close your eyes or stare at a spot on the ceiling, but don't let your eyes start wandering around.

What you are going to do is fill your furnace of emotions and images, word by word. Say the first word of your speech aloud. Then think about what comes to mind with that word. Then say it again. Then think of some wackier or more dangerous meaning. Do this several times, repeating the word with each new image. What you are thinking or feeling need not have anything to do with what the word actually means. For example, if the text is "oh," all sorts of memories from your childhood might rise up. Let them.

You can think of both deriving images from the word and ascribing images to the word. Remember that an image can be anything—a person, a place, a feeling, a memory, a smell, a sound, a thought, a sense of injustice, a joke, a hallucination.

Go on to the next word, and do the same thing. Spend forty minutes doing about forty to a hundred words of the speech. You need not finish the entire speech in one session.

The process is rather intense, but by the end of it you will have owned those forty to a hundred words. Musicians do something like this, too, note by note, so you are not alone.

Since no one else is in the room, you can go to any emotional place you would like to go, and summon as personal, as frightening, or as funny a past experience as you wish. These are not choices; this is the muck and mire of experience with which you are simply stoking your furnace.

Continue the next day and the next until you get to the end of the speech. Some actors who have had great success with this exercise worked it every other day. As long as your program is regular and intense, you should be fine.

Then, start putting two and three words together to make sub-phrases, repeating each sub-phrase the way you did each word. A few sessions later, start putting together whole phrases, then entire sentences, then passages, then the whole speech.

Next time you play the speech in front of other people, do not repeat, or even think about, this exercise. The images and emotions will come automatically. Rather than force anything, trust that it will all be there, and if even a tenth of it is, you will be quite overpowering. (I have seen it time and again: jaws will drop with amazement at how much you have to say. This exercise has turned students into actors—paid actors—quickly.)

Exercise: Placing Imagery. Sometimes you consciously keep your image private: for example, the thought of a person from your own life that you summon and map into a non-appearing character you mention in your dialogue. To make a private image public, though, invest some time and effort in locating it in the theater! Go further than pretending that the back row is the road to Moscow, that the ghost of your father is in the balcony, or that the ceiling is a starlit sky with the moon smiling down on you. Place the images there: More than just connecting to your space, charge it. As with sense memory, do more than imagine in your mind's eye—actually create and place the image right there. (See Sense Memory exercise, p. 89.) And make it intimate and potent so that it cannot help but generate a spark from you when you look there.

Example. In *Henry IV Part II,* Lady Percy is a widow. Her husband Hotspur was slain in Part I and does not appear in Part II. The memory of the deceased must fill not just her mind, but also her gut. Then her Hotspur can automatically spur her on as she begs her father-in-law, "O yet, for God's sake, go not to these wars!" (II.3)

Even better, though, if the relationship between Lady and Lord could fill the space and involve the audience—and it can. One Lady Percy I coached chose a rich, private image for her husband and then placed him in a specific area of the audience—before she walked on the stage. As the scene progressed, her Hotspur acted on her and made her call on "him, O wondrous him" (at which point she saw him) to stop the war. She did not have to think, overact, or even try to emote; but neither she nor the audience could hold back the tears.

Exercise: Private Textual Images. Remember that exercises using nonsensical text (see p. 87) ask you to mean something real, other than the sounds you say. You can exploit this principle to fill a scene with real life instantly, even during the middle of a performance.

Say you happen to develop a secret infatuation for the costar with whom you also just happen to be playing a love scene. Simply "fall out of character" (on the inside only) and "into yourself" without anyone knowing, and bestow a wash of sudden truth onto what you say. If anyone notices, it will only be to wonder "what's going on between those two?" (I knew one Nathan Detroit who proposed to his Adelaide onstage in *Guys and Dolls!*)

You can also ascribe light and capricious textual images to your dialogue—like discussion of weather, fashion, politics, or asking someone out on a date—as long as they are specific and you really try to communicate them. The more specific, the better. If they are not actually appropriate for your character, but they work, you need not let anyone know; in fact, no other actor need ever hear what you are really thinking. Straddling two worlds of inner life at once demands double the concentration. Obviously, if you are prone to going up on your lines, you may not want to try this in performance. (I have seen actors accidentally state their private images aloud. Oops.)

Variation 1. Here is a rather cheap but oft-used technique that is particularly effective: Try meaning the words "I love you" with each line of text. When your scene partner is a stranger, this is a great method to simulate prior intimate knowledge of each other (e.g., cold readings at an audition).

Variation 2. A relaxation technique used by public speakers and corporate executives, especially when they have a tense board meeting to attend: Imagine that you see the other actors or the audience in their underwear or even naked. This helps you not only remain calm, but also maintain your sense of humor and warmth. Again, keep this adjustment secret so you come across not as loony but as colorful and winning.

An image can even be an action. I have already discussed the technique of assigning a strong verb, or action statement, to your dialogue. (See Subtext, Action Statements, Attributed Verbs, pp. 42-43.) Try going for a more specific or drastic action, like getting the other character out of that chair, making her cry, or making her love you, even when the line does not talk about chairs, tears, or love. If it doesn't work, try another choice.

When attributing verbs, for example, instead of merely *arguing*, try to *belittle, humor, defend, attack*. Instead of *interesting* the other character, try to *seduce, sparkle, captivate, hypnotize*. Transform *say, state,* or *report* into *mesmerize, rationalize, campaign, conspire*, or even *earn a promotion*. Some directors and actors collect lists of such verbs. [15]

Adeptness at this technique is invaluable to today's actor. When you become expert at playing these actions with your entire will, then you can deliver a line with no spin whatsoever, or throw it away, yet still accomplish your action and be very interesting.

Never **merely** *say the line; always do something with it, even when throwing the line away.*

Beware of thinking that an image can be a quality or an adjective. These are not really playable as such: to apply an adjustment in the form "*to be +* adjective" results in exclusively result-oriented acting, which I am not advocating. If a director ever gives you a note like "be funnier" or "be suspicious," what you must really do is find how to get to the point where you must be funnier or suspicious. So transform the adjective into something active and actable: a circumstance, verb, action statement, or other appropriate adjustment. In this way, an adjective can still inspire.

Exercise: Remember the V's. I often recommend that actors "remember the V's." Many words in English that start with V happen to involve extremes. So don't hesitate to try acting a bit more vulgar, visceral, vivid, vivacious, vital, vibrant, voracious, vile, voluptuous, evil, violent, volatile, verminous, villainous, vulnerable, vindictive, vicious, vigilant, vigorous, vincible or invincible, vitriolic, vituperative, vocal, vociferous, vague, volcanic, voluble, valiant. These V-words should help you automatically act from the groin.

Again, you can't play the quality, but use the adjective to trigger an actable adjustment. To make your character more *vulnerable*, for instance, you might assume the adjustment "I am a deer, and headlights are shining on me." If *voluptuous* is your goal, you could try acting from your hips and lips; or dab a little perfume on some secret spot of your body. To play *verminous*, turn into a worm—in every possible way. (See Animal Work, pp. 147-148) Some of the words in the list are a little more difficult to access, but use your imagination.

Example. You are playing Birdie in Lillian Hellman's *The Little Foxes.* The director asks that your character be more "vague." What do you do?

Vague might inspire you to try obsessing on some idyllic fantasy (use a very personal one) as a buffer to the evil surrounding you. When your tyrannical husband scolds you, you will already have retreated elsewhere to the land of daisies and sunshine in your mind. The result could be a character who is appropriately withdrawn, batty, timorous, birdlike—vague.

The same principle applies to all sorts of notes that directors give actors.

Turn the director's note into an adjustment that is actable.

Outer-to-Inner Techniques

So far, I have focused largely on inner life. But the practical actor embraces the outer-to-inner process, too, for whatever works is useable.

**The physical informs the psychological as
the psychological informs the physical.**

This reciprocity occurs in life, too: a study of a decade or two ago revealed
that the sheer act of smiling tended to make people happier. In *The King
and I*, Anna instructs her son Louis to hold "head erect . . . , strike a care-
less pose," and "whistle a happy tune." As a result, "You may be as brave/
As you make believe you are." Posture and melody engender courage.

By the time of performance the distinction between inner-to-outer and
outer-to-inner work should disappear as your character becomes a living,
breathing organism. *Organic* suggests that the inner and the outer are fused
into one.

In effect, the outer-to-inner process involves variations on the following
scheme:

1. To start, make some choice to get your juices flowing with respect
    to one particular quality.
2. Let this one quality influence the rest of your characterization.
3. Finally, determine whether the quality is appropriate, compelling,
    and/or worthwhile.

The choice may function as a catalyst and be more valuable for how it affects
other qualities than for itself. (See Scoring, pp. 22-30.)

Olivier, for instance, talked about the importance of the nose. This is
the organ through which actors *re*spire, so it makes sense (at least lin-
guistically) that it would help to *in*spire the role. Finding the character's
walk may lead you to his voice and feelings, and vice versa. Try out a few
different walks until you hit upon the one that seems to fit. Then you integrate the physicality with the personality, the strut with the superiority.

To get your character from point X to point Y, don't necessarily work
on X and Y, but find the characteristic which, when you adjust it, will just
happen to bring you from X to Y. A director will often avoid even mention-
ing X and Y lest he make actors self-conscious about desired results.

You have probably put this principle into practice already. Regular exercise—jogging, swimming, working out—improves not only physical, but
also mental health; dance class gives you better posture and movement, but
also coordination and confidence. And if you do your voice and speech exercises every day, you should end up naturally speaking better and supporting
from your diaphragm; but you might also gain poise.

Exercise: Character Study. Ever searching for images and experiences, and always a student of human nature, the actor engages in the constant practice of character study by observing people. Inner life and even psychological history are revealed in a person's body, walk, demeanor, face, voice, and breathing. We manifest externally the very private things we would most like to conceal; the actor's job is to note how.

Before the rehearsal period starts, try to find your character in the real world. Spend a few hours watching people in some public place. When you finally spot someone who strikes your fancy as rather close to your role, don't stop to think why, at least not right away. Just keep watching and observing. If you can follow him, do so. Then, try to *become* him. Mirror his deportment, his gait, and even the contours of his face. Imagine his thoughts. If possible, try to duplicate his voice.

Maintain his physicality for a while and see if you invariably start to change on the inside as well. You may catch a quick glimpse of his thoughts, even of his past. In a sudden stroke, while trying to become him, you might feel as if you actually know him.

An otherwise normal female with a markedly concave posture may be shy and insecure about her body. She may have been overweight as a child, or prematurely developed as an adolescent, and has overcompensated, hunching over as a defense against unwanted attention. Try hunching over yourself and soon you too may start to feel shy and insecure about your body.

You have surely known someone with a certain smart-alecky look on his face and a cocky swagger to his walk. Find someone like this to observe closely, and then try walking that way. After a while you will start to feel cocky. Eventually it will be unclear (and unimportant) whether feeling cocky makes you act cocky, or vice versa.

Exercise: Animal Work. All of Aesop's and La Fontaine's fables were really about human beings. The animal world provides a rich source of metaphors for both fabulist and actor. Think of what makes a person a cat, a fox, or a kangaroo: it's not just the physicality. Try your character as a frog, for example, and your face, voice, thoughts, and personality will start to "hop," too. Plus your relationships with other characters will change as they react to your frog adjustment.

When you finally apply it to your character, avoid playing a frog *instead* of the human being. Rather, try making your character a human being who happens to be secretly a frog (unless you are playing a frog). Making sure others can guess what animal you are is a fine goal when playing a game, but it is not the point here; quite the contrary, the eventual goal is not to let anyone else even suspect that you are an animal at all.

In other words, as with all work, avoid serving your animal instead of playing your action, your given circumstances, your objective, and so on. In *The Importance of Being Earnest*, your Jack may be a jack rabbit, but he must also behave impeccably.

Building from the Neutral

There is a danger that some of your personal baggage—inappropriate to a role—will show. Sometimes you may not want to start with "yourself," then, but first establish the *neutral* as the basis for your character: in other words, build from scratch. To do this, you strip away your own baggage, both physical and psychological. Remember that we wear all our emotional history literally; every trauma in our past has been transformed into a tension in our bodies or a line in our faces. The ability to start from the neutral puts you in control of which of your own warts and woes you will apply to your characterization.

If you have had the physical and vocal training to return to the neutral, you have at your disposal a physical warm-up that removes body tensions and aligns your spine. (See appendix 2 for warm-up.) By layering on attributes one at a time, you will eventually be able to play any character, no matter how exotic.

Exercise: Masque Work. What I call *masque work* involves applying a set of character adjustments without necessarily using an actual mask (though the technique is also valuable in a masked production). Early in rehearsals, I have actors assume a bold, perhaps even exaggerated, adjustment for each of the following four aspects of their characterization:

Masque adjustments
- *physical;*
- *facial;*
- *vocal; and*
- *psychological;*

and also take on a signatory

- *costume piece or prop.*

These five elements create a heightened sketch of the role that is simple yet clear.

Example. Think of that parlor drama where you are playing Reginald's male secretary. First, try a masque: You need that monocle and clipboard (prop); you raise your eyebrows to look down at everyone superciliously (facial adjustment); you speak in a high, nasal voice (vocal); you have a hidden secret: that your older brother got the entire inheritance and you want to kill him, since you are broke. (This secret could come from the text of the play or not.)

Now think of other techniques to experiment with. Let us say that in the script's agenda, your character looks for dirt to blackmail someone. You could move so as not to be noticed at all, or perhaps in the exact opposite manner: overdeliberately, as if you have nothing to hide (physical adjustment). Or, ferret around like a ferret (animal work).

While you may dream up these adjustments out of the air, better to go out into the world and find this person in a mall or country club (character study). So your adjustment might be just to play this guy you observed, who defied any description other than that look in his eye as he puffed a cigarette and gave you a glimpse into his sad, confident, creepy soul. But you don't have to play sad, confident, or creepy, which are qualities—play the guy you studied!

Creating a role this way will be invaluable to highly theatrical or *epic staging* (see below). When you portray several characters in a production, for example, you can switch quickly from one to another without the emotional traces of one lingering into the next. Thus mimes, clowns, and storytellers can play all the parts without leaving the stage; think of Lily Tomlin, Robin Williams, and Dario Fo.

Masque work need not come off as caricature or cartoon, but can work within whatever style you wish, from naturalistic to highly theatrical. Make all your choices organic and you will be telling the story believably, vividly, and economically.

Subtlety

These techniques constitute the de rigeur craft of the exciting actor. But take a look at Daniel Day-Lewis, first in *My Beautiful Launderette*, then in *A Room with a View*, then in *My Left Foot*, and finally in *The Last of the Mohicans*. They are all him acting, yet you don't see him acting: you see the character. Again, the highest craft remains invisible.

To integrate these techniques invisibly, try not to let anyone know that you are enlisting any technique at all. Not all choices need to read: your approach to the role may be a solution for you, but you do not necessarily want to solve it completely for the audience. An outlandish choice rendered subtly can be far more intriguing than a meek choice overdone. If you plaster the word *coffee* on a mug in big, bold letters, you'll be clear, sure, but it won't get the audience to wonder what's in that mug. Instead, invite the audience to approach, sniff, and taste. Your result: a "natural theatricality" that happens to be very interesting. In fact, you will be amazed at how subtle you can be, yet still be effective and compelling, as long as you remember the audience—without letting them know.

THE ENSEMBLE AT PLAY

Moving on to rehearsal techniques and exercises, I now address both the director and an ensemble of actors.

Inspiration

As the old vaudeville bit goes:

> — A brilliant idea, a brilliant idea . . .
> — What?
> — That's what we need: a brilliant idea!

How to get one? Certainly you tax your creativity to the utmost. But even more, you must have the courage to forget yourself and yield to that other mysterious force, that most unmanageable, diaphanous ingredient of the drama: inspiration.

I am not talking about the inspiration of a particular performance, the thing that visited Olivier and made everything organic, seamless, and magical (see Magic and Frustration, pp. 83-84). Here I mean the process of coming up with an inspired interpretation or production, distilled from strokes of brilliance during the rehearsal period. Much like the other variety of inspiration, this kind visits in unexpected spurts, or brainstorms, frequently when you the actor are not trying to come up with any particularly new ideas: in the doing, rather than in the thinking about; in letting it happen, rather than in working it to death; and sometimes even when you stop doing it at all. For instance, I have often noticed actors suddenly fall into character for the first time during a break at rehearsal—when not working on doing so. Inspiration drops in the same way. While gazing on an apple tree as a piece of fruit falls, you suddenly think up an idea as complex as Newton's theory of gravitation or a gesture as simple as *rising on that line*.

Of course Newton had had a thought or two before that brainstorm.

Einstein, when asked if his theory of relativity came slowly or all at once, answered: "I came up with it all at once—after thinking about it the whole of my life."[16] A lot of perspiration is needed to generate a drop of inspiration.

The actor and director confront a challenge quite different from the scientist's or playwright's: how to come up with many ideas quickly, and, in particular, with ideas that matter—that tell the story better than any other idea that may be out there. No one can provide you with this *how*. The process of coming up with the stuff in the first place is a mystery common to all acts of creation. Fortunately, help is available.

Creativity craves a form. The sonnet and haiku forms, for example, help to inspire great poetry by restricting the poet to a certain pattern. How do limits help?

To understand how inspiration works, think of doing a crossword puzzle. You need a nine-letter word for *pleasure*. No idea. But when you start getting some of the letters from the transverse clues, you are suddenly confronting the following image:

$$\_ \_ J \_ Y \_ \_ \_ \_$$

and later:

$$E \_ J \_ Y \_ \_ N T$$

Now you certainly have it. Undoubtedly you experienced great enjoyment in the process, too, for there is always something exhilarating about coming up with a right answer or a useable idea.

Limitation creates an avenue for inspiration.

So to help inspire the blocking of a scene, try, say, letting your character cross exactly three times. Or make yourself keep moving at all times: either with one actor constantly circling the other, or with both circling each other, as if in a wrestling ring.

If you are playing a king, try never crossing toward another character, but rather, always beckon others to you (you do outrank them, after all). The same principle could apply to aristocrats, employers, politicians, bishops, headmasters.

Other limitations you might think of imposing:

- One person chases the other, until the director gives a signal, at which point the pursued becomes the pursuer.
- Only one person can be seated at a time, so if the standing person sits, the sitting person rises (finding the reason to do so) within five seconds or so.
- All motion is circular.
- Every line of text starts on the last word of the previous line, not after.
- Each speaker moves when speaking, but keeps still when silent, or vice versa.
- One actor mirrors what the other actor does—yet doesn't let that other actor notice.

And so forth. These approaches do not provide inspiration itself, but increase its likelihood. Although you may not adhere to your limitation in the final staging, all sorts of insight may come as you rehearse.

This list forms the beginning of a menu for structured improvisation.

Structured Improvisation

An improv is like a painter's small preparatory sketch before he starts on his canvas. If your director calls for a phase of improvisation, which may be particularly valuable early in the rehearsal period, keep in mind that it constitutes exploratory groundwork, not performing the play. You later return to the precise words and specific circumstances of the script.

Like other acting tools, structured improvisation abets your creativity through some particular aspect you focus on. Its goal may be identifiable, like blocking, or one of the V's; or it may be some ineffable quality you are trying to attain. (Remember, if our goal is to get from X to Y, we might not even mention X or Y.)

Variations of structured improvisation include:

On the scene/ on the text:

Example: The above list of limitations would belong in this category, like "Go through the scene, but keep moving at all times."

Goal: Developing blocking or physical life.

Example: Trying the scene with a wacky adjustment such as "You are all stand-up comedians," or "You are all six years old."

Goal: Broadening your palette of colors, freeing up your sense of abandon, or infusing humor or wonder into your work.

Example:	The speed-through.
Goal:	Mental energy, accuracy, pace.
Example:	The First Reading exercise (p. 92) and similar ones that embrace the present reality as well as the play's reality.
Goal:	Developing the sense of present truth.
Example:	The Filling the Tank exercise (pp. 141-142): "Go through the scene and say the text, but lying on your backs and breathing deeply."
Goal:	Relaxation; depth of inner life.
Example:	Overdoing each reaction.
Goal:	Augmenting and crystallizing those reactions; listening.

On the scene/ off the text:

Example:	Paraphrasing dialogue in your own words (particularly helpful when introducing novices to Shakespeare or classical actors to contemporary naturalness).
Goal:	Owning the text circumstances; making sure of meaning and structure.
Example:	Voicing your inner monologue during the scene.
Goal:	Owning the subtext, or establishing it.
Example:	The dance-through (p. 105).
Goal:	Maximum physical expression and variety.

Off the scene/ on the text:

Example:	The Folding Laundry exercise (p. 96).
Goal:	Natural, relaxed connection and delivery.

This category also technically includes any isolated text work you do, like diction or projection exercises.

Off the scene/ off the text/ in character:

Example:	Improvising an unscripted encounter between the characters, like their first meeting.
Goal:	Conjuring the characters' extended lives.

I leave it to you to expand the list with ideas of your own. Don't worry about the categories except insofar as they might inspire you to come up with a new structure to try. The more experienced an actor you become, the less time you are likely to have for improvs, but the less you will probably need them.

Abandon

There is something outlandish in even the most naturalistic of dramas, so why censor yourself in your rehearsal play? It is the wacky, even ludicrous notion that generally gives birth to the next masterpiece. *Drama occurs where the world of the plausible meets the world of the outrageous.* The last line of *Hedda Gabler*, after all, is "People don't do such things." That undreamed of, unimaginable event is why the playwright wrote the play.

So become a creative radical, irascible and incorrigible. Even choices that don't work today may lead to inspired ones tomorrow. And any work of genius is dangerously close to becoming a flop: The one becomes the other by adjusting a single element that makes the whole concept click—on or off. It only makes sense that some rehearsal exercises border on silliness. Silliness is often the gatekeeper of inspiration.

Working on problem scenes with abandon might just reveal their mystery. If you find yourself falling into the trap of merely repeating your performance—freezing it—experiment with ways to get out of your rut: expand your repertoire of colors, emotions, and line deliveries to keep your work fresh and alive. Here are a few ice breakers:

Sound Textures: Tempo-Rhythms and Music. Building on Stanislavski's tempo-rhythms as a way of imparting texture to the scene, try a rehearsal where you (or company members not in the scene) bang drums, beat the floor, clap hands, or make other percussive sounds during the dialogue. You might try a scene accompanied by some favorite music, live or recorded, and see how your work is affected. Music is a tremendous resource for evoking surprising sensibilities and physicalities. (To this day, my spine automatically aligns itself whenever I hear Benny Goodman.) Music may be abstract, but it is specifically abstract; whether highly rhythmic or pastoral, melancholy or comic, it carries emotion and affects pace, tone, and so on, without verbal content.

But tempo-rhythms can inform the staging of a scene as well as the feeling: In the 1999 revival of *Annie Get Your Gun*, during the shooting contest the ensemble kept thwacking their bandanas in unison, rhythmically, as the tension mounted.

Salutary Nonsense. Try a scene with nonsensical props in your hands, like Nerf® bats. Or try it as a pillow fight. Or try augmenting the circumstances of the scene with some nonsensical scenario: as if you are a cartoon character, or walking in molasses. Keep devising structures of salutary nonsense until you find what works for you. And make them *juicy*, for priming the pump of inspiration requires lubrication.

Example. In scene 5 of *A Little Night Music*, the Countess is introduced in a quick dialogue at breakfast with her philandering husband, Carl-Magnus. It starts:

Charlotte: How was Miss Desirée Armfeldt? In good health, I trust?
Carl-Magnus: Charlotte, my dear. I have exactly five hours.
Charlotte: (*Deadpan*) Five hours this time? Last time it was four. I'm gaining ground.

And on it goes. After trying the scene a few ways, we came across the device of having them pinch, poke, or prick each other with each hurtful line about his assignation with Desirée. In the eventual staging, she actually thwacked him as she caressed him, twisting his earlobe, biting his lip, digging her nails into his flesh. Next time I'll bring Nerf® bats to the first rehearsal. . . .

Adjustments like these need not be total nonsense, of course. Try a scene with a *secret object* hidden in your pocket that is charged with personal meaning, such as a lucky charm or a letter from a loved one. Or even simpler, put the set pieces in a different arrangement, to break up the monotony and help you look at your character's world afresh.

SIMPLICITY

Some of these games are so much fun that you might be tempted to hang on to them even when they're a far cry from what the story needs. Genius is a twofold process, entailing both *idea fluency* and *discrimination*. The former involves the capacity to generate a lot of ideas; the latter, knowing when to throw them out.

Choices are worth keeping when they serve the piece as a whole. If they do not, they are extraneous and must be eliminated. Too many ideas—even brilliant ones—will obfuscate the story. In a naturalistic play, beware of choices that call attention to themselves: theatricality is best rendered invisible.

I frequently cite Picasso's line drawing *Back of a Woman* to demonstrate Economy. With just two strokes of black ink on a bare white background, he not only gets the viewer to see the woman, but invites him to have a relationship with her (if he is alive and breathing).

If a painting needs seven brush strokes, our job is to find those seven. Eight are too many, six are too few.

Our arrangement of those brush strokes invites the audience to complete the picture; we need not complete it for them.

Too much analysis too close to opening night can stultify. Simplicity releases inspiration: so simplify. As rehearsals progress, you can achieve this simplicity gradually with your lines. Once you have filled every word and moment, then forget about filling every word and moment and instead play the phrase. Once you have filled the phrases, then forget about them (at least consciously) to play the speeches. Then the scene. And so on. In this way you need not juggle a hundred images to take you through the sundry legs of the roller-coaster ride, but only one or two incredibly bright or powerful ones, which will generate all the bumps and loops automatically.

Which one or two things do you keep in mind? Usually you go back to playing the action, and allow everything else that you want the character to be, to just be. Reminding yourself of your local objective before an entrance may help to give the next scene the drive that it needs, but sometimes your character should not even be conscious of his own ulterior designs. Your super-objective will frequently be most effective when your bones are more aware of it than your brain is.

Exercise. Once the play is blocked and rehearsed, try this: simply sit down and read the script again, like a first reading. If there is time for the cast to do this together, even better. This helps to cut through the complexity you have been working on so you can once again clearly see the simple story that you want the audience to follow. It also helps you spot bits of mislearned text so you can be word-perfect. You may think an erroneous "of" or "and" here and there doesn't matter, but the difference makes all the difference. Practice does not necessarily make perfect: Practice makes permanent. Practicing errors, then, makes the errors permanent.

Exercise: The Crystallizing Phrase. Vivien Leigh used a valuable device to simplify. She would choose a crystallizing phrase to serve as a password to unlock the full richness of the role automatically. For *Streetcar*, she chose a line of Stella's from Scene 8: "You didn't know Blanche as a girl. Nobody, nobody, was tender and trusting as she was." For *Gone with the Wind*: "I always wanted to be like [Mother], calm and kind. I certainly have turned out disappointing!"[17] You can see that for either Blanche or Scarlett, the entire character can be released by these phrases.

So by the time you reach performance week, reduce the creative load so that you can play simply, cleanly, and accurately. Trust your audience to see the fullness of your characterization, just as they see the entire back of Picasso's woman.

Assume your audience is smart.

OVERT THEATRICS

On the other hand, sometimes a playwright calls for a highly theatrical production. In children's theater you may play the Fox or the Cricket to Pinocchio's puppet, and in Shaffer's *Equus* or the stage adaptation of Orwell's *Animal Farm*, your character may literally be a beast, too. Since your work wants to remain animal work per se, you can let the audience in on the theatrical fun.

Theatrical events, or theatrics, are moments when the script or staging acknowledges the theatrical circumstance that we are in a theater, here and now. Every rise or drop of the curtain, and every aside or soliloquy, constitute a theatrical event.

Theatrics include celebration, like song, dance, and pageantry; slapstick humor (with sound effects); actor-generated effects, like changing costume onstage; or more technical effects like fog machines, strobe lights, choreographed scene changes. The *theatrical arch*—the string of theatrical events—entails:

- *how the story is told;*
- *how the play is staged;*
- *where the play takes place and where the audience is located geographically—visual point of view;*
- *how audience rapport is manipulated—psychological point of view.*

In a big-budget musical, for example, scene changes might be awe-inspiring as flats fly up and down, wagons move in and out, and lights dazzle. Each scene change constitutes a theatrical event, since it relocates the audience. If bereft of flies, wagons, and a budget, a saloon wench flipping a placard so that it now reads, "Meanwhile, back at the ranch . . . " can be used as a theatrical contrivance. Since her action does not advance the plot (though it does advance the story), she strives to be as entertaining as possible; a rim shot from the drummer helps.

A theatrical event means a change in the theatrical universe. Remember, event = change: but the character you are changing may be— your audience.

A take to the back row is the most elementary form of actor-generated theatrics. Soliloquies and asides acknowledge the audience too, of course, almost like short French scenes delimited by "enter audience" and "exit audience." What they are entering and exiting, though, is not the world of the play, but a character's inner life. As with other French scenes, then, try to make the action continuous, seamless and smooth (see Smoothness, pp. 30-31).

As a matter of fact, once you have invited the audience to enter your mind during an aside, they stay there, to a certain extent, for the rest of the play.

A character who speaks in direct address to the audience on any one occasion can resume that relationship at any time.

Example. From I.1 to III.2, Hamlet is almost the only character in his play to speak directly to the audience. (Polonius and Claudius have a quick aside or two, and Ophelia has twelve lines alone.) Starting in III.3, Claudius starts to soliloquize at length, too: in a way, he tries to "take the play away" from the title character.

Hamlet has already forged a relationship with the audience that allows them to hear his thoughts. Once this rapport has been established, he can exploit it at any time, even when he is not in direct address, by just looking at the audience as if to ask, "Can you believe that?"

Claudius cannot attempt this intimate psychological rapport with the audience until the first time he addresses them, in III.3. Why? Because Shakespeare withholds proof that he really killed Hamlet Senior until the end of III.2. (The guilty conscience suggested by Claudius's "O heavy burthen!" (III.1.54) could have come simply from marrying his sister-in-law.) If the audience were Claudius's intimates, then they would know the truth too soon. He may play the audience as citizens of Denmark, but not as his trusted confidantes, until his jig is up. Once that jig is up, he next appears with a soliloquy confirming his guilt (and praying for help, by the way—need I ask from whom?).

After the murder mystery has been solved, the play bounces between Hamlet's and Claudius's points of view, the intrigue now involving how each plots the other's doom. But before III.3, Shakespeare needs the audience to see Claudius through Hamlet's eyes.

The rule of thumb is that in direct address, a character tells the audience the truth. As he goes back and forth between a scene and his asides, the audience essentially changes location: from the safe hiding place of eavesdroppers, to a "psychological place" inside the mind of a character, where they can hear the thoughts heard by no one else onstage. Their point of view changes from objective to subjective.

A character who appears only in direct address is, by definition, a narrator, or chorus. Beware of thinking of the chorus as merely narrating, or of narration as being other than action. He does perform an action—on the audience. How he narrates will set up, or even express, the theme.

Note that *theatrics convey thematics.* If your production of *Medea* has the entire set collapse at the end, as in Jonathan Kent's revival with Diana Rigg, this theatrical event suggests some postulate like, "When people kill their children, civilization crumbles: literally, walls fall down."

But beware of a lot of cool ideas for their own sake, too many of which can cloud more important issues. If you can't justify the theatrics as something supporting the theme, think twice. The drama should build to the point where those walls *must* fall down.

The same principles of theatricality that playwrights and directors use fall within the province of the actor. When the height of the action rises to such a peak that it can no longer be contained by the staging conventions so far established, a character can violate those conventions by breaking through the fourth wall, for example. Keep this in mind, however:

> ### *A character addresses the audience, crosses to the audience, or blatantly enlists the audience's participation when he or she needs them.*

Remember Jack Benny: he could not answer the question, "Your money or your life, Mr. Benny?" without help—hence, his appeal to the spectators.

Another age-old staging rule that your character may break, particularly at the climax: never put your back to the audience in a proscenium theater. This is really only an application of the fundamental actor's mandate to share what you are doing, to take the audience along with you. If the best way to share is to break the rule, then you have most likely arrived at a dramatic peak that warrants turning your back to the audience.

Example. This is exactly what Charles Busch did in *The Lady in Question* when the Lady (Busch in drag) recognized her nemesis from long ago. Standing down-center, facing upstage, her back arched like a cat's when attacked. It was a marvelous theatrical gesture, perfectly suited to the moment.

You can also try wearing masks or bright makeup, playing with the audience in the audience, or changing clothes right onstage.

For additional ideas, see Theatrics in appendix 3. It's like children's theater, which makes sense because, remember, you want to get your audience wondering like a child on Christmas morning.

A note to directors: in rehearsal, experiment with all sorts of theatrical ideas. But again, those you keep should be the ones the characters—or the production—must. In other words, integrate your theatrics into the dramatic action and the theme. If Macbeth were to enter from the audience at the top of the show, the production would suggest, thematically, that he started out as one of the people. Theatrics = Thematics.

> *There should always be a thematic reason for any theatrical choice—even for something as small as where an entrance is made.*

Epic Staging: Point of View of the Storyteller

Many of these techniques come from epic theater. Although this genre was developed (by Erwin Piscator and Bertolt Brecht roughly in the 1920s and '30s) as a reaction against Stanislavski-based naturalism, over time its techniques have become standard staging devices. In the '60s and '70s it was common practice to put the cast on the stage, watching the action. Jean Anouilh opened his *Antigone* this way as early as 1946. *Nicholas Nickleby* (1980–81) capitalized on this, an actor rising from a bench upstage and crossing to center to become a character; actors even chatted with the audience at the beginning and end of intermissions. In *Equus* (1973–74) and *Copenhagen* (2000) some of the audience was placed on the stage. Peter Brook's production of *Marat/Sade* (1965–66), available on video, represents the epitome of epic theater, theatricality, and playing the audience.

In broad application, epic theater boils down to inviting the audience to recognize the actor as storyteller. As a rehearsal technique, Brecht had his actors state their character names and speak some stage directions before delivering their lines. So in *Caucasian Chalk Circle*, the actor playing Grusha might say, "Then Grusha says" or even "Then Grusha said, wearily. . . ." Try it when in rehearsals for even a naturalistic play, and you should get a rather invisible result of heightened stage life.

Exercise: *Objective Narration*. Have everyone in the cast, one at a time, tell the story of the play from an objective point of view, like a narrator of a novel speaking in the third person. This will be particularly valuable if someone goes up on a line and part of a scene is accidentally skipped, for you must know the necessary story information in order to improvise some way of conveying it to the audience.

Exercise: *Subjective Narration*. Next, let everyone in the cast try telling the story in the first person ("I . . ."), from a subjective (each character's) point of view.

Exercise: *Trading Places*. Have a run-through where everyone in the com pany exchanges roles with someone else. Looking at the play from someone else's point of view can help keep you from forgetting the audience's as you crystallize that of your own character. What results is a marked clarity in the company as to how all the parts of the story fit together.

Weird Worlds

Some plays depict landscapes of hell, purgatory, and outer space, inhabited by angels, ghosts, witches, and gods. To help you create these weird worlds onstage, try some of the following.

Exercise: *Worlds*. Draw an imaginary line across the middle of the floor to divide the room into two spaces. When one company member is so inspired, he crosses that line with some activity that establishes a particular theatrical world. Maybe his world is one where everyone hops up and down on one leg at a time. When a second person thinks she gets it, she joins the world. She may not have correctly grasped the first actor's actual intent, but that is all right: Instead of hopping up and down, she may secure one arm behind her back, consistent with her notion of everyone's lacking a limb. So she alters the world as she adds to it. Then a third actor joins, and more, until the world is finally established.

All sorts of worlds can emerge:

- where everyone sings instead of talks;
- where the wind never stops;
- where every creature is winged;
- where everyone travels in slow motion.

You get the idea: it's behaving silly consistently, without discussing how—just doing it.

Later, when you approach a playwright's ludicrous world, it will hardly be daunting to create a texture where newlyweds talk like pussycats (Ionesco's *The Future is in Eggs*) or corpses tell their life stories (*Our Town* and Masters's *Spoon River Anthology*). Our job is *to render the ludicrous plausible and the plausible, extraordinary*. We do the first of these by inviting the audience to play in the same theatrical world as ours.

The next few exercises are actually variations on the Worlds exercise:

Machines. The entire ensemble creates a machine—a particular world with integrated components—one human cog at a time. First, one person goes into the playing area and performs some repetitive, periodic movement and sound. When inspired, a second person joins with a different movement and sound, but with the same period, working in conjunction with the first person. One person is the piston, another the crank, a few more are gears that turn, and so forth. The machine need not derive from one in real life, but can be a product of sheer imagination.

The Machine is like a standard Sound and Movement exercise (see pp. 93-96) that is cumulative, each periodic gesture building on, instead of replacing, the previous one.

Start with a compact machine, with every person touching, or adjacent to, someone else in the machine. Then graduate to a disjoined one where the components do not actually touch but are connected as if by gravity or magnetism. The solar system is a machine, after all, as is an atom.

The Machines exercise may lead to actual staging. I had three actors play the arras (curtain) behind which Polonius hid during a set-free production of *Hamlet*. Certainly the three witches in *Macbeth* are an ersatz machine. They literally perform work, too: casting spells and conjuring hallucinations.

Conductors. The Conductor builds on connection exercises like Ball Tossing 101 (see p. 93) to develop ensemble staging for an actual scene. Think of everyone involved in this first Conductor exercise as lined up in sequence like molecules along an electrical wire, or billiard balls in a row. The charge that one person initiates will go through each person in turn until it arrives at the end.

First, line the company up in an established order. People need not assemble in a straight line, and some people can stand while others sit. You can use sound and movement, nonsensical text, or memorized text-bites from a play. Person A performs a sound and movement (or textual) gesture, to which person B reacts in his unplanned response, which then causes person C to react, and so on down the line to the last person. Then you can reverse direction.

Next, keep the same order of actors, but spread them around the room. Concentration must be heightened to keep track of the next person since he will not be in line.

Another sort of conductor has the entire company reacting to the same impulse simultaneously, as a unit. Let everyone be a tree in a forest and have an exterior source (a selected actor or the director) "be" the wind that blows; all trees must shake in the same breeze. Or let everyone be popcorn kernels in the bottom of a hot pan. Everyone reacts to the same hot oil, though they will actually pop one at a time, unexpectedly. Or put everyone on an imaginary train, and have it start, stop, shake, and turn with the ensemble acting in unison to achieve these effects. A director can conduct the journey by devising some motions to indicate starting, stopping, going uphill or downhill, and veering left or right, so that the ensemble can react as a unit. But with practice, the ensemble may not need an outside conductor.

Remember that scene in *The Music Man* where Harold Hill is on the train and hears gossip about himself from all the townspeople riding the train? The reeling is conveyed by the acting ensemble as a unit. The patter and orchestration have been expressly designed for such theatrical staging, all executed by actors and musicians instead of through technical effects. In other plays, an entire village will react as a unit to something or someone approaching from afar, like a storm, the Inspector General, or Conrad Birdie breezing in on his motorcycle.

A kick line in a musical exploits both kinds of conductors: all legs might go up in unison, or one after another, down the line. (Ball Tossing 101 and Sound and Movement are conductors, too, by the way.)

Ensemble Animals. A variation of the Machine is the Living Machine, or Ensemble Animal. Think of Dorothy and her three friends skipping down the yellow brick road, arms linked. They developed a communal stride and a melody to go with it—in effect, a Song and Movement.

Let the company divide into a few groups to come up with their own ensemble animals, complete with head, abdomen, tail, wings, or whatever. Figure out how the animal travels, turns, sits, stands, and performs a task.

The quickest and easiest animal, and perhaps the most useful for an ensemble's coordination, is the centipede. Especially if you have young or shy actors, it is important to get everyone's front flush against the next person's back. Start by having each person hug the one in front so you actually become one mass of flesh. Then walk around. The head takes the lead and figures out how to signal to the rest of the organism when it is going to stop or start. Everyone's feet must advance in sync, or some will get kicked. (Mutual trust should already have been established before starting this exercise.)

If your ensemble can play a centipede, a regiment of soldiers will be easy. I exploited this technique to create two communal legions of fairies in *A Midsummer Night's Dream*. In the first fairy scene (II.1), as Titania and Oberon talked about their wars, the ensemble moved liquescently as two phantasmic phalanxes, in sync with the words and windstorms of their leaders. In Max Reinhardt's film of the play, you can see a similar fairy horde, not unlike a colony of ants.

The skill is highly applicable to farce or burlesque. A Marx Brothers-type shadowing of every movement of some stuck-up rich guy will be much more effective if you can play right under and perfectly in sync with him, instead of two feet away.

The Mirror. Two actors playing on either side of an imaginary mirror is a standard theater game in intro acting classes. But have you thought about times when you might actually use it in performance?

In *Come Back to the Five & Dime, Jimmy Dean, Jimmy Dean,* the reunion of friends takes place in the same scene as the flashback of their last meeting together two decades before. Different performers portray the same characters twenty years apart. Color-coded clothes might help, but if both Sissies reach for a soda at the same time, and Joe and Joanne remove their sunglasses simultaneously, in mirror images on either side of the stage, you've heightened the theatrics—and the clarity.

The Mirror can give a stylistic boost in many ways. Non-identical actors paired in *Comedy of Errors* can synchronize their physical life so that the audience sees them as identical twins. Imagine two lovers in different spaces onstage, going through identical sighing motions: quite demonstrably, they are meant for each other. They may even be facing each other onstage, when in reality they could be in different rooms or different countries (*Sea Marks*).

Variation: Thought Balloons and Voice-overs. While one actor tells a story about another character, both can go through the motions of the story. In effect, one character "plays" the other's thought balloon, as in a comic strip. In *As You Like It*, while my First Lord told and enacted the story of Jaques crying over the wounded stag, the audience saw Jaques himself go through the scene in flashback (II.1).

Similarly, the audience might like to hear Hamlet's voice saying the words of his own letter to Ophelia, even though he is not supposed to be onstage at the time it is read.

The ways you can play in rehearsal and come up with more staging devices are limited only by your imagination. This ensemble work, even if discarded, is a wonderful way to get a company acting as one. After all, what is a courtroom of spectators or a square full of villagers but a social animal, a living machine, and a conductor, all at once?

THE AUDIENCE AT PLAY

One way to heighten the theatricality of a moment is by extending Stanislavski's siphon metaphor to include the audience (see The Siphon, pp. 84-85). First you fill your tank, then you gently siphon emotion (or whatever) organically. Siphoning is not the actor's goal, though, but rather how he does it; what he does is get the audience wet. Better to get them wet somehow than not at all for fear of forcing something. And as long as your tank is full, you need not limit yourself to using a siphon when you also have a jet spray at your disposal—and you do.

Example A. I saw David Hare's play *Amy's View* from the front row, and literally got wet when Judi Dench had water poured on her, like a baptism, in the last short scene of the play. But after the rising tension and revelation of the previous scene, it was refreshing. The plot was concluded, but the baptism was the theatrical event of the evening.

Example B. In the New York production of the musical *Angry Housewives*, when the title characters finally formed their rock band, they sang "Eat Your Fuckin' Corn Flakes" and the front few rows had a boxful or two of corn flakes thrown on them. It was great fun because we in the audience had shared a sense of complicity with the growing plight of the characters, and had also shared in all the camp leading up to that moment. The heat was on—the anger of the *Housewives*—and the jet spray in this case was corn flakes.

These, of course, are unusually literal, highly theatrical illustrations of the point. Generally, your interplay with the audience wants to be less overt and more subliminal; usually you spray them not with water or corn flakes, but with the dramatic juice of the play. Note also that both of these instances occur late in their respective plays; audience rapport (and zaniness, in *Housewives*) had grown to the point where spraying the spectator was more fun than annoying.

But sometimes we might want to persuade the audience to turn the hose on themselves, and we can. How?

The audience is like a pedestrian on a sweltering summer afternoon. If he passes by a sprinkler watering someone's lawn, what possesses him to hop right through the spray to cool off? For one, the unbearable heat and humidity. For two, the sense of play, or abandon, that the heat engenders. Seeing that sprinkler, the withered pedestrian suddenly has a means to cool down.

The heat of a play's principal conflict is like the scorching summer day. If we apply it properly and encourage the audience's sense of play, they will act like a puddle-splashing six-year-old and, on a caprice, opt for getting wet. This is the pinnacle of theatricality: not just making the audience feel like playing with you, but actually getting them to do so. And all of the methods of this book are here to help.

Example. Check out the Porter's soliloquy from Macbeth II.3:

> *Knocking within.*
> Here's a knocking indeed! If a man were porter of hell-gate, he should have old turning the key. [*Knocking within*] Knock, knock, knock! Who's there i' the name of Beelzebub. Here's a farmer (1), that hanged himself on th' expectation of plenty: come in time; have napkins enow about you; here you'll sweat for 't. [*Knocking within*] Knock, knock! Who's there, in th'other devil's name? Faith, here's an equivocator (2), that could swear in both the scales against either scale; who committed treason enough for God's sake, yet could not equivocate to heaven: O, come in, equivocator. [*Knocking within*] Knock, knock, knock! Who's there? Faith, here's an English tailor (3) come hither, for stealing out of a French hose: come in, tailor; here you may roast your goose. [*Knocking within*] Knock, knock; never at quiet! What are you? But this place is too cold for hell. (4) I'll devil-porter it no further (5): I had thought to have let in some of all professions, that go the primrose way to the everlasting bonfire. [*Knocking within*] Anon, anon! I pray you, remember the porter.

Someone knocking on the gate of the castle wakes him. "Who is it?" he wonders as he rubs his eyes. But as he comes to, in his daft and drunken stupor, he suddenly sees—an audience! Why should he open the gate right away when he has a captive audience at his disposal? The situation looks ripe for a comic turn.

During the first part of the speech, my hung over Porter went so far as to relieve his bladder off the upstage edge of the stage, back to the audience. Someone hidden below actually poured water from a pitcher into a pot, so that the audience could complete the image of what was happening. (There are high theatrics and low theatrics; this is depth of a different sort.)

Note the digs at the "farmer," the "equivocator" and the "tailor" (1–3). Why, this amounts to social commentary. So you can bet he cast these roles from among the spectators, and re-inspired his lines by seeing those people in the audience every night. He would see the first, the farmer, in one of the back rows, and the last, the tailor, in the front, exploiting the principle of increasingly infectious interplay. (See Casting the Audience and Casting *to* the Audience, pp. 13-19.)

My production took place outdoors in the mountains where even in summer it gets very cold at night, so each playgoer is lent a blanket. When our Porter said "But this place is too cold for hell" (4), by applying the principle that the play takes place in the audience's present time, he had no problem getting them to agree with him—it was indeed "too cold for hell."

Then, while he dissed the tailor, he stole a wink at the woman sitting in the next seat. When the shivering cold made him decide to "devil-porter it no further" (5), he would see if he could squeeze in next to her, and share her blanket with her. Such staging is dangerous without a welcome from the audience. At some performances he would have to alter his plans. When the entire front row was really "cold"—unwelcoming—he would snuggle on the floor instead. Occasionally he could get away with nestling his head in some lady's lap, and then directing the line to that place—as if her lap were "too cold for hell" (very low theatrics).

As the staging was recorded in the prompt book, he was not obliged to sit on somebody's lap every night, but had to rely on his stage smarts to judge his rapport with each crowd. And he would not necessarily cross to the same seat two nights in a row, because to treat any audience as if they were last night's would be a lie. When there were no empty seats, but a very festive and welcoming audience, he would find somewhere to squeeze in. The entire front row would adjust to make way for him, each person displacing the next one down the line like cascading dominoes. The payoff was hilarious, for:

REAL PROBLEMS ARE FUNNIER!

The Porter played not just with but *among* the audience, inviting them to become his jungle gym. This heightened, unabashed theatrical play came right after Macbeth had murdered Duncan and essentially sold his soul to the devil. The dramatic heat was on, the audience needed a break from it, and the Porter provided the relief of the jet spray.

The occasions when you will be able to play with the audience as aggressively as the Porter, or the angry housewives, will most likely be few and far between. A lot of elements must be in place to earn that precious impropriety: complicity, mounting heat, the need for relief, increasingly infectious interplay, and an actor with enough chutzpah and charm to get away with it.

CHAPTER 7
LANGUAGE

Another big difference between acting for the stage and for the camera: the repertoire. Stage plays are quite simply thicker with words than film or television scripts. The classical repertoire (as well as many new plays) demands that the practical actor become a master of language. Here, then, is a survey of how to glean the most from the words on the page. These techniques apply to writers from Aeschylus to Zindel, but let us start with the playwright whose richness of language is unmatched.

Many American actors think of Shakespeare as unnecessarily hard; others, as hardly necessary. Yet so many movie stars jump to get cast in relatively low-paying productions of his plays, all over the country. Why? Because Shakespeare makes you a better actor in every way. He makes you more sensitive to all sorts of clues in the text—rhythm, poetry, philosophy. He offers, and demands, an unparalleled depth and breadth of character. The climber attempts Mount Everest because it's there; the actor tackles Shakespeare because it's *all* there. The young non-Shakespearean actor may not be able to fathom what we mean by Mamet's rhythm or Tennessee Williams's poetry; the Shakespearean actor cannot fathom this lack of understanding.

The truth is that acting Shakespeare is not harder, but easier. It's the homework that's harder. After a while, your relationship to the text will be one not of work at all, but of a most sublime sort of play—wordplay.

WORDS

The dauntless actor approaches what's on a page as a playground of possibilities. Your goal:

Personalize *everything about your role, including the words:* *Earn and own every one.*

Remember, the playwright's words are the actor's best clues to character. Ask yourself why your character speaks exactly as he does, using such long or short sentences, or exotic words, or poetic imagery. Suddenly whole worlds of information open up, from a general sense of taste and values to the precise pattern of thinking and feeling.

Once onstage, the actor effectively becomes the author of his own character's dialogue, each role with its own style of speaking. "Style not only reveals the spirit of the man but reveals his identity."[18] Dialogue has been carefully crafted as the most perfect revelation of that identity. In the best plays—certainly in all of Shakespeare's—text and character are inseparable.

Personalizing does not mean mumbling, nor interpolating (changing or adding words). Every deviation from text deviates from thought, action, and character: Interpolation is sin. For your character is defined not only by what he says (and does), but also by precisely how he says it. You might think you're in character when using words of your own, as in some improvisations; but if it's the right character, then you have gotten to the point where you must, and can only, say exactly the character's words. Paraphrasing may be a valuable exercise, but the character does not need an exercise to mean precisely what he says: he does mean it.

To interpolate in verse destroys the verse, of course. Could you seriously say, "To be or not, you know, to be—well, that's the question"? Adding one syllable would detract from Hamlet's heightened lucidity. And even muddled characters must speak precisely as the playwright has prescribed for optimal effect.

Prose is just as carefully selected. Sloughing a line of a Neil Simon or Noël Coward play will invariably lose a laugh. David Mamet's dialogue is so rhythmic that you cannot alter it without losing part of the point.

In other words, *honesty requires accuracy*. This may tax your brain to the limit, but fortunately, accuracy not only requires augmented mental energy, it also helps you attain it.

Spoken vs. Written

Spoken language is the music through which a person or a culture conveys meaning aloud. The English spoken in Ireland has a different lilt from that of Texas, Jamaica, or India, reflecting each culture's uniqueness. These distinctions largely disappear in the written word; you can read an Australian author without ever having heard an Australian.

For an actor, the spoken word also conveys personality. Try recording conversations, and then transcribing them to paper. Later, read the transcription before listening to the recording again. You will see how live dialogue betrays specific meaning you would not necessarily associate with the written word. The speaker's delivery can bend, stretch, and shape a word's meaning even to the point where it implies its opposite (e.g., "how interesting" for "I'm bored"). As an interpreter of text, you reverse the process: take dialogue from the page and re-create that conversation. All that bending, stretching, and shaping of the written word will make it sound believable.

Dramatic dialogue is intended to be enhanced by the performer's interpretation before reaching its audience. Scripts play better than they read because they should: it is how you play with the words that makes them live.

There are two components to the meaning of any word, whether written or spoken: the denotative and the connotative. The first is the literal meaning, or definition; the second is what the word suggests. *Overweight* denotes *fat;* but the former has a rather neutral connotation, the latter a pejorative one. *Pleasingly plump*, on the other hand, suggests a positive quality.

Connotation, then, is the capacity of words to call to mind something that is not there. Does this sound familiar? It is the essence of art. (See The Art of Acting, pp. xi-xii.)

Language is abstract art.

Its very sounds connote intangible emotions, attitudes, values, and so forth. The more poetic the language, the greater its connotative aspect.

Example. Hamlet refers to death by using the euphemism "the undiscovered country from whose bourn no traveller returns" (III.1, the "To be or not to be" speech; *bourn* means milestone or border stone, hence, frontier). He is trying to neutralize death's horrors because he wants to confront it. Contrast this with Claudio, Isabella's brother in *Measure for Measure*, who has already been sentenced to death and wants her to help him avoid it:

> Ay, but to die, and go we know not where,
> To lie in cold obstruction, and to rot,
> This sensible warm motion to become
> A kneaded clod; and the delighted spirit
> To bathe in fiery floods or to reside
> In thrilling region of thick-ribbèd ice. . . . (III.1)

"Kneaded clod," "fiery floods," and "thick-ribbèd ice" are dreary, negative expressions. Claudio is scared out of his wits—and acting like it. Hamlet is daunted too, but wants to be brave enough to choose death when honor is at stake; Claudio would rather live even if in shame.

Since spoken language takes place over time rather than on a canvas, words are not merely brush strokes, but events. The flow of dialogue is like a steady current of electricity from actor to audience, with certain words generating sparks along the way. Some have already been charged by the playwright; others will cause a spark because of the potency with which the actor charges them.

How does the actor do this? Do you decide to inject a little excitement here and there and thus say one word louder, another one longer, and yet a third with a pause before it? Well, come to think of it, this is precisely what you do, in addition to ten thousand other choices. You have to do it well, however: do not make these decisions capriciously, nor execute them clumsily.

To charge your text, the first step is being able to recognize *when* the linguistic events occur. The second is deciding what to do with them. Then you deliver the language with personal stakes so high as to render it compelling.

Some of what follows might seem like a review of—shudder—grammar. But grammatical savvy is one of the most valuable tools an actor can have. Grammar, after all, is mental logic. It is also a component of style, and so constitutes one of the ways in which a culture organizes its conception of the universe; a character's particular usage reveals her relationship to that universe. As Strunk and White might say, "Grammar is Revelation."

Besides, what follows is not the same grammar you may have slept through in school: it is stuff that is actable. So read on!

EXTRA MEANING

Hamlet and Claudio's use of poetry offers a good dose of connotative meaning: they imply as much as they say. In contemporary street talk (listen to your recordings again), any word is fair game for being charged with such extra meaning, dependent on nothing more than the speaker's personality and whim. So feel free to impute specialized richness to any word in a speech, and if it works, congratulations. But you can rehearse more efficiently once you realize that not all words are created equal.

Of the eight parts of speech, four of them carry most of the meaning in daily conversation—nouns, verbs, adjectives, and adverbs. The other four—prepositions, interjections, pronouns, and conjunctions—have virtually no meaning except insofar as they relate to other words. I use the term *cipher* to refer to such a word. A cipher may signal a hint from the author that says, in effect, "Actor, invest here." By definition, the true cipher has no denotative, but only connotative meaning, requiring the actor to assign his own meaning. The key is to be specific, personal, creative, varied, and active.

Every *proper noun* (or name) is a cipher. "John" your kid brother means something entirely different from "John" the king of England.

Exercise. Ask a friend to tell you the name of someone he knows, whom you do not know, and who means a lot to him in some way. Then watch everything he does other than simply say the person's name: he may smile, or have a snide glint in his eye. You will at least be able to tell if he likes this mysterious person, and you may be able to tell a lot more. If you have a roomful of friends do this (at a rehearsal, in class, or at a party), one stubborn guinea pig may catch on and try to stifle his image so as not to give away any private information. But five seconds later, when you move on to someone else, take a look back, and you will notice the irrepressible smile or glint in the eye emerging as a delayed reaction.

So in life a proper name always invokes an actual person. When you encounter proper names in dialogue, make sure to be just as personal in your imagery as you would be in life.

Exercise. Take a speech from a foreign or period play with lots of arcane references to people, places, and other proper nouns. Then replace the playwright's choices for proper names with those of people or places you (and the people listening) know. Suddenly the passage comes alive with personal interest and even laughter.[19] Your character should be just as involved with every person, place, or title used in the play.

A *pronoun* takes the place of another noun, its antecedent. To be clear and believable, have a specific and rich personal image of what or whom you are talking about, complete with attitude and emotional history. With the plural pronouns *we, you,* and *they,* experiment with incorporating the audience: "we" could become "the audience and I," for example, perhaps in opposition to the other character onstage.

The special pronoun *thou* is not used in exactly the same way as *you.* Like *tu* in romance languages, the English *thou* is singular and informal, and refers to:

- an individual of lesser rank or age, like a child or servant;
- any animal;
- a spouse, lover, or close friend, particularly in private;
- an inanimate object or personified abstraction ("My country 'tis of thee");
- God or any other spirit, including a dead person.

Why is all this important for an actor to know? Because the use of *thou, thee, thy* or *thine* conveys important, actable information.

Example. At the end of *Hamlet*, Horatio holds the dying prince and addresses him: "Good night, sweet prince; and flights of angels sing thee to thy rest." (V.2) His use of *thee* and *thy* reveals that Hamlet has just died. As the crown prince, Hamlet would have to be referred to as *you*, which Horatio has done throughout the play ("You will lose, my lord," line 209). As soon as Horatio says "thee," all other characters onstage can convey this new information to the audience through their reactions. (Both of my Horatios also closed the prince's eyes gently while holding him, so that the audience, too, would realize Hamlet had died.)

For more examples, look at Duke Frederick in *As You Like It*, I.3 (he progresses from "Thou art a fool" to "You are a fool" within seven lines) and Lady Anne and Richard in *Richard III*, I.2. When characters change from *you* to *thou* while talking to the same person, it means that their relationship is changing: you figure out why.

Interjections are the part of speech that you can have the most fun with, for they by definition are extreme and exclamatory. Be careful to need them, however, so they come off as organic rather than as merely histrionic.

Example. As the Chorus, you start *Henry V* with the line "O for a muse of fire." (See appendix 1 for complete text.) Your pre-beat had better be a good deal more specific and personal than "I am about to introduce the story," for that is a given. The "O" comes out of frustration at not having such a muse handy; you humbly yet passionately ask the audience to compensate by enlisting their imagination to complement the meager storytelling skills of actors and playwright. Make your "O" so fiery with personal urgency that it wakes up the entire audience, and makes your Chorus unique.

Sometimes speech is best delivered by letting *conjunctions* remain mere function words which connect the other parts of the sentence. But incorporating a strong sense of a colon into your "AND:" can make yours the greatest tale ever told.

Example. I once directed a new play where one character used the word *and* so often in a scene that the actor asked me to approach the playwright about eliminating some of the *and's*. In the scene in question, her character is twelve years old, has just rediscovered her best friend from age seven, and is now filling her in on everything that has happened in the past few years. So I suggested, "Try owning the word as if you think it is the most magnificent word in the English language." This compelled her not only to relish her words, but also to make each part of her story even more exciting than those *and*'s. Within a day, she was hard-pressed to consider eliminating a single one.

Prepositions are usually unstressed words—but not necessarily. By emphasizing one of them you are implying "Not the opposite preposition." If your text consists of saying to another character, "Look under the tree," and the character being addressed has just looked above the tree, then you probably deliver your line, "Look *under* the tree," as opposed to above it, to make your point clear.

Listen to BBC (or even some American) news broadcasts for examples of the stress on the little word *to*: it betrays the slightly affected, disinterested quality of one who is reporting a fact rather than experiencing it. Or it might convey sincerity that is suspect:

Example. "I am very grateful to her, of course," says the President in the opening scene from *The Madwoman of Chaillot* when he tells the Baron all that his mother sacrificed for him. Since the President is one of the evil people, he is most likely *un*grateful. So the actor might want to try the affected delivery, "I am very grateful *to* her, of course," undermining sincerity with nonchalance.

Modals are auxiliary verbs like *will, would, shall, should, might, may, can, could.* If the reason something *may* happen is particularly significant, these words can carry tremendous meaning. Note that in the absence of a main verb, a modal always implies an unsaid one. "I *could*, but I don't know whether I *will* or not" means little until you decide what you could do, and under what conditions: ". . . if I had enough money" differs from ". . . if you gave me a kiss" (usually).

In Shakespeare's day, remember that usage had not yet been standardized. From time to time a preposition or a modal could carry the force of a verb, as in "to the breach," which implies *go* or *advance* to the breach. "Would that he were gone" = "I would prefer it if he were gone."

Another deviation from contemporary grammar: Lysander, in *Midsummer*, I.1, tells Demetrius, "You have her father's love, Demetrius,/ Let me have Hermia's; do *you* marry *him*." This last phrase is not a question, but an imperative, constructed so as to contrast "do you marry him" with "let *me* have *Hermia*." (Today the "you" is omitted: "you go home" becomes "go home.")

As you can see, grammar conveys worlds of intentions.

Will vs. shall: the future imperative. In absolutely proper English, the use of the auxiliary *will* or *shall* determines what kind of future tense is being used. The simple future, or future indicative, would apply to facts that are quite simply going to happen, for which no one need interpose his will. (Example: "The sun will rise tomorrow.") The future imperative (or emphatic future) is used when a statement is not necessarily true, but someone's will must be interposed to make it come true: "You've been late every day for the last twenty years, but tomorrow morning, by gum or by golly, you *shall* get to work on time or you'll have to answer for it." The speaker expects "you" not to get to work on time and wants to change things.

The future indicative:		The future imperative:	
I shall	We shall	I will	We will
You will	You will	You shall	You shall
He/She/It will	They will	He/She/It shall	They shall

"We shall overcome" was such a radical catch phrase in the 1960s not least because, being the simple future, it invited no argument. From the point of view of the speaker, it was simply going to happen, no battle required. These are *not* fighting words, but the irrefutable prophecy of the righteous.

Since the future imperative involves imposing one's will—implementing an objective—it is a great source of actable information. It should give the listener a wee spark of suspense as to whether the will of the speaker will be achieved or not.

Example A. In *Much Ado About Nothing* (see Thought Groups, pp. 53-55), Benedick must exert some effort to make the following happen in II.3:

I will be horribly in love with her!

"I will" is the future imperative. The point is not that he is in love with Beatrice (which he is, but he's been lying to himself), or that he simply will be, but that it will take effort for him to be. To bare his heart, he must bear his heart. "Will" lying in a *stressed position* (to be discussed in Verse, p. 194), helps the actor drive home the point of just how difficult it is going to be for him to love her.

Example B. In IV.2 of *A Midsummer Night's Dream*, the plot accelerates to its conclusion as the machinations of all four couples are resolved to the status of "happily ever after." With the future imperative, Theseus counters the will of Hermia's father Egeus—and the ancient law of Athens—and aborts the hunting party:

Egeus, I **will overbear** your will;	(1)
For in the temple, by and by, with us	
These couples **shall** eternally be knit.	(2)
And, for the morning now is something worn,	
Our purpos'd hunting **shall** be set aside. . . .	(3)

He is not stating what he already knows will happen. He is compelling:

1. himself: "I will overbear your will" (1)—and this takes some nerve and effort on his part, for to violate the law, he risks consequences he was not willing to face in I.1;
2. the other two couples: "these couples shall be knit" (2)—as if to say "it is my will that they be knit"; and
3. the hunting party: "hunting shall be set aside" (3)—because "I say so."

More than merely active, these be fightin' words, if conciliatory ones.

Quasi-Ciphers

Quasi-ciphers convey some meaning of their own, but have a connotative aspect far more meaningful than their denotative. Paramount among these is *love,* whose meaning is really defined by its subject and object. "Romeo loves Juliet" suggests a whole different concept from "I love peanut butter," or "you should love your country."

Similar are the *appellations* your character uses for other characters or things. Sobriquets like "my dear," or epithets like "that woman," can and should be charged with personal experience and attitude.

Some types of words, such as *numbers,* are naturally quasi-ciphers. "Seventeen" conveys one image when it answers the question "how old are you," another in response to "how many times have you been married?" Note your mental process in daily conversation: except in mathematics, we virtually never use words for numbers without a concrete image popping up in our brain. *Colors, flavors,* and other *varieties* share this property.

Example. Ophelia is mad in her last scene in *Hamlet*:

> There's rosemary, that's for remembrance—pray you, love, re-
> member—and there is pansies, that's for thoughts. . . . There's
> fennel for you, and columbines. There's rue for you, and here's
> some for me; we may call it herb of grace-a-Sundays. Oh you must
> wear your rue with a difference. There's a daisy. I would give you
> some violets, but they withered all when my father died. They say
> [he] made a good end. . . . (IV.5)

If all that Ophelia does is hand out flowers, this can become a boring mad
scene indeed. But if each flower is endowed with a pointed symbolic meaning, then there will be "method in her madness." Shakespeare even spells
out the meaning of the first two flowers for us, to make sure we notice her
ulterior agenda. So to whom does she give each flower, and to what end?
Ophelia's field is wide open for who gets the flower rue. Is she giving the
rue to Claudius, who is particularly ruthless? (*Ruth* is an old noun form of
the verb *rue*, which still suggests contrition or regret.) Although the modern
spectator may not know the hidden significance of fennel (flattery), col-
umbines (ingratitude), or the others she mentions, the choice and reaction
of each recipient can at least intrigue the audience with the sense that *something* else is going on. It is open to interpretation whether Ophelia is even
giving out flowers at all: being insane, she may hand out straws, strands of
hair, or nothing but blame.

Lists

A word expressing a color, flavor, flower, or other variety is an item from an
understood list. When a character uses a list, the playwright is asking the
actor to imbue it with dramatic growth, so no two elements should be
treated quite the same. Consider a list, then, as a progression with a beginning, middle, and end that is always growing in some aspect. That final
element generally constitutes an *arrival,* or climax.

> **Treating lists**
> * explore *connotative as well as denotative meanings of each
>   element;*
> * invest *in and* personalize *the character's experience and attitude
>   toward each of the list's elements;*
> * distinguish *the elements from one another; and*
> * build *to an arrival or climax.*

Often a speech's entire structure is that of a list.

Example. Jaques's Seven Ages of Man speech in *As You Like It* (see appendix 1 for complete text) really consists of two intertwined lists of the same seven elements. The list that names each age is charged with attitude and tone by a second, modifying list:

Ages	Modifiers
infant	mewling and puking
schoolboy	whining
lover	sighing and woeful
soldier	jealous, sudden, quick in quarrel
justice	round, severe, formal, wise, modern
pantaloon	well-saved, shrunk shank
second childishness	mere oblivion sans every thing

This list of modifiers is not merely the social theory of a pundit, but attitudes that have culminated from life experience. "And your experience has made you sad," Rosalind tells him in IV.1, yet another great acting note from Shakespeare. So as Jaques, personalize your attitude toward each age with heated images, perhaps from your own life. God forbid the audience should be impressed with just your diction!

Staging choices can help the audience grasp the structure of such a speech. My Jaques proceeded around the stage with each of the seven ages, converting the crawling infant to kneeling schoolboy to daunting soldier and so on: the shriveled old man of the seventh stage returned to the same ground from whence the infant was born. The effect was evocative of Escher's drawing *Metamorphosis*—the fish turning into the bird turning back into the fish.

Repetition

When a playwright repeats a word over and over, he creates a "list of re-iterations" that essentially transforms the word into a cipher. Repetition saps a word or phrase of its meaning and reduces it to mere sound; *you* give it growing significance. By the last iteration, since the audience has already heard the word several times, how has the action or idea been furthered? Not by the stagnating words, but by what you do with those words.

When Lear cries, "Howl, howl, howl" (V.3), or Macbeth, "Tomorrow and tomorrow and tomorrow" (V.5), the actor had better be at a different place at each "howl" or "tomorrow" along the way. The last iteration should be the richest one, to catapult him into the rest of his text, which in both of these cases is a long speech. By the last "howl" or "tomorrow," the word has become a sound-symbol conveying what the *actor* wants it to mean.

In trying to make the progression of meaning clear, beware of overacting: punching words, pushing images, or telegraphing choices. Dramatic growth may be subtle; it does not necessarily require more emotion or imagery at all. In Macbeth's case it might be a surge of emptiness, as "Tomorrow" is *the* existential speech of the play, a sublime expression of the pointlessness of life.

Example. In *Othello*, Emilia is privy to her husband's involvement with Desdemona's handkerchief, yet she does not mention it. Her silence presents one of the play's mysteries, for which the production must find some solution. When she finally does thaw out enough to talk, she is tongue-tied, stammering "my husband" over and over:

Othello:	Thy husband knew it all.
Emilia:	My husband!
Othello:	Thy husband.
Emilia:	That she was false to wedlock?
Othello:	Ay, with Cassio. Nay, had she been true,
	If heaven would make me such another world
	Of one entire and perfect chrysolite,
	I'd not have sold her for it.
Emilia:	My husband!
Othello:	Ay, 'twas he that told me first:
	An honest man he is, and hates the slime
	That sticks on filthy deeds.
Emilia:	My husband!
Othello:	What needs this iteration, woman? I say thy husband. (V.2)

Emilia's horror surges as Iago's treachery dawns on her. She can only babble the same two words over and over. She may even be in a state of shock, the words "my husband" (which interrupts Othello's rhythm) becoming the mantra of her anguish.

How does she build from the beginning to the end of this passage? The specifics are up to the actor, but here is a hint: during this passage she stammers ineptly, but by the end of the scene she has resolved to (1) risk her own life ("Do thy worst") in order to (2) turn in Othello for murder and (3) turn in her husband Iago, who will promptly kill her. You can decide at what moment she acquires that resolve, but since her very next word is "O," it is a prime candidate.

Motifs: Anaphora and Epistrophe

When a verbal motif appears at the beginning of a passage, it is called *anaphora*. Almost every sentence in the opening passages of the King James Bible begins with the word *and*; government proclamations often start each clause with *whereas*. The use of anaphora lends an officious, scriptural, or mythical quality to speech. In dramatic dialogue, it imparts a sense something like a town crier issuing a proclamation. Since it is a repeated phrase, give it new meaning with each iteration.

The complement of anaphora is called *epistrophe*, which is when the repeated text *follows* each successive passage—again, for growing effect.

Example. Marc Antony's "Friends, Romans, Countrymen" speech in *Julius Caesar* III.2:

The noble Brutus	
Hath told you Caesar was ambitious:	(1)
If it were so, it was a grievous fault,	
And grievously hath Caesar answer'd it.	
Here, under leave of Brutus and the rest,—	
For Brutus is an honourable man;	(1a)
So are they all, all honourable men,—	(1b)
Come I to speak in Caesar's funeral.	
He was my friend, faithful and just to me:	
But Brutus says he was ambitious;	(2)
And Brutus is an honourable man.	(2a)
He hath brought many captives home to Rome,	
Whose ransoms did the general coffers fill:	
Did this in Caesar seem ambitious?	
When that the poor have cried, Caesar hath wept;	
Ambition should be made of sterner stuff:	
Yet Brutus says he was ambitious;	(3)
And Brutus is an honourable man.	(3a)

You all did see that on the Lupercal
I thrice presented him a kingly crown,
Which he did thrice refuse: was this ambition?
Yet Brutus says he was ambitious;   (4)
And, sure, he is an honourable man.   (4a)

Three times Antony says verbatim ". . . Brutus is an honourable man"
(1–3) and once "he is an honourable man" (4). The irony in the reuttered
compliment actually vilifies Brutus. Do you hear the subversiveness in
Antony's voice as he styles the murderers "all, all honourable men" (1b)?
Make sure your audience does, too.

Anaphora and epistrophe also appear in shorter phrases:

Duke Frederick: Thou art thy father's daughter; there's enough.
Rosalind: So was I when your Highness took his dukedom;
                  So was I when your Highness banish'd him:
                          (*As You Like It*, I.3.55–57)

Rosalind challenges the Duke's banishment of her without actually arguing.
No "but" is required; she simply states the facts. But the anaphora makes
her regal and wins the audience.
    Motifs like anaphora and epistrophe elevate the speaker, suggest that
there is something unsaid going on, and incite the listener to action.

EXTRAORDINARY LANGUAGE

At the other end of the spectrum from ciphers lie extraordinary words and
language, which suggest something rich or exotic simply by the act of being
said aloud. Words you do not use in daily vernacular are easy to recognize.
Your job is to put them into your natural speech.
    Natural does not mean *ordinary:* avoid the pitfall of diminishing
extraordinary language to render it casual; instead, rise up to the extraordinary. A particular panache is required of Cyrano de Bergerac for him to use
the word *panache*.

> **Extraordinary language signals the actor to create
> the extraordinary inner life that generates it.**

To start with, then, circle (in pencil) any words you do not use every day; then find a way to make them yours.

Example. A quick glance at the opening Chorus speech of *Henry V* (see appendix 1 for complete text) reveals the following extraordinary words which require both defining and personalizing:

port	deportment, as in demeanor, appearance
gentles	Ladies and Gentlemen, but probably a little more flattering
cockpit	enclosed place of activity: literally, the Globe theater, which, besides dramas, also sported cockfighting (literally a *cock pit*)
vasty	two-syllable, somewhat histrionic version of *vast*
casques	helmets (French cognate)
affright	frighten, but slightly more elegant
ciphers	nothings; also, figures that stand for something else (actors!)
accompt	accomplishment, or account—or both
girdle	restraint, but with the sense of actively restraining something that exerts pressure from within
asunder	histrionic term for splitting "into separate parts" (Bert Lahr used it in *The Wizard of Oz*'s "Courage" number)
puissance	French cognate for "power" or "ability"
deck	"be-deck," decorate, or dress up fancily, as in "deck the halls. . . ."

Every time you say one of these words, let the listener know that it is special. Why pretend otherwise? After all, your word choices are *tactics* you enlist in trying to cast a spell over the audience. This objective is what makes your

Chorus wax so theatrical that you need those exact words.

To take the audience through your extraordinary language, let your inner dialogue (p. 19) be something like "This is a cool word, audience—get it?" Then the audience is that much more likely to get it.

Figurative Phrases, Platitude, Epigram

Playwrights have ways of using ordinary words so as to render them extraordinary. *Figurative phrases* convey more than just literal meaning, often the very opposite. Be on the lookout for irony (the most brazen example being "And Brutus is an honourable man," again from Marc Antony's speech in *Julius Caesar*), sarcasm, understatement, euphemism, hyperbole (exaggeration), and the like. When the language is extreme and the meaning is clear, you might want to try not necessarily acting extreme or punching the figurative meaning, but rather letting the language do its own work; try it cool, in other words, and see if it works.

There are other kinds of phrases I never learned about in school that permeate dramatic literature. *Platitude* refers to observations the speaker deems so flat-out true that they may have even become trite (*plat-* = flat). They may be universal statements about the condition of society, mankind, or men and women. As an example: "Drink has always been the bane of the working classes." Characters who use platitudes are probably self-righteous, possibly right, and particularly self-important.

Epigram, a synonym for *quip* or *witticism*, requires a special delivery when it is a platitude with a twist, some aspect having been turned upside-down for wry, comic, or satirical effect. The best example is Wilde's inversion of the above platitude: "Work has always been the bane of the drinking classes." This line could be delivered theatrically by casting the audience as either the drinking classes or as those intolerant of them. (See Casting the Audience, p. 13.) Note that the listener puts two and two together to figure it out, and that the humor makes way for the sting. Characters who use epigrams populate the works of Oscar Wilde, Noël Coward, George S. Kaufman, George Bernard Shaw, and other notable wits.

Florid Speech

Did Shakespeare's contemporaries actually expound their philosophy in long-winded wit or discursive iambic pentameter? To a certain extent, yes. When Shakespeare was hitting London, England had just defeated the Spanish Armada (1588). Virtuosic English constituted a form of patriotism. Courtiers and the literati would use speech to preen in front of each other and the visiting Spanish dignitaries; the more florid the speech, the greater the prowess of the speaker—sexual, political, or social. In the movie *Elizabeth* (1998), Joseph Fiennes's ability to rhapsodize in sonnet form got him access to the queen (he wasn't playing Shakespeare this time). And the tradition has trickled down to today: think of dueling rappers or slam competitions.

Speech that is grammatically florid actually tends to be more like street talk. We don't conceive conversation in simple, clear sentences, but in ideas, which can tumble one after the other faster than we can talk (as your recordings of overheard conversation have shown you). A character delivering a convoluted speech with interrelated phrases and sub-phrases has probably arrived at an inspired state of thinking, higher and clearer than the norm. Like grammar, the structure of speech is a source of revelation. The key lies in what holds the speech together, how its sections are interrelated. So look between the lines.

Shape of speech defines thought and action—character—just as content does. Extraordinary shape signals extraordinary thought and action. Here you finally realize the value of that unit on sentence diagramming back in English class. For those who never made those "sentence trees" that show how the words relate, think of a computer's drives, directories, folders, and files; the organization actually makes the computer user-friendly. Likewise, grammar makes complicated speech actable.

Punctuation

Again, try to transcribe recordings of real-life conversation and see how tricky it is. You will need periods and commas as grammatical separators to help keep thoughts straight for the reader, but they will not necessarily correspond to the speaker's slowing down or pausing.

Punctuation does not mean pause.

When playwrights write their characters' dialogue, they do it not to be read but to be heard. In a script, punctuation may not be grammatically correct, but will help you make sense of a convoluted passage for the listener on the first hearing.

Note how frequently colons and semicolons appear throughout Shakespeare, particularly in the *First Folio* (the first compilation of just about all of his plays, whose publication was overseen by some of his acting company). These are not stops, but propulsions onward. Many editors change colons and semicolons to dashes, commas, or periods for readers; Shakespeare tailored his punctuation for actors. (If the plays were first transcribed by Shakespeare's actors from memory, then clearly the punctuation reflects an actor's craft.)

Example. Here is Calpurnia's speech from *Julius Caesar,* II.2, in the First Folio. I have updated the spelling, but not the punctuation.

> *Caesar,* I never stood on Ceremonies,
> Yet now they fright me: There is one within,
> Besides the things that we have heard and seen,
> Recounts most horrid fights seen by the Watch.
> A Lioness hath whelped in the streets,
> And Graves have yawn'd, and yielded up their dead;
> Fierce fiery Warriors fight upon the Clouds
> In Ranks and Squadrons, and right form of War
> Which drizzled blood upon the Capitol:
> The noise of Battle hurtled in the Ayre:
> Horses do neigh, and dying men did groan,
> And Ghosts did shriek and squall about the streets.
> O *Caesar,* these things are beyond all use,
> And I do fear them.

Can you see how the colons and semicolon make the forward motion of her thoughts easier? I will let you find the three periods yourself, an effective device for identifying the sentences—hence, the thought groups. Note, too, the capitalization, and the italics on Caesar's name, inveigling the actor to charge both this word and her relationship to her husband. (Proper names and many nouns are capitalized throughout the *First Folio*, by the way, reminding the actor to charge them all.)

So punctuation, even the period, does not mean "let your voice come down in pitch"—which is something a reader might do at the end of a sentence, but not necessarily an actor.

Punctuation Marks = Mental Sparks

Your character's intent is like a ball you keep juggling, and must not drop. Punctuation helps you keep it in the air. (See discussion of semi-colons, colons, ellipses, and dashes in Pauses, p. 48 and Thought Groups, pp. 54-55.)

Antecedents

To keep that ball in the air, keep the antecedents straight, too: know what you are referring to at any given moment. In life we do it all the time naturally, but with rich text it is important to identify the antecedent when it is ambiguous. I have often asked an experienced actor, "what's your antecedent there?" to find that she has made an understandable and easily correctable error. Suddenly the speech makes more sense to her and to her listener.

Every verb and pronoun has an antecedent, stated or implied.

Example. During his Queen Mab speech in *Romeo and Juliet* (I.4), Mercutio goes on and on in long, giddy lists. He betrays not only a great sense of fun and teasing, but also a tremendous intellect, thinking in long, florid outline form to poke fun at Romeo.

> O, then, I see Queen Mab hath been with you.
> She is the fairies' midwife, and she comes
> In shape no bigger than an agate-stone
> On the fore-finger of an alderman,
> Drawn with a team of little atomies   (1)
> Athwart men's noses as they lie asleep: . . .   (2)

For eleven more lines he lists additional descriptions of her appearance. You can analyze the speech's antecedents to determine (1) what is "drawn with a team. . ." in the fifth line; and (2) what or who is the antecedent of "they" in the last line, there being four preceding plural nouns ("fairies," "atomies," "men," and "noses").

The past participle "drawn" does not modify the preceding nouns "alderman" or "fore-finger," which would not make sense; its subject might be "agate-stone," or perhaps "shape," but both of these lie in a descriptive clause, and are not the main topic. On inspection, it pretty clearly refers to "she," Queen Mab herself. Mercutio's image is of tiny Mab riding a jewel-sized chariot, "drawn" through the air by a "team" of little atomies (tiny fairies the size of atoms): "She comes . . . drawn . . . athwart men's noses. . . ."

"They" refers to the "men" over whose noses she travels, unless you can make a case for the immediately preceding noun, "noses," as "sleeping."

Yes, sometimes a poet is purposely ambiguous: locate those ambiguities and you are halfway to solving the mystery.

Parallel Structure

Parallel structure is a key ingredient of florid speech. The simplest examples are in nursery rhymes: ". . .That's what little girls are made of" parallels ". . .That's what little boys are made of." The contrast is between the words *girls* and *boys*. Technically, the variable part of the sentence is the *antithesis*; the repeated part, the *identity*.

Pope's famous line, "Man proposes, God disposes," is an example of a *double antithesis*, the identity being "-poses." With four words, Pope has constructed a perfect parallelogram of thought-provoking meaning.

Again, you get to make this meaning clear to your listener on one hearing. Stressing the identity tends to mislead the audience and confuse the meaning; the point of the parallel structure is its antithesis. Still, there are times you may not want to punch the antithesis: if there are many such contrasts in a short passage, or when a character wants to be cool about his point. And you will come across others, I am sure. (Rules are tools, not masters.) Still, give the antithesis the emphasis at least in intention, especially when you understate it in delivery.

As with antecedents, how one element corresponds to another is important to get straight. A character really on a roll, like Mercutio, even elides part of the identity, so the speaker must be clear as to what relates to what.

Example. Mercutio goes on to describe the fairy Queen's carriage in *Romeo and Juliet:*

> Her waggon-spokes made of long spinners' legs;
> The cover, of the wings of grasshoppers;
> Her traces, of the smallest spider's web;
> Her collars, of the moonshine's watery beams;
> Her whip, of cricket's bone; the lash, of film; . . .   (I.4)

The parallel structure here allows him not to repeat the identity "made" because it is clearly implied in every line after the first.

Later he uses *inverted* parallel structure:

> And in this state she gallops night by night
> Through lovers' brains, and then they dream of love;   (2)
> O'er courtiers' knees, that dream on court'sies straight;   (3)

O'er lawyers' fingers, who straight dream on fees;   (4)
O'er ladies' lips, who straight on kisses dream,   (5)
(Which oft the angry Mab with blisters plagues,   (6)
Because their breaths with sweetmeats tainted are:)   (7)
Sometime she gallops o'er a courtier's nose,   (8)
And then dreams he of smelling out a suit;   (9)
And sometime comes she with a tithe-pig's tail
Tickling a parson's nose as [he] lies asleep,
Then dreams he of another benefice: (12)
Sometime she driveth o'er a soldier's neck,   (13)
And then dreams he of cutting foreign throats,   (14)
Of breaches, ambuscadoes, Spanish blades,
Of healths five fathom deep; and then anon
Drums in his ear, at which he starts and wakes,
And being thus frighted swears a prayer or two
And sleeps again. . . .

In the third through fifth lines, he repeats the words *dream* and *straight*, but inverts the sequence. Why? To keep the speech fresh—to entertain.

Look at lines 2–5. Beacause he mentions each of Mab's "victims" at the same point in each line, we come to anticipate them. It's like rhyme: How many times have you completed a song before the singer?

Parallel structure also helps Mercutio go off on tangents. All he need do is establish a pattern, interrupt it (6–7), and then resume it (8). Remember that tangents betray personal experiences, attitudes, and passions: he has undoubtedly known blistered "ladies' lips" (5) and soldier's insomnia (13–20) himself!

Once you have analyzed the Queen Mab speech, try simply saying the text over and over. You will eventually start to think as quickly and clearly as Mercutio does. Sparks will fly: the deeper your meaning and the more charged your imagery, the brighter the sparks. You may find yourself becoming giddy automatically, just from saying the words aloud—and meaning them.

Structure conveys soul.

Though you must reach heights of intelligence, emotion, wit, or poetic sensibility to perform florid language, the words and their grammatical structure help take you to those heights organically. The process is reciprocal, then: you fulfill the text, and it fulfills you.

Half- and Hidden Antitheses

Antithesis can charge even the littlest word with a spark of meaning. Be on the lookout for incomplete and hidden antitheses. They suggest innuendo for you to make active:

Example. In *Troilus and Cressida*, III.2, Cressida tells Troilus, "Hard to seem won: but I was won, my lord. . . ." She is contrasting "seem won" with "was won": "won" provides the identity; and "seem" is contrasted with "was." Her meaning is that she really liked him all along, even when she did not seem to.

Frequently you will find only half an antithesis, the other half being implied. The speaker must compel the listener to make the comparison, especially when its second element is delayed, or hidden.

Example. Early in *The Tempest* (I.2):

Miranda:	Had I been any god of power, I would	
	Have sunk the sea within the earth, or ere	
	It should the good ship so have swallow'd and	
	The fraughting souls within her.	
Prospero:	Be collected:	(4)
	No more amazement: tell your piteous heart	
	There's no harm done.	
Miranda:	O, woe the day!	
Prospero:	No harm.	(6)
	I have done nothing but in care of thee. . . .	(7)

Look at the first line: "Had I been any god of power, I would/ Have sunk the sea" and saved the crew and the ship; she is contrasting herself with her father, essentially laying a guilt trip on him. (Who else caused the storm?) Yet she does not actually say "you." She just says what she'd do if she were a "god of power"—which her father the sorcerer actually is. The backhanded implication is so clear that it makes him defend himself with "I have done nothing" wrong. Is his defense a non sequitur, or does he hear Miranda's tacit indictment loud and clear? Obviously, the latter. So you, playing Miranda, bait him to provoke his defensiveness. Eventually, your "I" contrasts with Prospero's "I" much later. But meanwhile, by figuring out what she does not say, you have found the hidden antithesis and made the scene rife with conflict. (The fact that the first "I" lies in a stressed position helps you find this hidden antithesis; more about stresses in Verse, below.)

POETRY

Like the technical language of scientists or plumbers, poetry is the specialized language of characters who happen to be poets—or talk like them. Dialogue need not be in verse to be poetic, of course. If you are playing Blanche in *Streetcar*, Edmund in *Long Day's Journey*, or any character who speaks in verse, it will behoove you to participate in live poetry readings to make the world of poetical magic your natural speaking idiom. You may even go so far as to write poetry as a pastime; whether it is any good or not, it is *yours*—which is what you must transform poetic dialogue into when you play it.

Beyond becoming a poet yourself, recognizing poetical language is the first step in approaching how to deliver it. As with prose, this process involves locating linguistic events for which you find dramatic cause. First, as with any dialogue, simply mark any extraordinary language you may have. Second, identify figures of speech and poetic devices like irony, metaphor, personification—expressions that suggest something besides what they actually mean.

Example. Returning to the Chorus in *Henry V* (see appendix 1 for complete text), note the following poetic expressions:

the brightest heaven of invention	the idyllic state of a writer or artist, or the greatest work of artistic creation—both this play, and creativity itself (or the place where those gods of creativity, the Muses, dwell)
swelling scene	"growing action," suggesting the physical growth of more and more actors pouring onto the stage
at his heels/Leash'd in like hounds, should famine, sword and fire/ Crouch for employment	personification (actually "dog-ification") of three kinds of calamity
this unworthy scaffold	understatement for "this meager stage"

this wooden O	this round-shaped theater
a crooked figure	a humble euphemism for "actor"; but "figure" also suggests a sketch artist's stroke of the pencil
'tis your thoughts that now must . . .	personification of "thoughts"
into an hour-glass	into the time span of one hour

Again, every time you say one of the phrases from column A, communicate column B as well. As with any extraordinary language, acknowledge that you are waxing poetic: "act the footnotes" as the audience needs you to.

Musical Language

Playwrights exploit these sounds to imbue everyday words with meaning. Language, or abstract art, conveys significance by its sheer sounds. Playwrights exploit their sound to imbue everyday work with extra meaning. Pay careful attention to rhyme and other musical devices like:

Alliteration: Repetition of consonant sounds, as in "**P**eter **P**iper picked. . ." or "swelling scene."

Assonance: Repetition of vowel sounds, as in "**H**ere **fee**l **we**. . ."

Onomatopoeia: The imitation of sounds in nature or elsewhere, as in "babbling brook," "buzz saw," "the whoosh of the wind."

Tintinnabulation: A particular form of onomatopoeia mimicking the sound of bells, as in "ding-dong" or "tinkle tinkle."

Opera singers know that, in general:

Consonants convey information, while vowels carry emotion.

So a passage of consonants with short vowel sounds, which let the speaker clip along quickly, suggests thoughts or facts. Many long vowel sounds in a row suggest emotion bubbling over. They also require the speaker to slow down.

Long *O* sounds can convey the pain of a "moan":

Example. In *The Tempest*, Miranda says, "**O**, I have suffered," "**O** the cry. . . ," "**Poor souls**," "**O woe** the day," "**O** the heavens," "**O**, my heart bleeds," and "**O** good sir" (I.2). She is in excruciating pain for the victims of the storm, and Prospero has his hands full in trying to assuage her.

Long *ee* sounds, meanwhile, may convey glee or cheer:

Example. In *As You Like It* (II.1), when Duke Senior says "Here feel we but the penalty of Adam. . ." he is trying to cheer his fellow courtiers, who have been banished with him. They are despondent for the loss of their fortunes, while he, ever the optimist, demonstrates to them their newfound freedom from courtly demands. His subsequent alliteration in the same speech further supports his role as cheerleader: "**B**ooks in running **b**rooks,/ Sermons in stone. . ." These sounds convey action.

A barrage of *s* and *sh* might evoke a snake, as might *th, ch, f, h, l, t,* and *v*. Think of what a lot of *l*'s make your tongue do—or *k* sounds, for that matter. Very effective for a slimy character like Iago.

Example. Iago, in II.3 of *Othello*, soliloquizes:

> When devils will the blackest sins put on,
> They do suggest at first with heavenly shows,
> As I do now: for whiles this honest fool
> Plies Desdemona to repair his fortunes,
> And she for him pleads strongly to the Moor,
> I'll pour this pestilence into his ear,
> That she repeals him for her body's lust;
> And by how much she strives to do him good,
> She shall undo her credit with the Moor.
> So will I turn her virtue into pitch;
> And out of her own goodness make the net
> That shall enmesh them all.

What sibilance. Shakespeare's words are an overt note to the actor to play—or to become—the slithering serpent. Can you taste the action of the two *sh* sounds in the last line? Yum.

Think what sounds inherently suggest qualities like morbidity, violence, solace, warmth, lust, or fright.

**Sounds give actors mandates even stronger
than stage directions.**

VERSE

That antiseptic word, *scansion,* really involves a rather luscious process of stoking your creative furnace through the closest possible relationship to the text. But there is a lot more to interpreting verse than scansion, and a lot more to scansion than counting syllables. And again, it's all useable for the actor. Here, then, is my crash course on what the practical actor should know about verse.

Verse renders ordinary language extraordinary through placement of words. A word oddly placed is like a jolt: it piques or shocks the listener. Even the smallest word can become the most important in a line simply due to its location.

Shakespeare's poetry is generally *blank verse,* which means that *unrhymed iambic pentameter* is its point of departure—though he rhymes occasionally and he deviates often from the basic syllabic pattern. Iambic pentameter means that there are five *iambic feet* per line. An iambic foot, or *iamb,* is a combination of an unstressed syllable followed by a stressed syllable: "da-*dum.*" (A foot consists of 1–3 syllables, one of which is stressed. There are several patterns of feet in addition to iambs, but their names are unnecessary for our purposes.)

Not all verse is pentameter (five feet per line). A generation before Shakespeare, *tetrameter* (four feet per line) was the vogue, so occasionally when he wants language to sound old-fashioned, or like an incantation, he uses tetrameter, as in the *Macbeth* witches' "Double, double toil and trouble." The Prologue to *The Murder of Gonzago,* that play-within-a-play in Act III scene 2 of *Hamlet,* uses tetrameter to give the impression of old-school acting.

For us, | and for | our trag | edy,
Here stoop | ing to | your clem | ency,
We beg | your hear | ing pa | tiently.

There are two ways to deliver a stressed syllable: louder or longer. Longer is almost universally wiser onstage: punching syllables louder than others makes your delivery start to sound sing-songy.

We can chart a standard line of iambic pentameter as follows:

An unstressed syllable is indicated as: ˘

A stressed syllable is indicated as: ´

˘ ´	˘ ´	˘ ´	˘ ´	˘ ´
da *dum*	da *dum*	da *dum*	da *dum*	da *dum*
How an-	gri- ly	I taught	my brow	to frown

Occasionally there will be an eleventh, unstressed syllable, constituting a *feminine ending*:

˘ ´	˘ ´	˘ ´	˘ ´	˘ ´ ˘
da *dum*	da *dum*	da *dum*	da *dum*	da *dum* da
I come	to thee	for char-	i- ta-	ble li-cense.

The feminine line constitutes a variation rather than an exception.

When Shakespeare establishes a rhythmic pattern and then violates it, he invites the actor to investigate that violation and invest in some dramatic, emotional, or thematic reason that violation is warranted. Not all solutions need be big ones. And sometimes there is no reason but practicality: Note that in saying *charitable,* you really do not want to give the third syllable— *ta*—any undue stress. Likewise with the *ly* of *angrily* in the previous line. I call this type of syllable a *placeholder stress:* a syllable that may be slightly more stressed than the adjacent syllables, but not necessarily for an actable reason.

Step 1. *First try it regular.* See how the pattern of regular iambic pentameter fits your line:

da *dum*	da *dum*	da *dum*	da *dum*	da *dum*

Then ask yourself, "can I say the words this way and make sense?"

If so: Shakespeare is suggesting you try it that way. (Although you may not ultimately perform it like that, you know you *can*, and probably should.) Go to step 2.

If not: Go to step 3. In Desdemona's line "Not the world's mass of vanity could make me," the *the* cannot be stressed without confusing the listener (*Othello*, IV.2, discussed in step 3, below). It is clearly an irregular line.

Step 2. *Identify the unusual.* Next ask if there is anything unusual or surprising when you say the line as regular, such as a small word receiving an unexpected stress.

Step 2A. *If not,* then this is undoubtedly a line of regular iambic pentameter, as is "How **angrily** I **taught** my **brow** to **frown**," from I.2 of *The Two Gentlemen of Verona.* Julia has just sent her servant-and-counsel Lucetta away with a love letter addressed to herself. She later exclaims, "How churlishly I chid Lucetta hence." There is no reason to say this line any other way but regular. To stress *how* or *I* would de-emphasize *churl-* and *chid,* where more meaning lies. Trip along and say it as a regular line: "How **churl**ish**ly** I **chid** Lucetta **hence**."

In such regular lines, there are not necessarily any linguistic events, at least with respect to scansion. (Words constitute linguistic events for other reasons, such as Julia's alliterative *ch* sounds.) All other things being equal (no alliteration, punctuation, repetition, five-syllable word, or figurative phrase), the *last* stressed syllable of the line is generally the most important of the five. Give it a sense of arrival—sort of landing on it, or enhancing it with a special color, even as you keep talking (as you would with any poem). Other than for this last stress, you can say the line virtually like prose dialogue. Much better to err on the side of too prosaic a delivery, by the way, than one that's at all like a nursery rhyme. Your sense of the rhythm wants to be almost undetectable, heightening your speech rather than coming across as sing-songy. Shakespeare will generally use tetrameter or rhymed couplets when he wants this effect; unrhymed iambic pentameter is supposed to sound natural.

When Shakespeare places several regular lines in a row, he is suggesting that you clip along while you talk, without taking pauses or "acting moments." Try to speak relentlessly, in long phrases.

Example. Here is the rest of Julia's speech:

And yet I would I had o'erlook'd the letter:	(1)
It were a shame to call her back again,	
And pray her to a fault for which I chid her.	(3)
What fool is she, that knows I am a maid,	(4)
And would not force the letter to my view!	(5)
Since maids, in modesty, say 'no' to that	
Which they would have the profferer construe 'ay.'	(7)
Fie, fie, how wayward is this foolish love,	*
That, like a testy babe, will scratch the nurse,	

And presently, all humbled, kiss the rod!
How churlishly I chid Lucetta hence,
When willingly I would have had her here!
How angrily I taught my brow to frown,
When inward joy enforced my heart to smile!
My penance is, to call Lucetta back,
And ask remission for my folly past.
What, ho! Lucetta!   *

Only the two asterisked lines are necessarily irregular, suggesting that the actress clip along, speaking as she thinks without pausing or slowing down until she lands—with a particularly passionate arrival—on those two lines' "*Fie, fie,*" and "*What, ho!*" (The third line is feminine, and "profferer" in the seventh line might be said almost as "proff'rer.") Once you know what you are saying, delivering this speech becomes easy.

Step 2B. If there *is* something unusual in delivering the line as regular, even though you can do so clearly, then determine whether Shakespeare intended that unusual effect for some reason. Does he want the speaker to jar the listener with a certain word? Note particularly small words in stressed positions, like prepositions, articles, conjunctions, auxiliary verbs, modals, and the verb *to be*. If you treat this ordinary stressed word as an extraordinary one, the line may get clearer and richer; in this case, you have most likely uncovered more of the meaning of the line. On the other hand, if this treatment confuses the listener, the syllable might be a placeholder stress.

Example A. In lines 3 and 5 of Julia's speech from *Verona*, the word *to* appears both times as a mere placeholder stress. In line 4, the fact that *am* lies in a stressed position may encourage you to explore just how much she wants to defend her reputation as a virgin ("maid"). In the end, though, you will probably make it a placeholder stress, as Julia's conflict is with herself, not Lucetta.

But line (1) puts a particularly meaningful stress on the word *had:* "And yet I would I *had* o'erlook'd the letter" is half an antithesis; she contrasts wishing she had with the unstated (but evident) fact that she has not. Scansion helps you avoid even thinking about a delivery like "And *yet* I *would* I had *o'er-look'd* the *let*ter"—unnecessarily irregular and in this case even wrong (suggested doubly by the missing *v* in *o'erlooked*).

Example B. Arguably, the most famous line in Shakespeare is "To be, or not to be, that is the Question." (*First Folio* punctuation) Keeping it regular would put a stress on the small word *is:* "To be, or not to be, that *is* the Question." This scansion suggests that the sentence, though the first of the speech, is not the beginning of Hamlet's thought. Rather, he has been thinking for a while and finally realizes that the question of existence itself *is* the question. This implies a revelation, after having avoided "that being the question" for a couple of acts now. Here, trying the line regular points to a specific pre-beat, which inspires the speech.[20]

In fact, scanning the text any which way you want will lead to a more confusing delivery; it makes acting harder, not easier. The stresses that Shakespeare suggests (if they work) help make the speech clear to the listener on one hearing.

Example. When an actor playing Desdemona was working hard, but unclear, I reviewed her scansion with her. An asterisk below indicates an over-crowded line. By "overcrowded" I mean either an eleven-syllable line with the last syllable necessarily stressed (not a feminine ending), or a line of more than eleven syllables.

O good Iago,

What shall I do to win my lord again?	2
Good friend, go to him; for, by this light of heaven,	*
I know not how I lost him. Here I kneel:	3
If e'er my will did trespass 'gainst his love	1
Either in discourse of thought or actual deed,	*
Or that mine eyes, mine ears, or any sense,	2
Delighted them in any other form,	
Or that I do not yet, and ever did,	1
And ever will, though he do shake me off	1
To beggarly divorcement, love him dearly,	
Comfort forswear me! Unkindness may do much;	1*
And his unkindness may defeat my life,	1
But never taint my love. I cannot say 'whore':	2*
It doth abhor me now I speak the word;	2
To do the act that might th' addition earn	
Not the world's mass of vanity could make me. (IV.2.150 ff.)	1

Lo and behold, we found that she was stressing *me, mine,* and *I* unnecessarily, causing the listener to think "as opposed to who else?" Yet in the speech as written, there is no one to whom Desdemona is trying to contrast *me.* These capricious stresses were red herrings for the listener. I asked her why she did not try it regular at first, and she replied, "I just liked it this way." It might feel better to be talking about "me" and "my emotions," but the speech came off as whiny and self-indulgent, costing Desdemona the empathy of the listener.

Look carefully at the speech. It uses the words *I, my, mine,* and *me* seventeen times in as many lines, which I have tallied up for you to the right of the speech. Can you find one that lies in a stressed position? Try scanning the speech before reading on.

The answer: no, you cannot. Certainly this cannot be a coincidence, but is something Shakespeare carefully crafted. And the reason is stated in the last line of the speech: "not-vanity" is one of Desdemona's most important attributes, especially here in Act IV. The last word of the speech, *me,* is in a particularly unstressed position, the feminine ending, at which point Iago speaks.

Next time, the actor took her stress and focus off the word *me* and put them on Iago and her husband; and she struggled to be a champion instead of a victim. And without trying to, she cried. So did I.

Scansion provides a container for emotion, which increases the pressure so you can burst without effort.

You will find many ambiguities in scanning solutions, and several ways to scan the same line when it is not a regular one. But when it is a regular one, by all means, don't work so hard!

When the verse line can be regular, keep it regular unless there is a compelling reason not to. It makes acting easier.

Step 3. *When you cannot possibly make the line regular.* If you cannot say the line as regular iambic pentameter *and be clearly understood,* then Shakespeare has violated the iambic pentameter expressly. He has placed stresses in off-positions to call attention to certain words. Sometimes it is not so clear-cut which words to stress and which not to, and you have some choices to make.

Step 4. *Strive for five.* In making these choices, first try to find five stresses to maintain the pentameter. Count the total number of syllables. When there are as many as twelve or thirteen, then there may just have to be six or more stresses (not always, though). In Desdemona's asterisked lines (above), there are eleven or twelve syllables. In the fourth one, both *say* and *whore* should be stressed. Stressing *say* will help you convey the half-antithesis: she cannot say *whore* much less act like one. You must stress *whore* simply to be clear. This makes six stresses—an extraordinary line, indicating extraordinary inner life (not a feminine ending). The two stresses right next to each other slow down the whole line; betraying just how much "it doth ab*hor*" her to "say '*whore*.' "

In the last line, conversely, if you add a sixth stress to the word *me* at the end, you send the listener on a wild goose chase of logic: *me* as opposed to what other person (as discussed above)? Strive for five stresses here.

Not the ***world's mass*** of ***van***ity could ***make*** me.

The beginning of the line, as you can see, is irregular, for you must stress both *world's* and *mass* to make the words clear. The *y* of *vanity* is a place-holder stress and will emerge all by itself (requiring nothing of you but to speak clearly and not too fast). Some actors will stress *not* as well; acceptable but unnecessary, for if you strive for five *you need not work so hard*.

Step 5. *Investigate and invest.* Every departure from regular iambic pentameter indicates where to investigate and invest. Why should that stress be special, in acting terms? How does that word relate to other words? What is the speech's logic? What are the character's values? What is your action? All those irregularities invite you to invest in intensified personalization. And this is really the whole point of the scansion process: to help you own every word thoroughly.

When you come upon a line with several abnormal stresses (and/or a passage with several abnormal lines), then you have found a particularly climactic moment.

Shakespeare provides other rhythmic clues to help you scan:

Monosyllabic lines and words. If a line is made up entirely of monosyl-labic words, then you are invited to explore stressing any number—or even all of them. "***Howl, howl, howl*** . . ." is all stressed. *Monosyllabic imperative verbs*, in particular, are virtually always stressed. "***Come, fate, in***to the ***lists***. . ." has three stresses in a row. ("***Come, fate,*** in***to*** the ***lists***. . ." a possi-ble variation, but never "Come ***fate***, . . ." with the imperative verb unstressed.)

An entire line of ten monosyllabic words, or several such lines in sequence, indicates a peak or a climax. *"For 'tis your thoughts that now must deck our kings"* is the very statement of the task at hand, the Chorus's objec-tive, in the Prologue of *Henry V* (see appendix I for complete text). In such a monosyllabic line, all ten words may be stressed—or whichever six, seven, eight, or nine you prefer. (This principle encourages the Chorus to stress the antithesis between *your* and *our* as well as the already-stressed one between *thoughts* and *kings:* "For 'tis **your thoughts** that **now** must **deck our kings.**" An additional stress on *must* would be worth trying, as would one on *'tis.*)

This does not mean you get carried away with every monosyllabic line. In Desdemona's speech, "I know not how I lost him. Here I kneel" is a monosyllabic line, but many actors would treat it as regular (the word *I* is, after all, repeated; similarly, *him* lies in an unstressed position and does not introduce a new thought, and so is better left unstressed): "I **know** not **how** I **lost** him. **Here** I **kneel**." Others, however, might add a sixth stress on *not,* and perhaps even a seventh on the last *I* (which is a long vowel lying between two other long vowel sounds): "I **know not how** I **lost** him. **Here I kneel.**" If she's going to kneel, she may as well *talk* melodramatically for three syllables, too.

Suffice it to say that with monosyllabic lines, it's worth circling all ten words and investigating them with greater flexibility. After you do, you may then choose to go back and deliver a regular line that happens to be monosyllabic, as regular (which is my recommendation for the last example: "I **know** not **how** I **lost** him. **Here** I **kneel**").

Punctuation in verse is worth honoring; when extraordinary, find an actable reason. It may (or may not, as discussed earlier) be telling you to put the stress on the syllable directly after the punctuation mark, especially if it is a monosyllabic word followed by yet another punctuation mark or long vowel sound. A construction like " . . . : O," begs to be stressed more than if the comma were not there, as in Laertes's line from *Hamlet,* IV.7.165:

Drown'd! O, where?

If you do not stress all three syllables, the line sounds a bit silly, making it all the more difficult to plummet to the depths of grief. (See also Punctuation, pp. 185-187.)

Long vowel sounds are often stressed, especially when assonant in two adjacent monosyllabic words. Both the following pairs of long vowel sounds suggest two stresses, one for each syllable:

　　　′　　　′
No　　More

　　　′　　　′
Great Thane

Contraction. Words are shortened, or contracted, with an apostrophe to manipulate where the stress should fall: *'gainst* for *against*, *ta'en* for *taken*, *ne'er* and *e'er* for *never* and *ever*, and *th'* and *'t* for *the* and *it*, these last two taking no syllables. Sometimes the *e* of *the* (before a vowel) wants to be elided even if the editor (or the *First Folio*) does not do it for you. Banquo, in I.3 of *Macbeth*:

> How far is '**t** call'd to Forres? What are these
> So wither'd, and so wild in their attire,
> That look not like the **inhabitants o' the earth,**
> And yet are on '**t**? Live you? Or are you aught
> That man may question?

The two instances of *'t* for *it* are clear, but how can you make the third line ten syllables? By pronouncing *the* as if it were *th'* both times: "th'inhabi-tants" and "o'th'earth." Do you have to? No. But try it first.

Consonants. When consonants bump into each other, alliteratively or in thick blends, you are encouraged to slow down:

whi**ch sm**oked

With the clashing *k* sounds of "Mark, king of Scotland, mark:" from I.2 of *Macbeth*, try giving each surrounding syllable a stress:

*Ma*r**k**, **k**i*ng*

Note: The comma between the two *k*'s induces you to make two *k* sounds; but do not carry enunciation overboard: "I cannot tell" is spelled with two *t*'s but need only be said with one, unless extraordinary enunciation is otherwise warranted. Similarly, in "On this unworthy scaffol**d t**o bring forth," the *d* gets swallowed by the *t*, or else the listener cannot help but "catch you enunciating," which is dangerously close to catching you acting. Ditto with the *f* absorbing the *v* in Malcolm's "Hail, bra**ve fr**iend," in the same scene.

> ***Speak the way you speak, unless the* character *must articulate something in a peculiar way.***

Pace. In music, you adjust the tempo when you come across the words *ritardando* or *accelerando*; in verse, a half- or overcrowded line suggests similar dynamics. When a line has five stresses and more than ten syllables, it should generally take the same amount of time as a regular line. Shakespeare is suggesting that you talk faster, to fit all those syllables in.

Do not be confused: In other poetry, longer lines are sometimes said to slow down the rhythm—meaning the time between line endings, when you come to an arrival. In dramatic verse, you tend to keep the time between line endings uniform, and speed up or slow down the words to get there.

When a line has fewer than five stresses, and/or fewer than ten syllables, you are allowed to take the same amount of time that ten syllables would take. (Make sure it is not a shared line, however; see below.) This extra time is for your interpretation.

Fill out a short line by:
1. *pausing before the line;*
2. *pausing after the line;*
3. *taking pauses between words in the line; or*
4. *stretching vowels during the line.*

The last choice is often the most effective, as it gives color to the words rather than to the silences, which are harder to project.

Example. The Bleeding Sergeant has trouble speaking in I.2 of *Macbeth*. Without even reading the words you can see several lines that are shorter (though different editors divvy up the lines differently: check your *First Folio*):

> For brave Macbeth—well he deserves that name—
> Disdaining fortune, with his brandish'd steel,
> Which smoked with bloody execution,
> Like valour's minion carved out his passage
> Till he faced the slave;
> Which ne'er shook hands, nor bade farewell to him,
> Till he unseam'd him from the nave to the chaps,
> And fix'd his head upon our battlements.

"*Till he faced the slave*" could be treated as five doubly long stresses, since (1) it is a line of five monosyllabic words, and (2) it's a pretty exciting moment of the story that he's telling—a cliffhanger. In musical terms, think of each syllable as a half note, while in your regular lines each syllable is a quarter note.

Then later:

> If I say sooth, I must report they were
> As cannons overcharged with double cracks;
> So they
> Doubly redoubled strokes upon the foe:
> Except they meant to bathe in reeking wounds,
> Or memorize another Golgotha,
> I cannot tell—
> But I am faint; my gashes cry for help.

The two short lines here are different from the cliffhanger above. A line of only one or two stresses means that you have the remaining three or four beats for acting nonverbally: here, to gasp or choke or bleed—in the silences, you are *dying*. Briefing the king is more important to you than getting a doctor; then you faint.

When your character is in a heightened state of emotion but stays in iambic pentameter, Shakespeare suggests that your emotions are not totally out of control, but reined in by your intellect—at least enough so that you can be articulate. Balancing emotion and intellect is a constant concern for Shakespearean actors.

Irregular lead-in. When a stressed syllable follows two or more unstressed syllables, or two stressed syllables come in a row, one stress is made all the more extraordinary by its irregular lead-in, even if from the preceding line. Therefore, the first stress in a regular line after a feminine line, since it is preceded by two unstressed syllables, is extraordinary. In Julia's speech from Verona, note the special arrival of *fool* in line 4: " . . . for which I chid **her.**/ **What** *fool* is she . . . ". (Here, the two preceding unstressed syllables are marked by boldface.) If you feel you have to stress *what* then *fool* is still set up with an irregular lead-in, and rendered extraordinary by coming right after another stress, instead of after an unstressed syllable. Note Julia's ". . . '*ay*.'/ *Fie, fie* . . ." in lines 7–8: three stresses in a row.

Alternate syllabication. The same word can be pronounced "betroth-èd" or "betroth'd." Often you will see the accent or the apostrophe to help you, but not always. *Troilus* can have two or three syllables, depending on the rest of the line. In Shakespeare's day, the *-tion* ending could be said in two syllables or one, at least in verse.

Enjambment. If a sentence runs on to the next line (enjambment), still respect the end of the verse line, giving it at least a psychological mini-arrival, even while propelling yourself forward to the end of the grammatical sentence. Miranda's first speech (see p. 190) provides three examples of this. The enjambments help her keep Prospero from getting a word in until the fourth line.

Some sentences in Shakespeare last the length of a sonnet, fourteen lines: Keep talking, if you can.

Shared line. When two different characters share one complete line of verse, especially a regular line, Shakespeare is telling the second speaker, in no uncertain terms, to pick up the cue.

Example A. Prospero and Miranda (see p. 190 again) share lines 4 and 6, both of which happen to be regular. These two clues tell the actors to interrupt each other without pausing. Line 6 also happens to be monosyllabic, with an exclamation mark in the middle, so emoting may be allowed, but not pausing.

Example B. In *Macbeth* (II.2), four lines of dialogue are actually one line of verse:

Lady Macbeth:	Did not you speak?
Macbeth:	When?
Lady Macbeth:	Now.
Macbeth:	As I descended?
Lady Macbeth:	Ay.
Macbeth:	Hark . . .

It is the middle of the night. The title character has just killed King Duncan. The Lord and Lady are most assuredly not pausing during their shared line (which is either regular or has an extra stress on *When?*). If you save your pauses until after *ay,* and perhaps another after *hark,* you render them even more effective: what was that noise? Has someone seen them? Have they been caught?

There is almost no exception to the shared-line principle; but in the one out of hundred times that the staging does warrant a pause instead of picking up the cues, make sure it is tremendously exciting.

Caesuras. A caesura is the tiniest pause it takes the character to think. A *natural caesura* is the millisecond it takes the lips to go from completing one consonant to forming the next. The natural caesura is often found midline, where consonants (and phrases of thought) would otherwise collide, as in Jaques's "And so he plays his part. The sixth age shifts." You will often prefer taking the optional caesura. But to avoid a labored delivery, a natural caesura should generally take the least amount of time required for clarity of sound and thought: you should neither speak too fast nor seem to be stopping (except when your character *intends* a labored delivery).

Example. The last line of Jaques's famous speech (see appendix 1 for complete text) is:

Sans teeth, sans eyes, sans taste, sans every thing.

A natural caesura lies at each comma, and is probably required at the second, in order to articulate the two esses of "eyes, sans . . . " *Sans,* from French and now rare in English, needs time to be re-coined, by both speaker and listener. Then, to distinguish "every thing" (two words) from "everything," another caesura might be called for. Why did Shakespeare put so many possible caesuras in one line? Because the topic of conversation is old age, which the rhythm itself evokes by slowing down to a halt—and dying.

But if you don't want the audience to see you thinking so frequently, the above line can be said just as clearly with no pauses at all: just keep talking—clearly. You will soon see how short the required midline caesura can be. If you do take that millisecond, as with all pauses, make sure something is going on during it.

Keep thought and action moving forward through all pauses, including caesuras.

Editions. Check out several published versions of the play. Not everyone agrees on punctuation or even where a line ends. Refer to original texts—the *First Folio* in particular—as often as you can so that no editor comes between you and Shakespeare.

Priority. Most important, all this theory is to serve you. (Again, rules = tools ≠ masters.) If a particular performance impels you to say *"that* is the question," don't censor yourself, but go right ahead—especially if you have tried Shakespeare's suggestion first.

Putting it all together. When you finally perform:

Talk in phrases, not syllables.

And think in large groups of phrases, not one sentence at a time; then you will acquire a sense of momentum in your speech. (See Thought Groups, pp. 53-55.)

Just because scansion is highly analytical and technical does not mean that it cannot become organic and effortless, and provide the groundwork for a lot of spontaneous play. Invest intensely in your scansion *early* in the rehearsal period to make the poetry your own; then in performance you will be free to concentrate on other things. There are a limitless number of ways to deliver the same line, even with the same scansion. And all the words will be there to help you—now that you know how to let them.

Check out John Barton's series *Acting Shakespeare* on video. You can see great actors from the Royal Shakespeare Company—Judi Dench, Ian McKellen, Roger Rees, Ben Kingsley, Patrick Stewart, David Suchet—go through many of the same processes to render their work clear and compelling. The secrets of the masters are available for you to explore and exploit.

POETIC ACTION

When the poetry seems neither to further the dramatic action nor accomplish the characters' goals, try to uncover either:

1. why the play *has* to stop the plot for poetry; or
2. how the poetry actually does move the play forward with at least the same force as rhetoric.

Poeticizing

Sometimes a character engages in the *act* of poetry.

The sheer act of speaking or creating poetry is action: the act of poeticizing.

Heightened language is not simply a vehicle for writer and elocutionist to show off (though that may be involved). A character rhymes when he *has* to rhyme. Just as a fool or comedian is compelled to make others laugh, so must you investigate why your poetic characters are compelled to live in the world of poetry. The act of poeticizing can become an objective of its own.

Example. In *A Midsummer Night's Dream*, Hermia and Lysander mourn their lot:

Lysander:	How now, my love? why is your cheek so pale?
	How chance the roses there do fade so fast?
Hermia:	Belike for want of rain; which I could well
	Beteem them from the tempest of my eyes. (4)
Lysander:	Ay me! for aught that I could ever read,
	Could ever hear by tale or history,
	The course of true love never did run smooth;
	But either it was different in blood—
Hermia:	O cross! too high to be enthrall'd to [low]. (9)
Lysander:	Or else misgraffed in respect of years—
Hermia:	O spite! too old to be engag'd to young.
Lysander:	Or else it stood upon the choice of friends—
Hermia:	O hell, to choose love by another's eyes!
Lysander:	Or if there were a sympathy in choice, (14)
	War, death or sickness did lay siege to it, (15)
	Making it momenta[r]y as a sound,
	Swift as a shadow, short as any dream,
	Brief as the lightning in the collied night,
	That, in a spleen, unfolds, both heaven and earth;
	And ere a man hath power to say "Behold!"
	The jaws of darkness do devour it up:
	So quick bright things come to confusion. (I.1)

(Note the interwoven anaphora in lines 9–14, hers starting with *O*, his with *or*.) The lovers could be much briefer, but the world of prosaic brevity is not the one they inhabit; theirs is one of waxing poetic about their plight. (What else are they doing, after all?) Hermia actually performs the act of coining the phrase "the tempest of my eyes" (4) as the most perfect way of talking about her tears. Likewise, Lysander performs the act of personifying *war, death* and *sickness* so he can then attribute to them the verbal phrase, *lay siege* (15). They link themselves to all star-crossed lovers of yore with this histrionic show. Just as a character in a musical can't keep himself from breaking into song, Hermia and Lysander have to not be able to stop themselves.

Exaltation

A shift into heightened language is a tremendous clue to what is going on. Poetic language can signal that a higher plateau of inner life has been reached: an *exaltation* of some sort. When Oedipus, Lear, and Othello realize what they have done, or Don Giovanni finally goes to hell, then death is near, a new sort of life is about to begin, and/or a great truth is finally being faced—and their language soars.

In a musical, the transformation could come when a character falls in love ("She Likes Basketball" from *Promises, Promises*, or "Vanilla Ice Cream" from *She Loves Me*). In the title song from *Cabaret*, Sally Bowles turns into something of a goddess, an almost inhuman incarnation of the decrepit cabaret. (This type of exaltation is *apotheosis*, the elevation from human to god or god-like state.) To help make an exaltation in a straight play effective, think of it as a show-stopping number from a musical. The transformation is conveyed by the sublimity of the language—a character breaking into a spoken aria.

Exaltation can be recognized, too, when a character goes mad. Shakespeare tells us in *A Midsummer Night's Dream*, "The lunatic, lover and poet are of an imagination all compact." (V.1) What all three states of being have in common is more than imagination, however: all three are a little closer to godliness. As Blanche DuBois says when Mitch lights her cigarette and calms her down: "Sometimes there's God so quickly."

Example. What makes *A Streetcar Named Desire* is not what happens, which can be told in two sentences, but *how* it happens—poetically.

When Blanche is finally taken away in the last scene, she does not merely leave, she transforms. Earlier in the scene she tells Stella:

> I can smell the sea air. The rest of my time I'm going to spend on the sea. And when I die, I'm going to die on the sea. You know what I shall die of? I shall die of eating an unwashed grape one day out on the ocean. I will die—with my hand in the hand of some nice-looking ship's doctor, a very young one with a small blond mustache and a big silver watch. "Poor lady," they'll say, "the quinine did her no good. That unwashed grape has transported her soul to heaven." [*The cathedral chimes are heard*] And I'll be buried at sea sewn up in a clean white sack and dropped overboard—at noon—in the blaze of summer—and into an ocean as blue as [*Chimes again*] my first lover's eyes!

The phrase "transported her soul to heaven" suggests an apotheosis. (The chimes help, too.) But she's not there yet. Right now she needs the poetry to restore her illusions and dignity, at least to herself.

Enter the Doctor and Matron who must shatter that dignity. In a heartbeat, the play plummets from the sublime to the base. She resists the stranglehold of the Matron, but then the Doctor plays the part of her gentleman caller and tenderly helps her up, to which she responds with the famous line, "Whoever you are—I have always depended on the kindness of strangers." She has now been transported to her own heaven: that of madness, where a doctor is a gentleman, and strangers are kind.

For the actor playing Blanche, more is warranted than merely losing your mind. As you leave the stage, finally submitting to the Doctor, you become more lyrical, more beautiful, more dignified, more transcendent, more God-filled. You've already been beaten down to earth; now fly up to your own version of heaven, with poetry as your wings.

Throughout the play, Blanche has looked at the world through the eyes of lunatic, lover, and poet. The play succeeds if, by the last scene, the audience does, too.

CHAPTER 8
FROM CASTING TO CLOSING

Rehearsal situations vary in cast size and experience, length of rehearsal time, nature of the script, location of the audience, budget, production values, and technical requirements. It is almost never the case in the professional theater that your process is the focus of rehearsal; you simply have to be able to know how to work—and how to do homework. Experience will help you tailor that homework to complement what is going on in rehearsal, and to bridge the gap between yourself and the role.

During rehearsals and the run, keep honing, expanding, exploring: that way your connections will stay fresh and your character will keep growing.

> **Work on something at all times. Every rehearsal,
> run-through, or performance is an opportunity.**

A short rehearsal period need not prevent you from trying any ideas at all.

Let's trace a rehearsal period from the day you are cast to your last performance, to see how to take advantage of every opportunity, and to keep growing into the role as you confront problems that arise.

EVOLVING THE FORM

Approach to First Rehearsal

Before you meet the rest of the cast you know just about everything the playwright could possibly mean. You have a lot of personal stakes as well. Now it is time to interact with the other players and the director.

The Director

A director is not necessarily an acting coach. Moreover, in short rehearsal periods, there simply may not be time for the lengthy discussion, or hands-on coaching, that some actors crave. At any rate, it's not the director's job. Liv Ullmann once told of being directed by Ingmar Bergman, with whom she had been working for twenty years, so he knew her well. At the first rehearsal of an Ibsen play, he gave her a direction like "Sit in the armchair, and on such-and-such line cross to look out the window for the remainder of the speech." For some mysterious reason, the first time she tried this blocking, her face filled with tears. Now, that's blocking. His job was to come up with the form that would release the inner life; her job would be to perform it each subsequent time as freshly and potently as she had the first time.

A director stages in such a way that solutions to acting questions, like motivation, are there to find, not necessarily to discuss. And sometimes the motivation is clarity for the audience, which may not have been part of your consideration (until now).

Try to be aware of all the concerns a director is coordinating aside from your own. In addition to forging an ensemble, a director creates:

1. a *moral universe,*
2. an *aesthetic universe,* and
3. a *theatrical universe,* that provide
4. the essential way to *tell the story* in
5. an *integrated whole.*

(Think of *moral* here as applying not just to morality, but to *mores:* the set of behavior systems, values, laws, etc.) Some directors impose one of the five elements above at the expense of another; an over-designed aesthetic, for instance, can confuse rather than clarify. But a successful director creates a world where set, costumes, lights, sound, makeup, acting, blocking, and dialogue all work together.

"Act the set" may be a difficult directive for an actor to apprehend, but it is one of the underlying imperatives of a director, whether he says it that way or not, to help achieve the integrated whole. Such a notion may lie behind that note he gave you that you cannot begin to fathom, whether it's (1) "make those crosses parallel and perpendicular to the proscenium," (2) "lift your hand and place it in the door jamb," (3) "keep your elbows away from the sides of your body," or (4) "stand taller and directly under the center of this archway." All of these are notes that colleagues or I have given, respectively:

1. to Theseus's court entering and establishing the rigid formality of Athens in 1.1 of *A Midsummer Night's Dream*;
2. to Frederick joining Desirée in her digs in *A Little Night Music,* full of sexual tension and not knowing whether he belongs there or not;

3. to any number of female players in French farce (here, *A Flea in Her Ear*);
4. to Dracula.

By opening night, all these notes worked from the audience's perspective.

Not only is performance really for the audience, but so is rehearsal, ultimately: and before opening night, *the director is the proxy of the audience.* As you come to inhabit the theatrically-created universe, the blocking should start to feel right.

Blocking

Some directors stage in great detail right away, while others do not block for weeks. I generally prescribe entrances and exits, which to a great extent have been pre-figured with the set designer. Then I see if I can let the actors go from there with the ground rule "feel free to move when you *must.*" This is an idealized point of departure, since every actor applies the rule differently. Some actors will be less in character than others, and some will feel obliged to cross even when they do not really need to. So a director's blocking technique involves its own sort of discrimination, namely: (1) being able to tell when a gesture is spontaneous and right for the character, rather than a case of the actor trying too hard; and (2) being able to give direction that the actor would have found later anyway, when more in character.

The stop-and-go of a blocking rehearsal can be terribly frustrating, since it defers acting concerns for the sake of traffic. Still, exploit every opportunity, including a stop-and-go rehearsal, to work on Connection—not just for yourself, but to help everyone else, too. Ideally Connection, informed by Meaning and Stakes and distilled by Shape, generates the blocking. Get so that you almost never need to look at your script when other characters are talking:

Stay in the scene.

The director has to stage the relationships—what happens *between;* if noses stay down, he can only move actors around like pegs on a board. This is a rehearsal technique at which you simply must become proficient.

Mark your cues, not just your lines, in bright highlighter. Then learn them to know when to glance down for your next line, or, once off-book, when to call for a line. And get off-book as soon as you can—without memorizing *how* you are going to say your lines, of course.

Incidentally, rehearsal etiquette stipulates that until a star is off-script, no one is, until the announced off-book date. This may seem strange if you have only five or ten lines, but think about it for a minute. Everyone's paycheck rests on that star carrying the play. What could be more intimidating than for every rehearsal to demonstrate that the rest of the cast knows their lines better than he knows his? Lurking deep within every great actor is a terrified one: that's part of what makes him great. One goal of the rehearsal period is to turn that vulnerability into something glorious rather than neurotic. All hands contribute to this effort. So with rare exception, which you will have to play by ear, if the star has script in hand, you do too. It's courtesy.

What if the director has the whole show already blocked before the first rehearsal, a situation that some actors decry? Relax: He is only doing his job; he has not done yours. More specifically, he has not pre-solved everything you are supposed to do onstage, merely its form. It is up to you to fill it, see if it can work organically, and make it your own. This is what it means to be an actor, after all. The director may be weeks ahead of you in developing the shape of the play, and may even know your character better than you do—for now.

One conflict that comes up time and again: Actors invariably want to look at each other to connect, while the director needs them looking toward the audience so that they participate, too. When there is enough time, you can spend the first week or two connecting with your eyes, then gradually wean yourself from this habit to include the audience. That is how I try to rehearse with young actors. But if the director needs you to face the audience earlier, stay connected from the gut. If you need more eye contact with that other actor, go out for a beer. (I do not say this facetiously.)

It is wonderful when the director makes you feel respected, safe, and free to discuss anything. But this freedom is not the goal of rehearsal; it is a device to get results. (Heaven forbid I should ever say this aloud in rehearsal, though.) So play by ear whether or not it is advantageous to bring up a concern or indulge a brainstorm. Problems may be more apt to vanish by themselves when left unarticulated.

Throughout rehearsals, then, though it will be particularly difficult during a stop-and-go, try your best to remain relaxed, concentrated, connected, and open.

Work-Through

Breaking the Blocking

The primary goal of a work-through is to perfect the blocking whether collaborating or streamlining, polishing what's already been tried, or testing out something new. At this point in the rehearsal process, you expressly want to apply the principle: If it ain't broke, break it (p. 138). Depending on how protected your creative environment is, you can break it in safety and with abandon. Sometimes a work-through's goal is expressly to indulge that brainstorm you had.

But breaking the blocking does not mean that you try to break it because you think you have to, you do not trust it, or you want to assert your creativity. Best if it is your character who breaks it, to better attain his objective, stay truer to his passions and peeves, and the like. If you are not yet fully in character (e.g., still on book) there is little point in deviating from current blocking.

So start the work-through by seeing if the scene can work through, regenerating the blocking from listening, reacting, and playing actions, rather than by rote. If a new gesture emerges naturally, very likely your character has been compelled organically to break the blocking. This does not mean that the new gesture is better, though it may be. Director and actors reassess the moment to see if some sort of adjustment is required, either internal or external. Internal adjustments include things like psychological choices, while external ones refer to crosses, line delivery, or pace. A typical reassessment might involve some circumstance the actor has forgotten that his character would remember. I might tell an actor, "Remember, Hedda, that though you hate Mrs. Elvsted, you mustn't let her know that." Frequently, the actor simply needs to be reminded: "Remember the audience."

When the playwright is alive she may even change a line. I would hesitate to ask her to do so, however; not only does that betray a lack of faith in her craft, it also suggests that you can't fill the line that she has so painstakingly chosen. (See Problems that Defy Analysis, p. 57.) Besides, if it really is not the best one possible, your filling it thoroughly is a good way to make that evident.

Likewise, avoid undermining staging before you even try it, just because it does not yet feel right. A rehearsal is generally most effective when it builds on previous ones, not when it discards them; it typically takes three tries before any staging starts to gel, anyway.

And depending on the director, her blocking may have to be treated as sacrosanct as the text—almost certainly if you are an understudy or cast replacement going into a show after opening night. Of course, in a relaxed and friendly rehearsal environment, these lines are crossed all the time. But it helps to know what those lines are: text is the province of the playwright; blocking, that of the director.

As rehearsals progress, instinct starts to take over, and staging becomes fuller and more natural. You start to play the very life of the play.

Letting the Blocking Gel

Some directors—and great ones, too—treat the original staging as immutable, never changing a cross, devoting rehearsals to perfecting their form rather than modifying it. Remember that the designers and crew—even the producer—may need to see a full run-through by the end of the first week. It is everyone's job to get that run-through ready. Do not be miffed; do your job and make the staging work. To help you, trust the blocking as if it will be the most appropriate gesture for your character in the moment, even though you have yet to fully experience that moment.

As opening night approaches, you cannot necessarily explore changes, even in a flexible environment. Sure, the artist's temperament always struggles to perfect the form, but consistency engenders a confidence that lets a scene sizzle that much more when the audience shows up. I hesitate to use the word *frozen* for blocking that is in the book for good; nevertheless, the form must be set enough to allow the performance to gel. An indulgent director is not necessarily a good one: keeping actors on track may actually protect them from straying unproductively.

What if you get a director who is both untalented and a tyrant? Then I am not sure I can help you. You may have cause to summon more of your acting skills than anyone might be aware of.[21] Still, just as you hope your director will be able to get the best possible performance out of you, so do you want to enlist all your diplomacy to get the most out of him. He still serves as the eye of the audience, after all. Use tact if you want to keep your job.

Several actors have suggested evoking "actors' eccentricity" when given senseless staging: they say "thank you" cooperatively, do what they need to, and hope that the director never notices. Should he repeat his note, they are prepared with a cheerful, "Oh, that's what you meant." You be the judge of how far you can go before you might be replaced; stars can play the eccentric more easily than interns. But this tactic is a drastic measure, not a point of departure. Be careful not to scorn staging that may simply be ahead of you.

It's a funny business, dealing with fragile egos. But *the art of working with people* is *the art of the theater.*

At long last the blocking comes out the same each time: the process of developing it is essentially done, and the structure is set. This means that when the lighting designer watches a run-through, she will see, for the most part, the same traffic the audience will see. It does not necessarily mean that no changes are allowed ever again, however, for inspiration may yet drop in. There still may be a way to make the staging smoother or more exciting: find it if you can. The occasional show undergoes revision even after opening.

Late Rehearsals: Not Acting

The next week or so of rehearsal is both terrifying and wonderful. The script is out of your hands. Yikes. You know your lines, cues, and blocking, but not too well. You actually have to listen in order to come up with your next line or bit of staging. You quite naturally go through the scene as if for the first time, your mental gears having to turn as your character's.

This is when acting is easy—that is, not acting is easy. The hard part comes later, in remembering and simulating what this not acting was like even after a hundred performances.

Do not be surprised if the first run-through off-script feels absolutely horrible. It always does. Either nothing feels natural, or it takes five hours to get through. So what? It is nearly impossible to serve both pace and the organic at once: work on one thing at a time. The baby has just been born; it will take a while for it to learn to walk.

Pace

As you approach opening night, the pace you strive for will involve not just speed, but getting your character to the point where he must operate that quickly. Try to proceed as fast as your character must and your audience can. Be particularly aware of the second of these parameters. In many productions, actors simply speak too rapidly to be understood, or too slowly to be interesting. Finding the balance is no small accomplishment.

Especially in a pre-Ibsen play, words are the most expressive conveyor of substance and spirit. Remember, nonverbal communication is far more effective when it does not stop the words, but accompanies, colors, and propels them. And theatrical pace entails more than just speed; it involves *relentlessness*, and *variety* in color and tempo, to take the audience through a series of delights and thrills.

Generally, I recommend that pace become an express goal of rehearsal only once all the other aspects of acting are in place. If you go too fast when you're not really anchored to the text, like a rickety roller coaster, you are headed for derailment. One exception to this principle is when your character is partly defined by a certain quickness (with farces, pace is often essential to making the scene work at all). Another is when the producer or director needs to see a run-through early in the rehearsal process, obliging you to "put out" and sacrifice other qualities for some modicum of pace. Do not fret; you will get back to those other qualities later. But for the most part:

Pace is the final ingredient.

(Review also discussions of Pauses, Discursive Speech, and Thought Groups, pp. 47-55; RARE, pp. 100-102; and Punctuation, pp. 185-187, 201.)

The Principle of *Letting*

There comes a point at rehearsals when it's time to stop working and start playing: trust your technique. If you don't give your technique the chance to hold you up, it never will.

Let—*rather than* make—*it happen.*

This is not an easy principle to adhere to. Clearly you need a rehearsal environment that makes you feel safe to strive and free to fail. After all, only when your character might fail is real suspense generated. Acting well does not mean merely reproducing what you have rehearsed; rather, rehearsing well means setting up circumstances that compel your character to take action for the first time . . . in roughly the same way you did yesterday.

In acting class, you often find yourself working a scene for results, rather than trusting that your previous choices (or something better) will simply emerge. A similar phenomenon takes place in professional theater: you do not want the director to think you cannot retain blocking, so you repeat it faithfully to make sure you are not fired. This is a difficult consideration to balance. But remember that a scene is more than the sum of its words and blocking: its most important aspect is the something else it conveys. So being excessively result-oriented is not a good idea. Play the action anew, and let words and blocking reoccur because they have to. The trick, of course, is to get them to have to.

THE RUN

The night the audience arrives, the rehearsal cocoon is shattered. Your task is to simulate that aura of comfort and safety even now that the audience is present, to act with the same abandon you enjoyed during rehearsals, and even to invite the audience to join you inside the cocoon. You can, because the audience is your friend. If you let them into your play, they will help you automatically by providing a dose of spontaneity and unpredictability.

A pinch of unpredictability is the spice of performance.

But unpredictability should not be misconstrued as a license for sloppiness.

In fact, playing the audience with abandon requires more thorough rehearsal and more intense concentration; since they have not rehearsed, their reactions could actually throw you off. Stay relaxed. Concentrate. For a second or two you may have to rely on rote to take you to the next moment. Because you know that the form has worked, though, you can trust it, and soon get back in the scene. Your well-rehearsed lines and blocking let you act with both confidence and abandon.

To keep your work fresh over the run, keep your play fresh. The form may not be free, but what you do with and within it *is*. Much like the first rehearsal, every performance is about having not just a lot of answers, but also a slew of questions. Determine a creative agenda for each time you walk on that stage.

With a one- or two-week rehearsal period, you may barely have gotten the show blocked when the audience arrives; your stage manager may forbid you to change anything. Still, even after performances have begun, at least keep finding motivations for every bit of staging. As the run continues, get more inventive in giving yourself a specific creative agenda for each performance. Working on a physical aspect might open up new inner life, and vice versa. You may suddenly realize how capricious your character must be if you try something as small as acting with your toes.

The benefit of a long run is that you can truly forget the form and generate it anew. The danger is that you may take it for granted and simply repeat it by rote, losing the tingle of danger that it might not happen. Beware of falling into automatic pilot.

What if the other actor falls into automatic pilot? Unless the show calls for improvisation, keeping the performance fresh does not mean altering the blocking at will, which would throw off the other actors—and you want to throw them *on,* so to speak.

At a sit-down reading of a new play I attended, the heroine had to play an intimate scene with an inexperienced actor sitting next to her, who kept her nose in the script the whole time. So the heroine snapped her fingers under the novice's nose (in character, with appropriate dialogue) to get it out of her manuscript. That young actor woke up, and the scene started to sizzle.

The point was not to add the gesture to the permanent blocking (there was no blocking in the reading, anyway); it was to jump-start the scene. Your intent is to revitalize the form, not change it.

To wake up a scene, try any of the following ideas.

To keep your performance fresh:
- *try to establish eye contact with the other actor*
- *say a line with a radically different reading or gesture*
- *percuss (snapping, clapping, rolling fingers, hitting an object) differently*
- *squeeze a fellow actor's arm a little tighter*
- *reassess and strengthen objectives*
- *engage brighter images and bolder secrets*
- *re-read the play to discover something new (that was there all along)*
- *try out, subtly, a new physical, facial, or vocal adjustment*
- *hide a secret object in your pocket*
- *prep the pre-beat scene in the wings with the actor you enter with (improvising the dialogue offstage)*
- *do jumping jacks in the wings before entering*

As you develop your personal arsenal of devices, you will notice your fellow actors' performances adjusting slightly to your new choices. It's the first time every time.

The most important technique of all, of course, is to stay in the moment without knowing what is going to happen in the next moment; in other words, truly

- *listen*

to your fellow actors and to the audience. There is ample food to nourish the freshness of your performance, if only you look up, connect, and relish what is right in front of you.

Once you know how to work—and play—there is nothing like a long run for developing your theatrical instinct if, as you play the audience, you also accept what they give back to you. By acting on each other, actors and spectators give new life to each other. This communion of artist and audience promotes a continual replenishing of the soul of Mankind by offering not just a glimpse into a mirror of what the world is, but also a vision through a window of what it could be. This common insight strengthens the bonds that unite us all. To get the audience to laugh together, cry together, feel together, think together, realize the truth together, hope together, change together—that is the charge of the theater.

Together is the point. It is what makes the Theater our last best hope.

APPENDIX I
TEXTS USED IN THIS BOOK

AS YOU LIKE IT

Jaques's Seven Ages Speech
Act II, scene 7

> All the world's a stage,
> And all the men and women merely players:
> They have their exits and their entrances;
> And one man in his time plays many parts,
> His acts being seven ages. At first the infant,
> Mewling and puking in the nurse's arms.
> Then the whining school-boy, with his satchel
> And shining morning face, creeping like snail
> Unwillingly to school. And then the lover,
> Sighing like furnace, with a woeful ballad
> Made to his mistress' eyebrow. Then a soldier,
> Full of strange oaths, and bearded like the pard,
> Jealous in honour, sudden and quick in quarrel,
> Seeking the bubble reputation
> Even in the cannon's mouth. And then the justice,
> In fair round belly with good capon lined,
> With eyes severe and beard of formal cut,
> Full of wise saws and modern instances;
> And so he plays his part. The sixth age shifts
> Into the lean and slipper'd pantaloon,
> With spectacles on nose and pouch on side,
> His youthful hose, well saved, a world too wide
> For his shrunk shank; and his big manly voice,
> Turning again toward childish treble, pipes
> And whistles in his sound. Last scene of all,
> That ends this strange eventful history,
> Is second childishness and mere oblivion,
> Sans teeth, sans eyes, sans taste, sans every thing.

HENRY V

Chorus' Prologue
"O for a Muse of Fire"

O for a Muse of fire, that would ascend
The brightest heaven of invention,
A kingdom for a stage, princes to act
And monarchs to behold the swelling scene!
Then should the warlike Harry, like himself,
Assume the port of Mars; and at his heels,
Leash'd in like hounds, should famine, sword and fire
Crouch for employment. But pardon, gentles all,
The flat unraisèd spirits that have dared
On this unworthy scaffold to bring forth
So great an object: can this cockpit hold
The vasty fields of France? or may we cram
Within this wooden O the very casques
That did affright the air at Agincourt?
O, pardon! since a crooked figure may
Attest in little place a million;
And let us, ciphers to this great accompt,
On your imaginary forces work.
Suppose within the girdle of these walls
Are now confined two mighty monarchies,
Whose high uprearèd and abutting fronts
The perilous narrow ocean parts asunder:
Piece out our imperfections with your thoughts;
Into a thousand parts divide one man,
And make imaginary puissance;
Think, when we talk of horses, that you see them
Printing their proud hoofs i' the receiving earth;
For 'tis your thoughts that now must deck our kings,
Carry them here and there; jumping o'er times,
Turning th'accomplishment of many years
Into an hour-glass: for the which supply,
Admit me Chorus to this history;
Who prologue-like your humble patience pray,
Gently to hear, kindly to judge, our play.

APPENDIX II
THE WARM-UP

Disclaimer: Since I have not met you, I cannot take responsibility for introducing you to the actor's warm-up. What follows is but a reminder of its essentials, which you should already know from your training. If you have never worked with movement and voice specialists, then do get that training; if these exercises are done incorrectly, you can hurt yourself.

I cannot overstress the importance of a full physical, vocal, facial, relaxation, and spiritual warm-up before every rehearsal and performance. To perform to the max you must be flexed and lubricated to the max. Moreover, when you do not warm up (as you may have noticed), you have to work harder just to be interesting. You could have the most marvelous thoughts and emotions inside you, and yet nothing will read—at least, not effortlessly.

Never show up tired or unprepared. Design your daily regimen to maximize alertness and flexibility. This does not mean you can never go out for a beer after an evening performance; but if you have a 9:00 a.m. call, you will not want to have more than one beer. Or else go and be a film actor, where you typically get to the set by 6:00 a.m. just to wait.

Every warm-up, even a brief one, should encompass certain basics. Remember to breathe a lot when stretching to get the maximum amount of oxygen to the various parts of your body.

Every stretch has a proper rhythm of inhaling and exhaling:
Exhale with each stretching motion, inhale with each relaxing
motion. But don't hold your breath while holding the stretch:
keep breathing.

THE MINIMUM WARM-UP

Physical Stretching

In stretching, *go to the point of pain, but not beyond*. So be very gentle at first. If you do your physical stretching right after waking up in the morning, start with your neck, gently moving your head to the right, left, back, and front as far as it will go without hurting yourself. Then roll it around clockwise, then counterclockwise, flexing as far as you can. Don't forget to breathe a lot. Best to exhale on a sound, *mmm, fff,* or *sss,* to monitor your breathing.

All parts of the body are connected to the spine, so the required portion of your physical warmup is to flex, twist, and roll your spine.

Flex the Spine

Stand up straight, feet shoulder-width apart in second position. Now, reach with your right arm as far to the right as you can go. Make sure you are not leaning forward or backward, but that your body remains on a single plane. Hold the stretch for a few seconds, exhale a few times, then come back. Then reach further, pulling that right arm out even more with your left hand. Then lift both arms above your head to return to center, and change directions. Do this at least three or four times—or minutes, if necessary—on each side.

Twist the Spine

Version A. Stand up straight, feet shoulder-width apart. Palms facing each other, let the fingertips of each hand touch the wrist of the other, bending your arms at the elbows to do this. Then clasp the fingers of your left hand with the fingers of your right hand, bending your knuckles. Raise both arms to shoulder height. Now rotate from your waist, twisting to the right as far as you think you can go; at the same time, turn your head to the left. Hold the stretch, and then pull yourself around with your right hand even further—just a bit. Then back to center, and invert your hands to repeat the twist to the left, head turning to the right. Repeat a few times in each direction, going a little further each time.

Version B. There are corollary exercises to do on a bare floor, which use gravity to work out the kinks in your back gently. As long as you stretch only to the point of pain, you should be fine.

First, lie on your back with a pillow under your neck. Let your entire back sink into the floor, so no part of it is raised. Let your arms fall down by your side. Then, lift your knees as close to your chin as they can go. Open up your arms to "snow angel" position. Then turn your head to your right as you let your legs swing to your left. Return both head and legs to center and repeat, inverted.

You can vary this with (1) legs straight, extended out at a right angle from your body, or (2) your top leg straight and your bottom leg bent. Always breathe with each stretch, and return to center before changing directions.

Since this is a popular stretch, you should have no trouble finding a fellow actor (or movement specialist) to demonstrate it for you and check your spine in places you cannot.

Roll the Spine

Version A. The standing version of this exercise requires someone to help you your first time through it, because you cannot reach the knots in your own spine to feel for and massage them.

To prep: Stand up straight, arms down by your side, weight on the balls of your feet, which are shoulder-width apart. To help simulate this quickly to start, try standing on tiptoe; reach up in the air as high as you can (breathe!), and then let your heels drop back to the ground, keeping your weight over the balls of your feet. Then slowly let your arms fall to the side.

One vertebra at a time, you are going to roll down your spine, all the way to bending at your ankles. First, make sure your head is sitting on top of your spinal column. Flexing only at the neck, let your chin touch your chest, then lift your head up and back as far as you can go, then back down and up a few times. (Imagine the Tin Woodman treated with the oil can.) Make sure you flex only at the neck, keeping your spine in a straight line. Then, let your head—only your head—hang as far down as possible (directly down, not outward). Have a partner come and try to lift your head; it should be dead weight if you are really not holding it up.

Then, one vertebra at a time, descend, letting your head fall closer to your knees. Have your partner watch that you do not drop two vertebrae at a time. Go back and forth over sections of your spine that need to be unstuck. If you have knots, your partner should work them out (gently but firmly) with fingers or knuckles. Shoulders should sag directly down, not be held up, forward, or back.

You are not in a hurry to roll your spine all the way down. Your goal is to find and massage those knots so your spine is aligned and safe. Make sure that your spine stays totally aligned below the vertebra you are on at the moment. You should be standing erect except for the head, at first, and then except the head and one vertebra, then the head and two vertebrae, and so on down.

Once all the vertebrae have been rolled, bend at the waist, then knees, then ankles, arms loose and drooping. There is no need to keep your knees locked in straight position (that is another exercise entirely). Some people's arms will droop down as far as the floor, their heads below their knees; others' hands may dangle only as far as their knees.

Finally you have arrived all the way down, your spine totally rolled, and you are thoroughly relaxed with your weight still over the balls of your feet, breathing freely and fully. Now, slowly again, one vertebra at a time, you are going to reverse direction and stand back up. First, engage your ankles. Second, your knees. Third, put your hips on top of your legs.

Then, one at a time, pile each vertebra on top of each lower one until only your head rests on your chest, and then, gently, lift your head up to sit on top of your spinal column. Take your time. You will feel as if your head could keep going up to the sky. You may not be able to resist standing on tiptoe; do so. You may feel your pelvis tuck under you (which is where it should have been all along). Then let your heels come back down to the floor. Now your center of gravity lies over the balls of your feet. Remember this position: it means you are ready to act.

I recommend several spine rolls in your warm-up; each one will get easier as you work out the kinks in your back. The first time you do this spine roll (with a coach), it takes a good while. You may be surprised to discover how much tension the spine carries.

During a performance, many actors stand on tiptoe and reach skyward to help retuck their pelvises and realign their spines while waiting in the wings for their next entrance. You can, too.

Version B. If you do not have a partner but you have enough room, then you can do a corollary version on the floor. First, prep your back with a few gentle flexes and twists; if you start off too abruptly, you could hurt yourself. You may need a pillow under your neck.

Lie on your back, knees raised. With your hands by your ears (wrists flexed, fingers toward your waist), place your palms and feet on the floor. Then gently push your body up off the floor; gradually raise it until your stomach is in the air as far as it can go. Then, from your neck to your hips, let your vertebrae slowly sink into the floor one at a time, breathing deeply as you go. Repeat a few times.

Facial Stretch

These exercises are so often neglected, but so easy to do on the way to rehearsal. Just stretch out your face. In all sorts of directions. Think of it as pushing against a big boulder, making it as fat as you can. Then think of it as a wrinkled up raisin. Make it long and narrow, then short. Move it all to the right, then all to the left, then up, then down. Open your mouth wide, then wriggle it in various ways.

Then try engaging your plastic face while saying some text out loud. It may feel like mugging, but it is only an exercise. The trick is to get all your facial muscles relaxed and flexed so that they will convey your inner life effortlessly.

Vocal Warm-up

There are lots of detailed vocal exercises for you to check out, especially when working on a particular speech or song. Voice training gets you to support your breath from your diaphragm and produce sound in one continuous stream without any constraint in your throat. If you have never taken a voice class, you need to learn how to do this.

The voice box region, the back of the mouth, the throat, and the trachea are receptacles for tension that must be eliminated in order for you to release sound effectively onstage. It should be as if there were a pump (your diaphragm) and a ping-pong ball floating on top of a jet stream, and you send that ball out of your face (the sound you emit)—but there is no apparatus in between. Practice daily and it should become your natural means of producing sound.

Stretch your soft palate: Pretend to swallow a hard-boiled egg several times. The first time you do this, you will note how closed you normally keep your windpipe, as if to protect your insides from outside influences. To open it up makes us feel more vulnerable—because we are.

Vocal production can be quickly enhanced by repeating certain sounds over and over. Avoid monitoring whether you are producing sound correctly, which sends your focus, and hence the sound, back to yourself. To help alleviate this tendency:

- *Always have a particular person or point in the distance that you are talking to. If your vocal warm-up is with the ensemble,* then really talk to each other.
- *Always have something you are trying to communicate when you are using nonsense syllables.*

Though not every vocal coach will emphasize these principles, they are the secret to a doubly effective vocal warm-up, whether in speech or song. During the vocal warm-up you can tap your deepest, darkest secret, and reveal it even to your worst enemy, and because all you are saying is "ha ha ha" he need never know. Then, when you are playing Phaedra or Lear, you can be just as vulnerable and full, and still have your maximum vocal capacity at your disposal.

It is one thing to produce sound correctly when you are thinking of producing sound correctly; it is another when your heart is broken and you are crying or howling. The actor must be able to do the latter: you can't get "choked up" literally if you have to speak.

Bbbb: To practice avoiding the throat while producing sound, put your lips together and, supporting from your diaphragm, try a Bronx cheer without the tongue, idling like an electric lawn mower, *bbbb*. You'll find you won't be able to sustain the sound unless your diaphragm is engaged. Then, gradually open your lips to produce an *ah* sound, maintaining the same production as your *bbbb* sound.

Engage the diaphragm: Try the sounds *huh, ha, heh,* and *hey* over and over. Make sure the sound starts from your diaphragm. If you've done the *Bbbb* exercise, you should be able to feel when your diaphragm supports you properly.

Loosen your lower jaw: Jiggle your jaw a little with your hand to make sure that there is no tension there. Then let your jaw drop as you say *mah* or *my* over and over.

Send the sound out through your eyes: Try the syllables *nay* and *neh*. Feel free to sound acerbically nasal (still using the diaphragm). Point the sound as if you were aiming a dagger, hurling a javelin, or blowing a kiss to a distant point. This helps to ensure that you are using all the resonating chambers in your head. Phyllis Curtin (the singer and educator) once said to me, "sing through your eyes," for then you sing from your soul, and to someone or something you see. It makes all the difference when speaking, too.

Get to maximum breath: There are various ways to do this. If you are rehearsing a musical, certain singing exercises get you to maximum, each requiring more breath than the last.

Sing up and down five notes of the major scale, with one breath, on *la*.

Then go up and down the same five notes twice on one breath, then three times, and so on until you can go no further. Each time you inhale, use more breath than the last time.

When inhaling, do not think of taking in air, but of letting it in. Any asthmatic knows that if you try too hard to take a breath, you gag. What you want to do during your warm-up is increase your capacity for air; then when exhaling, you create a vacuum that instantly fills with air all by itself when you open the valve. If someone sees your shoulders rising when you inhale, you are working too hard. The lungs should expand outward, not the shoulders upward.

Alternatively, try exhaling on a sound with lips almost together, like *fff, sss, ththth,* or *bbb,* as long as you can—so long that you have to bend over to squeeze out more air. Have a friend gently push out the last traces. Then, simply release your valve to let the air back in. You will notice that a whole lot of air will come rushing in immediately all by itself. Repeat, expanding your capacity each time.

> ### *The trick to inhaling is to work on the exhaling;*
> ### *the inhaling takes care of itself.*

Finally, take a long, long speech and try it all on one breath—not as fast as you can, but with sensible phrasing.

Diction: It helps if you do a facial warm-up before you proceed to diction exercises. Take any speech from the play you are rehearsing and try over-enunciating every consonant—to the point where some of the muscles around your mouth, and your jaw, feel a little sore. No pain, no gain. This is not a psychological exercise: physically over-enunciate.

Try some tongue twisters, like Peter Piper. Collect tongue twisters to practice on your way to the theater when time is short.

Relaxation

I have found greater value in relaxation coming last in your warm-up, rather than first, so that you are already flexed, stretched, and at maximum breath. After your physical warm-up, then, try to steal at least a few minutes to lie down on your back with your eyes closed. Let sound out as you exhale. As you inhale, feel your back pressing into the floor and your ribcage expand. Try to let your mind empty of the day's vicissitudes. Breathe deeply, but don't work on taking more breath.

Relaxation entails the mental as well as the physical, so next, get spiritually centered: calm, together, connected, present. You will know what these words mean when you achieve them.

Your own training may have provided you with other relaxation exercises. Some actors meditate, and time their sessions around rehearsal or performance to best advantage, either right before, or a few hours earlier, or whatever works for them. This is because relaxation is as important as concentration onstage, and they always go together. If you are not relaxed, your instincts will never be engaged automatically, and no mystery is possible, only a reproduction of yesterday's performance.

APPENDIX III
LISTS AND MENUS

SOURCES OF ACTOR INFORMATION

Recall the list of sources from which an actor gleans information for his character (see chapter 2, pp. 32-34). For your reference, here is the comprehensive list:

What the play does mean:
- *what your character says;*
- *what your character does;*
- *what other characters say;*
- *what the playwright says;*
- *what the playwright tells you to go find out.*

What the play might mean:
- *what you happen to find out;*
- *what the playwright hints at;*
- *how your character says what he says (language);*
- *what your character does not say (silence) . . .*
- *. . . until later (delayed text);*
- *what your character knows;*
- *when your character finds out, decides or realizes;*

What the play means to you (Stakes):
- *what your character wants and how badly;*
- *what the playwright wants;*
- *what the "play" wants;*
- *what the production wants;*
- *what the ensemble wants;*
- *what the director wants;*
- *what you want.*

What the audience came for:
- *what the audience wants;*
- *what the audience needs;*
- *what the audience can stand; that is,*
- *what you can get away with.*

What your instinct tells you:
- *what you know about human nature;*
- *how a play works (dramatic craft);*
- *whatever works.*

Remember, though, that the freedom to explore whatever works requires a readiness to acknowledge what does not work; just because an idea is "cool" does not mean that you have gotten away with it.

SHAPING YOUR PERFORMANCE

To be a compelling storyteller, keep the audience involved. To help you accomplish this:

- *Identify the French scenes and find the event of each.*
- *Determine what kind of event it is:*
  - *If dramatic, make sure it changes at least one of the characters.*
  - *If thematic, make it act on the audience.*
- *To generate momentum, evoke:*
  - *Suspense about what is going to happen, or*
  - *Wonder about why, how, or where.*
- *Take the audience through the beginning, middle, and end of all phrases, from speeches and gestures to the entire through-line.*
- *Distinguish every moment from every other one.*
- *Render each moment so that it leads inevitably to the next.*
- *Find how the dramatic and thematic arches are actually one.*
- *Make rhetoric active.*
- *Entertain.*

THEATRICS

Some theatrics will be dictated by the text ("Lights, please!"); others may involve design and technical effects, casting choices, or result from the director's theatrical staging with the ensemble. Yet it's possible for even a lone actor to try a few of the following ideas, and let the director see how they work.

An actor can:
- *face the audience or talk to them directly even while addressing someone else*

- **ask for a blatant response from the audience**
- **gesture to the audience:** *"shh" or "keep clapping"*
- **address the audience as some other group:** *a church congregation, a jury*
- **enter from or exit through the audience**
- **play (sit or stand) in the audience**
- **play with the audience** *(as in children's theater)*
- **turn your back to the audience**
- **exit and enter to the wings while talking, bleeding the scene on and off stage** *(which extends the theatrical universe into the wings)*
- **walk through a previously established wall**
- **break through the fourth wall**
- **sit at the edge of the stage**
- **lean against the proscenium arch**
- **open a door or window (that is not really there)**
- **deal with an object on the fourth wall, inviting the audience to see it**
- **repeat a piece of business to call attention to it as business**
- **suddenly overact:** *e.g., physicalize more than you have to*
- **move in slow motion**
- **use the curtain as something in the play**
- **treat one prop as something else:** *coat tree = elm tree, chair = bush*
- **treat a prop or set piece in a suddenly new way:** *like suddenly lifting the heavy boulder that is really papier-mâché*
- **react to, or instigate, a light or sound cue** (Our Town)

The ensemble of actors can:
- **be introduced before characters are** (Rent, Kentucky Cycle)
- **stay onstage to witness scenes they are not in**
- **be blatantly miscast:** *as animals* (Equus), *characters of the opposite sex* (Cloud Nine, The Club), *non-humans (children's theater), even set pieces*
- **be blatantly multicast, one actor playing many roles or several actors playing the same role** (Come Back to the Five & Dime, Jimmy Dean, Jimmy Dean)
- **play themselves, or be called by their own names:** Godspell, *where only Jesus and Judas have character names*
- **generate sounds and other technical effects visibly:** *Eliza walking on a frozen river—a sheet—in (Uncle Tom's Cabin) segment from* The King and I
- **wear masks**

- **wear costumes, or parts of costumes, that their characters would not:** *the entire company in leotards or sneakers*
- **change costumes in full view of audience**
- **execute set changes visibly**
- **act out a story narrated by one character**

The staging or script can also incorporate:
- **a chorus**
- **direct address:** *narration, asides, soliloquies, commentary, or other choric functions like introducing the next scene* (Nicholas Nickleby) *or titling it* (Chicago, Threepenny Opera, *burlesque placard*)
- **voice-over** *(miked or not) or* **thought-balloons**
- **rhyme**
- **song and dance** *(all musical theater uses theatrics)*
- **acrobatics**
- **mime**
- **sudden changes of venue:** *flashback, montage, split-screen action, or any kind of memory or stream-of-consciousness transition*
- **sound, musical scoring, or surrealistic lighting to accompany scenes**

Once you have explored and exhausted the above possibilities during your rehearsal process, and thrown away what does not help tell the story, your work is done. Now go out and play!

ENDNOTES

Introduction

1. Tony Kushner *(Angels in America)*, Elizabeth Egloff *(The Swan)*, and Craig Lucas *(Prelude to a Kiss)*.

2. E.H. Gombrich, *The Story of Art* (New York: Phaidon Press Limited, 1978), p. 4.

Chapter One

3. John Ayto, *Dictionary of Word Origins* (New York: Little, Brown and Company, 1990).

4. Citations from *The Madwoman of Chaillot* are from the Maurice Valency adaptation.

5. Constantin Stanislavski, *Creating A Role* (New York: Theatre Arts, 1961), p. 255.

6. From *3 Plays by Ibsen* (New York: Dell Publishing, 1958), pp. 38 ff. Translator unaccredited.

Chapter Two

7. The use of brackets around text suggests words that are not actually the author's but the translator's or editor's. But other translations feature these same two bracketed pauses, so it's likely that Chekhov himself called for them.

8. *American Heritage Dictionary*.

Chapter Three

9. I happened to see this production the night Margaret Hall went on for Nancy Marchand.

Chapter Four

10. Constantin Stanislavski, *An Actor Prepares* (New York: Theater Arts, 1936), ch. 5, sec. 5, pp. 77ff.

11. Leonard Bernstein's phrase, I am told.

Chapter Five

12. Richard Wilbur translation.

13. I am indebted to Maria Aitken's video on Restoration Comedy performance for her slalom image, although I use it differently here.

14. *American Heritage Dictionary.*

Chapter Six

15. Judith Weston's excellent book, *Directing Actors: Creating Memorable Performances for Film and Television* (Studio City, CA: Michael Wiese Productions, 1996) is geared primarily toward on-camera work, but I recommend it if only for the appendices in which she lists action verbs.

16. National Public Radio, Morning Edition, June 18, 1999.

17. See Gavin Lambert, *GWTW: The Making of Gone with the Wind* (Boston-Toronto: Little, Brown and Company, 1973), p. 94.

Chapter Seven

18. William Strunk, Jr. and E. B. White, *The Elements of Style* (New York: Macmillan Publishing Co., Inc., Third Edition, 1979), p. 68.

19. With indebtedness again to Maria Aitken's video on Restoration Comedy performance, although this is an age-old technique.

20. Robert Cohen, in his fine book *Acting in Shakespeare* (Mountain View, CA: Mayfield Publishing Company, 1991), suggests that the semi-colon requires a caesura: ". . . *that* is the question." I do not think that a semi-colon *requires* a caesura, nor that you must land on the next syllable with a stress, but that you have a choice. Cicely Berry, voice coach for the Royal Shakespeare Company, agrees with me in her equally fine book, *The Actor and the Text* (New York: Applause Theatre & Cinema Books, 1992), p. 232. But needless to say, this line is so rich that many interpretations are possible—and justifiable.

Chapter Eight

21. If physical safety is compromised, however, do not be craven. The adage "the show must go on" is superseded by the one that says *life* must go on. By all means, find a way to speak up. First go to the person at the root of the problem. If no redress is offered, keep going up the line to his superior and then his superior's superior. Non-profits may be financially liable for damages that result from an accident; that could shut a theater down. Actor ≠ victim!

SOURCES

American Heritage Dictionary. New York: American Heritage Publishing Company, 1975.

Anonymous. *The Diamond Sutra* from *Sacred Texts of the World: A Universal Anthology*. Ninian Smart and Richard D. Hecht, eds. New York: Crossroad Publishing Company, 1982.

Anouilh, Jean. *Antigone* in *Jean Anouilh (Five Plays) Vol. I*. New York: Hill and Wang, 1958.

Aristotle. *The Poetics*. Chicago: University of Chicago Press, 1999.

Ayto, John. *Dictionary of Word Origins*. New York: Little, Brown and Company, 1990.

Beaumarchais. *The Barber of Seville* in *The Chief European Dramatists*. Brander Matthews, ed. New York: Houghton Mifflin Company, 1916.

Beckett, Samuel. *Waiting for Godot*. New York: Grove Press, 1954.

Berry, Cicely. *The Actor and the Text*. New York: Applause Books, 1992.

Camus, Albert. *The Myth of Sisyphus and other Essays*. Justin O'Brien, trans. New York: Random House/Vintage Books, 1955.

Chekhov, Anton. *The Seagull* in *Four Great Plays by Chekhov*. Translator unaccredited. New York: Bantam Books, 1958.

Chekhov, Anton. *Uncle Vanya* in *The Oxford Chekhov*. Ronald Hingley, trans. New York: Oxford University Press, 1964.

Churchill, Caryl. *Cloud Nine*. New York: Samuel French, 1979.

Cohen, Robert. *Acting in Shakespeare*. Mountain View, CA: Mayfield Publishing Company, 1991.

Congreve, William. *The Way of the World* in *Cavalcade of Comedy*. Louis Kronenberger, ed. New York: Simon and Schuster, 1953.

Edgar, David. *The Life and Adventures of Nicholas Nickleby* in *Plays: 2*. London: Methuen Drama, 1990.

Genêt, Jean. *The Balcony* in *Seven Plays of the Modern Theater*. New York: Grove Press, 1962.

Giraudoux, Jean. *The Madwoman of Chaillot*. Maurice Valency, adapt. New York: Random House, 1947.

Gogol, Nikolay. *The Inspector General* in *Great Russian Plays* (see Turgenev).

Gombrich, E. H. *The Story of Art*. New York: Phaidon Press Limited, 1978.

Goodrich, Frances and Albert Hackett. *The Diary of Anne Frank*. New York: Dramatists Play Service, 1986.

Hammerstein II, Oscar and Richard Rodgers. *6 Plays by Rodgers and Hammerstein*. New York: Random House, 1951.

Hellman, Lillian. *The Little Foxes* in *The Collected Plays*. Boston: Little, Brown and Company, 1972.

Ibsen, Henrik. *3 Plays by Ibsen*. Translator unaccredited. New York: Dell Publishing, 1958.

Inge, William. *Bus Stop*. New York: Random House, 1955.

Inge, William. *Picnic*. New York: Bantam Books, 1953.

Ionesco, Eugene. *Jack or the Submission* in *Four Plays*. Donald M. Allen, trans. New York: Grove Press, 1958.

Ionesco, Eugene. *The Future is in Eggs* in *Rhinoceros and Other Plays*. Derek Prouse, trans. New York: Grove Press, 1960.

Jarry, Alfred. *The Ubu Plays*. Cyril Connolly and Simon Watson Taylor, translators. New York: Grove Press, 1969.

Kanin, Garson. *Born Yesterday*. New York: Viking Press, 1946.

Lambert, Gavin. *GWTW: The Making of Gone with the Wind*. Boston: Little, Brown and Company, 1973.

Lerner, Alan Jay and Frederick Loewe. *My Fair Lady: A Musical Play in 2 Acts*. New York: Signet Books, 1958.

Lorca, Federico García. *The House of Bernarda Alba* in *Three Tragedies of Lorca*. New York: New Directions Books, 1947.

Miller, Arthur. *All My Sons* in *Best American Plays: Third Series 1945-1951*. John Gassner, ed. New York: Crown Publishers, 1952.

Miller, Arthur. *Death of A Salesman* in *The Portable Arthur Miller*. New York: The Viking Press, 1973.

Miller, Arthur. *Timbends*. New York: Grove Press, 1987.

Mitchell, Margaret. *Gone with the Wind*. New York: Macmillan Publishers, 1936.

Molière, *The School for Wives and The Learned Ladies*. Richard Wilbur, translator. New York: Harcourt Brace Company/A Harvest Book, 1991.

O'Neill, Eugene. *Long Day's Journey into Night*. New Haven: Yale University Press, 1956.

Pool, Daniel. *What Jane Austen Ate and Charles Dickens Knew*. New York: Simon & Schuster, 1993.

Sartre, Jean-Paul. *No Exit and Three Other Plays*. New York: Vintage Books, 1958.

Shakespeare, William. *Mr. William Shakespeares Comedies, Histories, & Tragedies: A Facsimile edition prepared by Helge Kökeritz*. New Haven: Yale University Press, 1955.

Shakespeare, William. *The Complete Works of William Shakespeare*. William Aldis Wright, ed. Philadelphia: The Blakiston Company, 1936.

Shaw, George Bernard. *Complete Plays with Prefaces*. New York: Dodd, Mead & Company, 1963.

Simon, Neil. *The Sunshine Boys*. New York: Samuel French, 1973.

Stanislavski, Constantin. *An Actor Prepares*. Elizabeth Reynolds Hapgood, trans. New York: Theatre Arts, 1936.

Stanislavski, Constantin. *Creating A Role*. Elizabeth Reynolds Hapgood, trans. New York: Theatre Arts, 1961.

Stoppard, Tom. *Arcadia*. London: Faber and Faber Limited, 1993.

Strunk, Jr., William and E. B. White, *The Elements of Style, 3d Edition*. New York: Macmillan Publishing Company, 1979.

Turgenev, Ivan. *A Month in the Country* in *Great Russian Plays*. New York: Dell Publishing, 1960.

Weston, Judith. *Directing Actors: Creating Memorable Performances for Film and Television*. Studio City, CA: Michael Wiese Productions, 1996.

Wheeler, Hugh and Stephen Sondheim, *A Little Night Music* in *Great Musicals of the American Musical Theatre, v. 2,* Stanley Richards, ed. Radnor, PA: Chilton Book Company, 1976.

Wilde, Oscar. *The Importance of Being Earnest* and *Lady Windermere's Fan* in *Plays*. London: Collins, 1954.

Wildeblood, Joan and Peter Brinson. *The Polite World*. New York: Oxford University Press, 1965.

Williams, Emlyn. *Night Must Fall* from *Famous Plays of Crime and Detection*. Van H. Cartmell and Bennett Cerf, compilers. Philadelphia: The Blakiston Company, 1946.

Williams, Tennessee, *Memoirs*. New York: Bantam Books, 1976.

Williams, Tennessee. *A Streetcar Named Desire*. New York: Signet Books/New American Library, 1947.

Williams, Tennessee. *Camino Real* in *Famous American Plays of the 1950s*. New York: Dell Publishing, 1970.

INDEX

abandon, 33, 99, 152, 154-155, 166, 215, 219

Abe Lincoln in Illinois (Sherwood), 62

Aborted Speech, exercise, 127

absurd, theater of the, 48, 73-75

academic, compared to artist, xi, 33, 58

accuracy, 83, 153, 156, 157, 169-170, 184

Ackerman, Peter, *Things You Shouldn't Say Past Midnight*, 19

acting editions, 36

Acting in Shakespeare (Cohen), 237

action, 6-7, 8, 38, 39, 44, 62, 64, 65, 71, 76, 97, 98, 100, 101, 105, 108, 111, 113, 117, 125, 126, 144, 148, 156, 170, 180, 182, 185, 193-194, 200, 206, 215, 218, *see also* scoring

  dramatic, 23, 34, 36, 46, 50, 55, 68-69, 122, 136, 138, 160

  inner or psychological, 22-24, 42, 50-51

  physical, 22-24, 26, 36

  poetic, 207-210

  reciprocal, 46

  rising, 118, 159

  theatrical, 23, 159

action statements, 42-43, 144-145

Actor and the Text, The (Berry), 237

actor training, ix-x, 22, 30, 148, 224

adjectives, 144-145, 172

adjustments, 37-39, 43, 90, 104, 139, 144, 148-149, 152-153, 155, 215, 220

  actable, 144-145

adverbs, 101, 172

Aesop, 147

  Aesop Effect, 12

"AH!", defined, 115-116

Aitken, Maria, 113 (see note), 173 (see note), 236, 237

Albee, Edward, 73

alienating the audience, 72

All My Sons (Miller), 64, 121-122

allegory, 63-64, 120

alliteration, 192, 193, 196, 202

ambiguity, 37, 38, 56, 79, 187-188, 199

Amy's View (Hare), 165-166

anacrusis, defined, 118-119

analysis, 32-37, 57, 62, 109, 120, 156

analysis, actable

  defined, 32-33

anaphora, 181-182, 208

ancillary characters, 70, 71-73

"AND SO...?", principle of, 115-116, 134

Angels in America (Kushner), x (see note), 236

Angry Housewives (musical), 165-166, 168

Animal Farm (Orwell), 157

Animal Work, exercise, 145, 147-148, 149, 157, *see also* Ensemble Animals

Annie Get Your Gun (musical), 154

Anouilh, Jean, *Antigone*, 160

antecedent, grammatical, 173, 187-188

anticipation, 43-44, 98, 99, 100

  anticipation, audience's, 51, 52, 57, 111, 116, 128, 136, 137, 189, *see also* suspense

Antigone (Anouilh), 160

antithesis, 188, 201

  antithesis, half- and hidden, 190, 197, 199

Anything Goes (musical), 11, 64

apostrophe, figurative device, 15

apostrophe, punctuation mark, 202, 204

apotheosis, 209-210

appellations, 177

arc of suspense, 116

Arcadia (Stoppard), 123-124

arcane references, exercise, 173